He Said, She Says

He Said, She Says

An RSVP to the Male Text

Edited by
Mica Howe and
Sarah Appleton Aguiar

Madison • Teaneck
Fairleigh Dickinson University Press
London: Associated University Presses

Associated University Presses
440 Forsgate Drive
Cranbury, NJ 08512

Associated University Presses
16 Barter Street
London WC1A 2AH, England

Associated University Presses
P.O. Box 338, Port Credit
Mississauga, Ontario
Canada L5G 4L8

The paper used in this publication meets the requirements of the American National Standard for Permanence of Paper for Printed Library Materials Z39.48–1984.

Library of Congress Cataloging-in-Publication Data

He said, she says : an RSVP to the male text / edited by Mica Howe and Sarah Appleton Aguiar.
    p. cm.
    Includes bibliographical references and index.
    ISBN 0-8386-3915-1 (alk. paper)
    1. American literature—Women authors—History and criticism.
2. Feminism and   literature—United States—History—20th century.
3. American literature—Male authors—History and criticism—Theory, ec.   4. Women and literature—United States—History—20th century.
5. American literature—20th century—History and criticism.
6. Feminist fiction, American—History and criticism.   7. Feminist literary criticism—United States.   8. Authorship—Sex differences.
9. Sex role in literature.   10. Women in literature. I. Howe, Mica, 1959– II. Aguiar, Sarah Appleton, 1957–
    PS228.F45 H4   2001
    810.9'9287—dc21   2001023669

PRINTED IN THE UNITED STATES OF AMERICA

Contents

IV. Politically Re-Correct

Acknowledgments

WE WOULD FIRST LIKE TO THANK OUR EDITORS HARRY KEYISHIAN and Julien Yoseloff, who encouraged this project and offered invaluable guidance. We are also grateful for the expert advice of Danielle Burnham, the production editor. Many colleagues, friends, and family have also offered insightful contributions. Sarah would especially like to thank Murray State University colleagues Carol Osborne, Jane Etheridge, Kevin Binfield, Squire Babcock, Mike Morgan, Laura Dawkins, Ann Neelon, and Roy Helton. She would also like to acknowledge the vitality and support of her students, especially Leslie Rowland and Alyson McNutt English. Mica would like to thank Staci Settle, Lisa Mandeel, Janice Morgan, León Bodevin, and Connie Blanchard. We are particularly grateful for the encouragement of our department chairpersons Peter F. Murphy (English and Philosophy) and Meg Brown (Modern Languages), and the past and present Deans of the College of Humanistic Studies, Kenneth Wolf and Sandra Jordan.

Sarah's list of inspirational people includes: Lynn Z. Bloom, Jacqueline Sweeton, Suki Bisbing, Charles Wilson, Cheryl Doherty Decter, Kathleen Guglielmi, Richard and Janice Normand, Daniel Day Appleton, and of course, Mica. She thanks her husband, Jesse, and her children, Sam and Jill. These are the people from whom spring the principal joys of her life.

Mica would like to thank her husband, Dave, and her sons Joshua and Wesley, for their love and support, her friends, Leslie Veach, Miriam Andrews, Guiomar Fages, Susan Brown, and most of all, Sarah. She also thanks her parents, Sarah Mica and Bob Kubicek, her brother Stan and his family, and Herb and Sue Howe. Finally, her gratitude goes to John VanDyck, Monnie VanDyck, and Marty Rushing.

Sarah would like to thank the Modern Language Association and the Margaret Atwood Society for providing her with the opportunity to present original versions of her paper. Mica would like to thank the University of las Américas in Cholula-Puebla, México, in conjunction with the Popular Culture Association and the American Culture Association, where she presented her paper included in this book.

Introduction

Mica Howe and Sarah Appleton Aguiar

> Re-Vision—the act of looking back, of seeing with fresh eyes,
> of entering an old text from a new critical direction—is for
> women more than a chapter in cultural history; it is an act of
> survival.
>
> —Adrienne Rich

ADRIENNE RICH'S MUCH-QUOTED CALL FOR WOMEN'S REVISIONS OF literary texts, and history as well, has galvanized a generation of feminist authors to reply with texts of their own. The importance of these emerging female voices responding to the traditionally male canon cannot be overlooked because, as women gain their places within and without literary heritage, their voices enlarge, contest, and re-animate the tradition itself. Not to be content with creating their own canon, women authors have also engaged in the task of recreating the existing body of canonized male texts, offering within their work meta-critical perspectives of the purloined originals. And as the essays in this volume demonstrate, the range of re-visioning has transcended the purely literary texts; women's responses are reaching beyond the "story" and into the primal bases for narrative: the philosophies, theologies, psychologies, politics, and archetypal geneses that comprise the origins of narrative itself.

Thus, this volume seeks to accomplish three critical tasks: to continue the established project of interrogating male texts, to ascertain the subjectivity of the often objectified female characters in the male texts, and to contest the validating influence of those texts. Moreover, the narrative (re)versions that are articulated in these pages are not meant to supplant the original discourses, whether literary, political, social, or political; they are meant to widen the scholarly discussions of literary meaning.

While such notable feminist critics as Judith Fetterley, Elaine Showalter, Nina Baym, and many, many others have endowed literary studies with several decades of fresh interpretations of

9

canonized male texts—particularly noting the flat dimensions of stereotypified female characters—this volume articulates a feminist inclination toward reconceptualization derived at the primary narrative level, revising the text itself.

"Re-vision can be represented in two ways," according to Peter Erickson, "a conciliatory mode that urges moderation and balance or an oppositional mode that insists on a more uncompromising critical perspective" (167). And while some of the essays in this collection seek to balance viewpoints skewed by male narratives, others challenge the foundations of the narratives themselves. For the feminist author, revision serves the triple purpose of renewing an established narrative, extending the boundaries of the female character's subjectivity inhabiting the text, and, to quote Nancy A. Walker, "to expose or upset the paradigms of authority inherent in the texts they appropriate" (7). In addition, as Molly Hite recognizes, feminist revisionists evoke strategies which involve "emphasizing conventionally marginalized characters and themes, in this way re-centering the value structure of the narrative" (2). Thus, for the feminist author, "conciliatory revision" is an oxymoron of untenable dimensions; the very nature of the feminist response is oppositional, political, and laden with implications of resistance to the allure of "authenticity" in narrative. At the same time, however, the refashioned texts seek not to wholly demote the original narrative; a feminist revision draws upon the original narrative even as it challenges it. Feminist revisions are then, as Walker contends, "not only a way of subverting the traditional text, but also of laying claim to it, entering into dialogue with it on an equal plane" (5).

Reflecting the imperative position of oppositional revision, *He Said, She Says* brings together a myriad of perspectives recovering such primal narratives as the Bible, the Torah, mythology, traditional literary texts, male depictions of female sexuality, patriarchal Marxism, American democracy, and multiculturalism. This collection is, as the title implies, an RSVP to the traditionally male or "marked" history of writing; it is a series of essays covering a broad scope of the (m)other half of a conversation that normally stands as a phallocentric monologue. These essays address exclusions that are in the male literary canon, exclusions that, as Walker contends, are "a telling part of culture" because such silencing of the female text becomes part of the very "formation" of culture itself (18). The texts that comprise the various aspects of this RSVP are interdisciplinary answers—or calls for conversations—in which different understandings and interpretations are defined concerning male writings and the relations and connections between what man has said and how woman responds.

Literary revisions of earlier works are, of course, nothing new. Hite, for instance, recognizes that all writings, in a sense, "obscure and encode other stories" (4). Classic myths, originally derived from the oral tradition, have found their way into numerous written works. The Romans liberally borrowed from the ancient Greeks; likewise, contemporary fairy tales have their roots in a variety of cultural traditions. In fact, Jungian archetypal criticism suggests that all stories can find their genesis in a limited number of primal narratives.

Indeed, diverse authors have long refashioned literature to present a revised philosophical viewpoint or to enable readers to reconsider the interpretations of the original story. Most of Shakespeare's plays, for example, are revisions of earlier works—revisions that validate the Elizabethan age and Protestant ethics. James Joyce's *Ulysses* presents a proletariat perception of *The Odyssey*, Homer's epic legend; John Steinbeck, in *East of Eden*, recreates the biblical tale of Cain and Abel, questioning the traditional Christian interpretation of evil, and J. M. Coetzee's *Foe* reworks Daniel DeFoe's *Robinson Crusoe* from a postcolonial perspective.

Revision, then, can always be viewed as a political act; yet, revision also does not seek to eradicate the original text with its recitation. As each refashioned narrative subverts the earlier narrative, it presents its own text as *an* authority, not *the* authority. That is, revisions simultaneously undermine and reinforce the authority of the established text by, paradoxically, using that text as its basis of authority. The revision cannot supplant the original text; it needs the original text on which to base its own existence and credibility. This reliance upon—yet subversion of—the male text reflects, as Walker notes, the feminist revisionist's role as "astute reader of narratives—both literal and cultural—that tell persistent stories about her. . . . To confront such texts is no small matter" (172).

Man's control and domination of the written language has trapped women inside a male truth which she no longer wants to unquestioningly accept, and feminist criticisms, although sometimes factious, basically agree that revision is empowering, whether it be to take control of (other)wise man's language or to create a separate feminine discourse. As noted, the feminist revisionist most often writes to recover a missing authenticity that may be lacking in the original work and to validate women's roles and philosophies. In this regard, feminist writers have engaged in numerous revisions to recover missing feminine voices and to present a counterpoint to the prevailing male voice. Yet, while the scope of feminist revisionings is primarily reactionary—active resistance to dominant texts, the revisions may also be complementary—supplementing, expanding, redirecting the texts they adopt.

In her 1972 essay, "What Can a Heroine Do? Or, Why Women Can't Write," Joanna Russ identified the ubiquitous portrayals of women most prevalent in male authored fiction:

> You will not find women [in the literature] but images of women: modest maidens, wicked temptresses, pretty school-marms, beautiful bitches, faithful wives, and so on. They exist only in relation to the protagonist (who is male). Moreover, look at them carefully and you will see that they don't really exist at all—at their best they are depictions of the social roles women are supposed to play and often do play, but they are public roles and not the private woman; at their worst they are gorgeous Cloudcuckooland fantasies about what men want, hate, or fear. (3)

Russ effectively articulates the voicelessness—as well as the lack of human subjectivity—of women characters in much of the traditional body of literature, their "absent presence" in the male text; her assessment points to the question, as Mieke Bal pointedly asks, how can women "rewrite themselves back into the history of ideology?" (132). One answer may lie in Alicia Ostricker's 1981 article, the aptly named "Thieves of Language," which hails the contemporary women—poets in this case—who have engaged in "revisionist mythmaking":

> Whenever a poet employs a figure or story previously accepted and defined by a culture, the poet is using myth, and the potential is always present that the use will be revisionist: that is, the figure or tale will be appropriated for altered ends, the old vessel filled with new wine, initially satisfying the thirst of the individual poet but ultimately making cultural change possible. (317)

Much of the revisionary literature written by women fills the old stereotypical female "vessels" with character portraits that are complex, individual, and unique conceptions. For example, as Sarah Appleton Aguiar's essay relates, feminist revisions of

King Lear focus upon the daughters' perspectives, presenting Lear not as a victim of inconceivable daughterly oppression, but rather as the instigator of his own defeat. Goneril, Regan, and even Cordelia are granted the power of telling their stories, extricating themselves from beneath the weight of centuries of their father's dominant role as teller of the tale.

After years of exhortations by feminist theorists for authors to retell the world from the women's perspective, and after many have heeded the call, assessments may be made as to the scope of the ongoing revisioning processes. This collection reflects the widening sphere of feminist literary revision; and while many authors have readapted classic literature—from myth to Shakespeare to postmodern canonized texts—the range has also broadened into the primal institutional discourses that shape sexuality, politics, and theology.

Part 1 of *He Said, She Says*, "Religious Re-Inscripture," delves into the ramifications for women in subscribing to the doctrines of phallocentric religion. In an interrogation of Judaism, Ruth Bienstock Anolik's "Appropriating the Golem, Possessing the Dybbuk" addresses, as she states, "contemporary Jewish writers who appropriate the religious figures of the Golem and the Dybbuk to address their own particular concerns of powerlessness and voicelessness." The supernatural Golem and Dybbuk, originating in the rabbinical literature, became part of the Jewish folktale tradition and have been reappropriated in works by Cynthia Ozick, Marge Piercy, Ellen Galford, and Judith Katz, to show how these figures may be feminized and thus resistant to the roles created for them by the male patriarchy.

"The Reclamation of the Feminine Divine: 'Walking in My Body Like a Queen' in Lee Smith's *Fair and Tender Ladies*" by Linda J. Byrd questions traditional Christian phallocentric religion as "a religion that places sacredness solely in the male domain." Byrd sees in Smith that the consistent use of goddess imagery to empower females reflects the character/author's personal quarrel with traditional Christianity and her struggle with the absence of the feminine divine. She points to Ivy Rowe as the novel's "sacred-sexual-maternal" protagonist who, as the original Great Mother Goddess, battles with what traditional Christianity teaches, discovering a feminine space in which to worship.

In their tacit critiques of phallocentric theology, the authors of the works that re-center traditional patriarchal religions place woman into, as Bracha Lichtenberg-Ettinger puts it, the "matrix" of theological centrality. Lichtenberg-Ettinger's "The Red Cow Effect: The Metramorphosis of Hallowing the Hollow and Hollowing the Hallow," an essay that is metatheoretical in nature, redefines feminist literary criticism in terms of psychoanalytic theory in a critique of Judaic patriarchy, examining the problems in translations of the Hebrew rite concerning the sacrifice of the red heifer. Lichtenberg-Ettinger gives a new definition to this rite from the point of view of a "she-cow" within her terms of a "feminine-matrixial" dimension, opposing the polar opposition relating to the Pure/Impure and proposes a third state of "im-purity" that is neither—yet paradoxically both—pure nor impure.

Part 2, "Sexual Re-Identification," discusses the response to and rewritings of women's male-appropriated sexuality. The essay "Signifyin(g) Sex: Gloria Naylor's *Bailey's Cafe* and Western Religious Tradition" by Lynn Alexander works with "the recovery of the term 'whore' by the very women against whom it is pejoratively leveled." She explores the biblical roots of what we consider today as the roles of "negative" female sexuality; Naylor's novel, based on the stories of Eve, Jezebel, Esther, Mary Magdalene, and Mary, revisits, revises, and ultimately establishes a means for women to reclaim their sexual histories from the male paradigm that classifies these women as either whores (Eve, Jezebel, Esther, Mary Magdalene) or icons of virginity (Mary). "Taking America as a Lover: Contemporary Women 'Engage' the American" by Merri Lisa Johnson explores the relationship between women writers and America in terms of the language of revision, and how "what arises between men and women—the many ways we negotiate our personal daily interactions—resembles and provides insights into the literary lineage inherited and interrogated by women writers in the American tradition." She proposes a new look at American literary history that attends to issues of similarity among male and female texts. In doing so she argues that women writers operate at the same level as male writers and reiterate central American mythologies such as individualism, the frontier imagination, and the Adamic namer. That these mythologies are always sexually encoded is one of the central premises of Johnson's text. In another examination of a predominant sexual mythology, Timothy McCracken's "Lolita Talks Back: Giving Voice to the Object" explores the subject position of the "Lolita" figure unfiltered through the male perspective. In his essay McCracken redefines the "Lolita Syndrome" by discussing texts that reclaim the *sub-*

ject Lolita from the *object* Lolita, demythologizing the romance attached to the icon and baldly recounting Lolita's experiences as molested child, not "nymphic" lover. Likewise, " 'I Will Not Wear that Coat': Cross-Dressing in the Works of Dorothy Allison" by Connie D. Griffin establishes that within her semi-autobiographical texts, Allison "slips in and out of genres like outfits she is trying on in order to elude the reification of textual representation, in order to enact the human joy and suffering behind the textual reading." Griffin proposes that "In disrobing herself of the limiting identity of incest victim forced upon her by her stepfather's desire, rage, and rape, Allison claims authority over her body." In each of these essays, the authors of the revised texts are seen to be striving toward subjectification of sexually and mythologically constituted female body.

Part 3, "Vintage Re-(Per)Versions," focuses on feminist revisions of mythological and classical literary narratives. Elise Earthman's essay "Instructions for Survival—or, Plans for Disaster? Young Adult Novels with Mythological Themes" examines young adult novels that re-envision traditional male texts from classical mythology, resetting their stories in the contemporary world. These young adult novels give voice to unvoiced female figures from mythology; as Earthman writes, "Many women readers have felt that it is not only 'the world' but mythology itself that has been oblivious to their particular presence." Her essay, while celebrating the female authors' entry into the texts of myth, notes the difficulties still facing these authors, difficulties that may result in insufficient revisions. Another essay that refocuses upon the impact of myth, "Galatea: Rewritten and Rewriting" by Ellen Peel, is a look at the powerful appeal of the myth of Pygmalion which is an allegory, she says, for the objectification and subordination of women in male-dominated society. Focusing upon a cross-generation sampling of revisions—*The Taming of the Shrew, Frankenstein*, "Adieu," The Sand-Man," "Sarrasine," *Pygmalion*, and *Mannequin*—Peel questions the retellings and their preservation of gender.

"(Dis)Obedient Daughters: (Dis)Inheriting the Kingdom of Lear" by Sarah Appleton Aguiar examines women-centered revisions of *King Lear*, revisions that focus on Lear's daughters: Cordelia and her two infamous, wicked older sisters, Goneril and Regan. The novels she examines, written by Margaret Atwood, Laura Esquivel, Anne Tyler, and Jane Smiley, re-value the differing women's perspectives of the tale's unfolding. Likewise, Beverly Curran's essay, "Mingling and Unmingling Opposites: Bending Genre and Gender in Ann-Marie MacDonald's *Goodnight Desdemona (Good Morning Juliet)*," articulates the Canadian playwright's uses of *Othello* and *Romeo and Juliet* in order to borrow from and "bend" the original text. The final essay in this section, " 'On Which [We] *Looked* Up at Her': Henry James's and Jane Campion's *Portrait(s) of a Lady*" by Jamie Barlowe, contends that Campion's revisionary film is an acknowledgment of the complex relationships between the hypothetical female spectator that her film constructs, the actual historically and culturally situated female viewer in the film's audience(s), and herself as an end-of-the-twentieth-century alternative feminist filmmaker reconsidering the nineteenth-century male author Henry James.

Politically Re-Correct is the final part of the collection, a part which emphasizes the merging of sociopolitical themes with a feminist or feminine perspective. "He Said *Che*, She Says *No*: Apocalyptic Discourse and Awakening in Chely Lima's *Confesiones Nocturnas*" by Mica Howe reclaims the power for women living within a patriarchal Marxist system through apocalyptic themes. Castro's Cuba is shown to be an apocryphal atmosphere where amidst the crumbling dictatorship, the protagonist is able to redefine herself through her own terms of feminist expression. The second essay, "Purloining *The Scarlet Letter*: Bharati Mukherjee and the Apocryphal Imagination" by Christian Moraru, is a look at a political strategy appropriated by marginalized writers to question and critique dominant discourses. *The Holder of the World* is the novel that Moraru uses to describe a rewriting that "turns out to be counter-writing." It is, he claims, an 'apocryphal' response to Hawthorne's original notions of gender, race, religion, and ethnicity. "To Speak with the Voices of Others: Kathy Acker and the Avant-Garde" by Svetlana Mintcheva addresses issues of power and sexuality in the novels *In Memoriam to Identity, My Mother: Demonology* and *Pussy: King of the Pirates* and finds that the avant-garde tradition which has been marked by male fantasy is now emerging in Acker as a more female-empowering text.

Revising the male text has, these essays contend, reinvigorated literature itself. "Narratives are essential to our sense of place in a human continuum," Walker writes, and the body of feminist revisionary texts that has emerged has contributed "wit, irreverence, and the freshness of vision" to our literary tradition (7).

WORKS CITED

Bal, Mieke. 1987. *Lethal Love: Feminist Literary Readings of Biblical Love Stories*. Bloomington: Indiana University Press.

Erickson, Peter. 1991. *Rewriting Shakespeare, Rewriting Ourselves*. Berkeley: University of California Press.

Hite, Molly. 1989. *The Other Side of the Story: Structures and Strategies of Contemporary Feminist Narratives*. Ithaca: Cornell University Press.

Ostriker, Alicia. 1985. Thieves of language: women poets and revisionist mythmaking. In *The New Feminist Criticism: Essays on Women, Literature, and Theory*, edited by Elaine Showalter, 314–38. New York: Pantheon Books.

Rich, Adrienne. 1972. When we dead awaken: writing as re-vision. *College English* 34:18–30.

Russ, Joanna. 1972. What can a heroine do? Or, why women can't write. In *Images of Women in Fiction: Feminist Perspectives*, edited by Susan K. Cornillon, 3–20. Bowling Green, OH: Bowling Green University Popular Press.

Walker, Nancy A. 1995. *The Disobedient Writer: Women and Narrative Tradition*. Austin: University of Texas Press.

He Said, She Says

Part 1
Religious Re-Inscripture

Appropriating the Golem, Possessing the Dybbuk: Female Retellings of Jewish Tales

RUTH BIENSTOCK ANOLIK

IT IS A COMMONPLACE OF CONTEMPORARY JEWISH DISCOURSE THAT in twentieth century America all Jews, including Jewish writers, are Jews by choice: with external obstacles to assimilation lifted, every Jew is free to leave, or stay within, the tradition. Jewish women writers who wrote earlier in the century tended to opt for the path to assimilation. Mary Antin and Anzia Yeziarska, for example, used their writing as a means to get out of their tradition. Contemporary Jewish women writers, like Allegra Goodman, Pearl Abraham, and Rachel Goldstein, however, are increasingly choosing to remain within their tradition, writing as Jewish Americans.

The choice to retain a Jewish identity poses a particular paradox and poignancy to the Jewish American woman writer: how to write within a heritage that traditionally disempowers and even silences her. The traditional role of the woman, developed in the Jewish culture of Eastern Europe, a culture with continuing power and influence upon a people committed to its past, is marked by constraints and limitations. Within the traditional paradigm exists a system of laws and customs, buttressed by the ritually impure state of the menstruating woman and the primacy of women's responsibilities to husband and children, that denies women access to the highest levels of Jewish observance available to men. Within the tradition, women do not count in a *minyan*, the quorum required for the most serious prayers, nor may they lead public prayer; they may not bear witness in a religious court or for a religious event like a wedding; they are prohibited from participating fully in various rituals and are also denied access to the highest levels of scholarship—until the 1970s the concept of a woman rabbi was impossible and is now a possibility only within the liberal wings of Judaism.

What is, perhaps, for the Jewish woman writer most telling

is that within this traditional paradigm, the access of women to language is limited. In Europe only the vernacular language Yiddish or the secular languages of the local populace were spoken by women (resulting in a canon of Yiddish texts read exclusively by women); the holy tongue, Hebrew, was used exclusively by male scholars. The principle of *kol isha*, still observed in traditional communities, is also a direct limitation of the voice of the woman (the literal meaning of the Hebrew words). Within the guidelines of this principle, the voice of the adult woman is so seductive that it may not be heard publicly.

Although much of Western culture has come to accept female power and the authority of women to create (Gilbert and Gubar, for example, identify the nineteenth century as the moment when English women writers experienced "anxiety of authorship"), the place of women within Jewish culture is still controversial, as the debate raging on this topic reveals ideological fault lines within the spectrum of Jewish observance. Contemporary Jewish women writing within their own tradition must, then, continue to grapple with the traditional powerlessness of women in Jewish culture, the curtailing of their authority and of their voice.

The response of some writers to the anxiety of authority[1] generated by these cultural tensions is to engage in a Bloomian misreading of the powerful texts of their tradition, particularly the folktales of the golem and the dybbuk. In appropriating and recreating these narratives in their own image, Jewish women writers open up a narrative space for the figure of the creative, powerful, and vocal woman. In revising and feminizing these narratives, Jewish women write themselves back into their tradition, appropriating the tradition and making it truly their own.

The figures of the dybbuk, the migrant soul that possesses the body of a living person, and the golem, a living creature made by men from clay, have long haunted Jewish folk tales. Both figures represent unnatural appropriation. The dybbuk supernaturally appropriates the body of another; the golem represents the human appropriation of the divine power to create life. In creating a golem, the rabbi violates the second commandment prohibition against creating graven images and subversively reenacts God's creation of man, vivifying a creature of clay through the power of the word. Both the golem and the dybbuk are, in fact, monsters of language (appropriate to a culture that valorizes the power of the word): the dybbuk manifests as a torrent of inappropriate language emanating from the possessed (usually female) body; the golem is (as was all of creation within Jewish cosmology) created by the power of the word.

These figures manifest generalized cultural anxieties of power, creation, and voice, anxieties that were not limited to women in Eastern European Jewish culture. The situation of all Jews, men *and* women, was circumscribed by outer forces of persecution and prejudice (significantly, both folk figures most powerfully captured the popular Jewish imagination in the sixteenth century when persecution of Jews in Europe increased) and by inner forces of God-imposed rules and constraints that limited and problematized the avenues of creative expression for all Jews.

In their appropriations and revisions of the golem story, Cynthia Ozick and Marge Piercy reconstruct the motif of the golem to appropriate the authority of creation (and sexuality, the basis of biological creation) for women. Rewriting the texts to include female figures of authority and power, Ozick and Piercy reveal the possibilities of female creation and power that are suppressed by the traditional golem stories.

The golem stories originated in the rabbinic literature and became part of the Jewish folktale tradition. They appear in many different versions in the folklore; the most famous of these is the legend (appearing centuries after the rabbi's death) of Rabbi Judah Loew, the Maharal of sixteenth-century Prague. The elements that recur in each version of the legend are: the golem, a large, powerful, humanoid, is created to save the Jewish people from some outward danger, including the blood libel; the golem, made from clay, is vivified by a powerful rabbi using the power of God's name inscribed on a piece of paper, inserted into the golem's mouth; the Hebrew letters *aleph mem taf, emet* (truth), are sometimes inscribed on his forehead.

The primary function of the golem is to save the Jewish people from danger. Some golems, however, assist with homely household duties like lighting the stoves of the Jews on the Sabbath and fetching water. It is this more mundane role that invites a reading of the figure of the golem as a veiled code for the woman in Jewish culture. In the Talmudic literature, the word "golem," which literally means "unformed substance," is associated with women; "Thus an unmarried woman is called a golem, since her nature is not fully rounded until she is married" (Minkin 43). The golem is frequently speechless, like women in traditional Jewish culture and, like women, is prohibited from participating fully in religious life; as Marge Piercy indicates in her golem novel, *He, She and It*, a golem, like a woman, is unable to participate in a *minyan* (113).

Critics note the displacement of anxieties relating to women onto the figure of the monster. Halberstam argues that the figure of the monster exists as the "infinitely interpretable" emblem of horror in response to the Other (20). In "The Laugh of the Medusa," Cixous locates the monstrous Other as the female Other, inhabiting a dark mysterious continent. In *Powers of Horror*, Kristeva delineates associations between the abjected mother and various sources of cultural horror. In addition, Gilbert and Gubar argue that nineteenth-century English women writers displace their own anxieties of authorship and authority onto the figure of the monster. In the light of these readings, it is possible to see that the golem folk tales simultaneously express and allay male anxieties toward women: the coded female character is monstrous but is ultimately subject to the linguistic power of the male rabbi. The golem is always reduced to clay when, as often happens in the tales, the growing power of the monster threatens to endanger the Jewish community, emblemizing, in this reading the fear of the unleashed women—the fear of the "rampant sexuality" that Rachel Adler argues functioned as "a metaphor for the disequilibrating potential of female power . . . [representing] to the rabbis all that is untamable, unpredictable and lawless in human beings."[2] The folk tale further works to limit the threat of female power by appropriating to the male rabbi the most powerful act available to women in traditional culture, the ability, based on biology and sexuality, to create life.

In *He, She, and It*, Marge Piercy tells her golem story through two interwoven narratives: the story of the creature made by Rabbi Judah Loew, the Maharal of sixteenth-century Prague, and a post-apocalyptic narrative of the creation of a cyborg. In the primary narrative, set in the twenty-first century world devastated by nuclear war, Shira, who loses her son to her former husband, returns to Tikva (Hebrew for hope), the Jewish free colony on what was the east coast of the United States. There she is enlisted in acculturating Yod, a cyborg: part human, part robot/computer,[3] who has been created by two scientists, one male, one female (Shira's grandmother). Piercy's story of her twenty-first-century golem is interspersed with a telling of the story of the golem of Prague, narrated by Malka, the scientist grandmother, who tells the story to Yod.

Piercy's version of the golem legend closely parallels its

source: her golem, like Joseph, Rabbi Loew's golem, is created to protect a beleaguered Jewish community. The name of Piercy's golem, Yod, recalls the name of Rabbi Loew's Golem. Yod is the name of the tenth letter of the Hebrew alphabet; given to the cyborg because he is the tenth in a series; Yod is also the first letter of Yosef, Joseph in Hebrew. Piercy evokes the anxieties of creation inherent in the folk tale. Her characters debate the morality of creating a humanlike creature; this act of creation is overtly illegal and subversive, forbidden by the powerful multis (corporation-like governments) who rule the world, and Shira, after the death of Yod, realizes that to recreate him would be wrong and destroys all the records that would make that recreation possible.

Piercy's retelling of the folk tale is, however, not merely an updating, a resetting of the tale in more modern times. In her narrative, she reworks the story, appropriating and rewriting the traditional narrative to include the possibilities of female power suppressed by the originals.[4] While the golem legends work to repress the power of female sexuality and deny the power of female creation, Piercy's narrative valorizes these female possibilities. Her narrative wrests the creation of the golem from the male rabbi and from the supernatural God; Piercy emphasizes that the cyborg Yod is created through science, not magic, and represents female as well as male generative power. Yod is created by a male scientist, programmed by a female scientist, Malka, and then acculturated by a woman, Shira.

Percy inverts the premises of the golem legend in insisting on the significance of the female principle of creation and in expanding the possibilities of female creation beyond the biological to the scientific and intellectual. She counters the rabbinic fear of the unleashed woman: Yod is more gentle, more civilized, more *human* because he is invested with the female principle. His nine precursors, earlier cyborgs created by the male scientist alone, were too violent and threatening and, like the golems of legend, had to be destroyed. Yod is a creature who successfully synthesizes opposites: human/machine, male/female.

Susan Niditch's reading of representations of Adam (the precursor of all golems, denoted a "golem," an unformed creature) in the rabbinic literature as a figure negotiating the tensions between the male/female, spiritual/physical indicates a precedent for this view of the golem figure as mediating polarities constructed by rabbinic culture. Although a machine, Yod sustains a sexual relationship with Shira; although physically male, he exhibits the sensibilities that Piercy attributes to women. In Yod, then, Piercy constructs a being who resists the polarizing categorization that rabbinic culture constructs to diminish women: her androgynous golem, unlike the originals may, in fact, participate in a *minyan* (as may Shira in the utopian, egalitarian Tikva).

The story of Shira and her child also supports Piercy's valorization of female authority to create and possess children. In Piercy's postapocalyptic, damaged, and male-dominated world, most of the population is infertile; only the inhabitants of free towns like Tikva, flourishing on the "unclaimed margin" (36) outside of the multis are able to bear children naturally (116). Shira's conception and birth of her son, Ari, is remarkable for being achieved without technological intervention, as a result of her sexuality and biology. Although Shira's husband, Josh, is awarded sole custody of Ari by the evil and patriarchal multi government and allowed to take him to a space station, the novel climaxes when Shira, with Yod's assistance, manages to steal Ari back, killing Josh in the process. At the end of the novel, when the male scientist and his records are also destroyed, the biological, natural, female-centered form of creating life prevails in Piercy's utopia.

Malka, the scientist grandmother, performs her own act of textual appropriation within the novel, retelling and revising the legend to valorize the female power to create life. Malka's retelling of the golem legend introduces a major female figure, one who is absent from all other versions of the tale. Malka invents a granddaughter for the Maharal, Chava, who is a midwife. Chava is a prototype of the female scientist, possessing knowledge that is unavailable to men. Most significantly, she is a woman who controls birth. The name Chava (Hebrew for Eve), evokes the female source of all human life and recalls that Eve's trangressive hunger for knowledge has been long associated with the dangers of the female. The figure of Chava promotes Piercy's valorization of the female-centered birth process and counters the male-centered process of golem formation. Chava's introduction into the golem tale emblemizes Piercy's introduction of the figure of the powerful, knowledgeable, and sexual woman into the tradition.

Cynthia Ozick's "Xanthippe and Puttermesser" (in *The Puttermesser Papers*) locates the female within *her* version of the golem story by inverting the genders of the original. Both the golem, Xanthippe, and her creator, the Jewish civil servant, Ruth Puttermesser, are female. It would, however, be reductive to read Ozick's retelling as an insistently feminist revision of the golem tales; the subtlety of her writing tends toward the ambiguously ironic rather than the insistently political.

Ozick's complicated, ironically skeptical stance toward feminism can be seen in her characterization of Puttermesser's feminism: "she was careful never too speak of 'man's' nature. She always said 'humankind' instead of 'mankind.' She always wrote 'he or she' instead of just 'he' " (24). The name Ozick gives her feminist protagonist can also be construed as an ironically ambivalent commentary on her politics: the name Puttermesser means "butter knife," a sly Freudian dig, perhaps, at her attempts to co-opt male power.

Ozick's ironic wit pervades her revision of the golem story, investing her retelling with a humor absent from the original legends and from Piercy's rather earnest retelling. Puttermesser creates her golem out of the earth in the flowerpots in her apartment. With the help of this golem, Puttermesser wrests power from the evil, but cleverly named, mayor of New York, Malachy ("Matt") Mavett,[5] and becomes mayor of New York herself. Under Mavett's rule, marked by patronage and corruption, New York has been, as Ozick explicitly indicates, as dark and threatening as medieval Prague. Puttermesser's informing text, however, is "that immigrant's dream of merit: justice, justice shalt thou pursue" (30). This passage, from Deuteronomy (16:20), significantly ends with the promise that just action will result in the inheritance of the land. When her pursuit of justice leads to her ascension as mayor, Puttermesser creates an earthly Paradise in New York. Gardens are planted, the subways are refurbished, "the youths who used to terrorize the subways put on fresh shirts and walk out into Central Park . . . they dance. They have formed themselves into dancing clubs, and crown one another's heads with clover pulled up from the sweet ground" (76).

Yet if Ozick's revision resists the overt feminism of Piercy's retelling and the gravitas of the original tales, these two elements do, nevertheless, manifest in her story, which is, as Xanthippe points out to Puttermesser, the story of the first female golem (43). The original golem folk tales are remarkable for being birth narratives from which mothers are completely absent; Ozick's revision of the golem story reveals a poignant longing for the possibility of a female presence within the line of tradition, that line in which all previous golem makers have been male.

Feminist critics have long noted the need of intellectually creative women for a tradition of women, the need to discover for themselves female precursors within their cultural tradition. Woolf argues for the necessity to female artists of female precursors and a female tradition (56), a necessity that informs later works as Moers's *Literary Women*, and Showalter's *A Literature of Their Own*. Critics note that the absence of a female tradition is emblemized in literature by an absence of mothers from literary texts. Rich, for example, in writing of Jane Eyre's motherlessness, cites Chesler's comment, " 'women are motherless children in a patriarchal society' " (91).

Ozick's retelling reinstates the mother and the daughter into the narrative. Puttermesser, distanced from her own uncomprehending mother, who writes from Florida of potential accountant suitors, dislocated by an intellectual tradition that disinherits her, and marginalized by a political system that disempowers her attempts to instate a female line. Puttermesser yearns for daughters: "She was not yet reconciled to childlessness. Sometimes the thought that she would never give birth tore her heart. She imagined daughters" and Xanthippe appears, unconsciously created by her creator (36). Xanthippe is Puttermesser's intellectual clone, knowing all that Puttermesser knows, desiring all that she desires. But Xanthippe, daughterlike, golemlike, resists Puttermesser's molding. Before Puttermesser breathes life into Xanthippe, she is able to remold and refine the features on her face, after her vivification, this is not possible; Xanthippe's features are set. Xanthippes's name, too, is a form of daughterly resistance, an instance of a daughter reforming a dynamic tradition; she resists Puttermesser's intention to name her Leah. The line ends, however, with Xanthippe, as Puttermesser, faithfully re-enacting the rabbinic ritual, resisting the calls of the previously silent Xanthippe to "my mother," returns Xanthippe to clay (99). The fantasies of Puttermesser and Ozick, to instate a female dynasty of mystical and political power, are fantasies that cannot, as yet, be sustained.

The fate of Xanthippe and her creator's fall from power, indicate Ozick's ambiguity toward her ambitious protagonist. In her creation as well as her destruction of the golem, Puttermesser appropriates the ancient mystical power of the rabbis, traditionally an exclusively male domain. (In becoming the first female mayor of New York, Puttermesser appropriates yet another

form of traditionally male power.) The technologies of her creation are an exact replica of the methodologies employed by the
rabbis in the folklore. In this, it is possible to identify Ozick's
strain of feminism: unlike Piercy, Ozick resists a valorization of
the traditional, biologically based female avenues to creation
and power and insists on female entry into traditionally male
domains of the mind.[6] Yet, in Ozick's formulation, this feminist
project cannot be sustained.

The ambiguity of Ozick's feminism surfaces in her representation of Xanthippe's rampant sexuality, the cause of Puttermesser's downfall (reminding the reader that Puttermesser's is
not the first Paradise to be lost because of female appetite.) In
this, Ozick explicates the fear of sexuality, and most specifically
female sexuality, that is a repressed presence in the original
golem folk tales. In Ozick's story, the sexuality of the golem
quite literally takes over. As Xanthippe grows, her body and her
sexual appetite grow too until, finally, Puttermesser is undone
by Xanthippe's insatiable sexual appetite. The golem ravishes
every commissioner of Puttermesser's utopian government;
succubus-like, she drains them of their powers, immobilizing
the administration, leading to the downfall of the earthly paradise that Puttermesser has instated as mayor of New York.
Ozick's narrative precisely follows the movement of the traditional golem stories: her golem, too, resists and threatens the
power of her creator. As in the folktales, as in Piercy's narrative
(in which the golem's transgressive resistance to the authority
of his male creator is also posited in sexual terms—he dares to
have a physical relationship with a woman), the golem's creator
is driven to destroy the uncontrollable, transgressive creation.
In couching this uncontrollable resistance in sexual terms,
Ozick reveals the anxieties that lie hidden within the folktales.
The feminist value of this explication is, however, ambivalent:
is Ozick's revision a critique or an affirmation of the traditional
Jewish anxieties toward unbridled female sexuality?

Ellen Galford,[7] in *The Dyke and the Dybbuk*, and Judith Katz,
in *Running Fiercely Toward a High Thin Sound*, recover and revise the figure of the dybbuk[8] as a means of instating the female
line, *their* line, into the patriarchal tradition. The transgressive
figure of the dybbuk (the word means "attachment"), deriving
from the Kabbalistic notion of transmigration of souls, first
seized the popular imagination in Jewish Eastern Europe in the
sixteenth century. The popular implications of this belief were
that any transgressive, deviant behavior (frequently that of

women [Schifrin 35]) could be attributed to spiritual possession, the victim subjected to rabbinical exorcism.

The most well-known representation of the dybbuk story is relatively recent; it is the early twentieth-century play by S. Ansky, who set out to recapture the already disappearing culture of the Jewish shtetl but who, in doing so, reinvented it. In Ansky's version of the folktale, Khonen, betrothed to Leah, dies of a broken heart when she is betrothed to another. He returns as a dybbuk to possess her and ultimately manages to bring her to him in death. In addition to providing a critique of the patriarchal politics and economics of arranged marriage, Ansky's representation explicates the traditional figure of the dybbuk as the emblem of the male voice speaking ventriloquistically through the female body, the figure of the male appropriation of the female voice. Ansky's reading of the folktale reveals that the dybbuk tales, like the golem legends, were a way of expressing and allaying anxiety toward uncontrollable women. The uncontrollable voice of the woman, the emblem of female sexuality in rabbinic culture, is revealed, in Ansky's play, to belong to a far less threatening figure: the male yeshiva student, who is, in fact expressing rights that *are* legitimately his. The woman possessed by the dybbuk, who appears to vocalize uncontrollably, is, in fact, silent; the powerful voice actually belongs to the possessing male. Ansky's play is, then, not about the wild power of women but of their subjugation.

It is in Katz and Galford's constructions of female dybbuks, speaking in female voices, that the voice of the woman (silent in the golem legends, silent in the dybbuk tales), is finally heard. Galford and Katz employ the ventriloquistic power of the dybbuk to explore and counter the traditional silencing of Jewish women and to seize the authority of the female voice and female sexuality that is emblemized by the female voice within Jewish culture. In their revisions of the dybbuk folktales, Katz and Galford construct dybbuks who are articulate, female, *and* lesbian. These reconstructions reinvent the legends and also work to interrogate the central texts that support the patriarchal and heterosexual structure of Jewish law and culture: the Torah; the Jewish Bible, in which the law first appears; and the Talmud, the code of Jewish law (and legends) that governs all aspects of traditional Jewish life.

In constructing dybbuks who speak in an authentically female voice, Katz and Galford pointedly interrogate the patriarchal texts and practices (including *kol ishah*) that constrain the

voice of the woman. The guidelines that dictate the public silence of women are derived from readings of *The Song of Solo-
mon*. The Talmudic statement based on these readings is: "qol
be-ishah ervah" (*Berakhot* 24a), the voice of a woman is *ervah*,
"indecent," "shameful," "lustful" and seductive (Taitz 46). Katz
and Galford remove the veils of shame and secrecy from the
figure of the speaking woman; they construct the female speaking subject as unashamedly and shamelessly indecent and lustful and also joyful and benign. They locate within their subjects
the "jouissance" that Cixous finds in the female monster: "You
only have to look at the Medusa straight on to see her. And she's
not deadly. She's beautiful and she's laughing" (885).

In representing the traditionally transgressive figure of the
dybbuk as a lesbian, Katz and Galford also interrogate rabbinic
proscriptions against female sexual expression. Lesbianism is
not explicitly mentioned in the Torah, nor does the Talmud condemn it forcefully: "The only two references to lesbianism in the
Talmud . . . agree that lesbianism does not constitute even an
act of promiscuity which would disqualify a woman from marriage to a priest. It is merely licentiousness, a condemnable act
but with no legal or punitive ramifications" (Biale 195). Although the rabbis interpret the statement in Leviticus 18:3:
"You shall not follow their laws" as forbidding all homosexual
behavior: "What did they used to do? A man would marry a
man, and a woman a woman" (*Sifra Acharei Mot* 9:8).[9] Maimon-
ides, who shares this interpretation, is relatively lenient in his
response to violations (*Mishneh Torah, Hilchut Issurei Bi'ah*
21:8); he suggests that men keep their wives from women who
engage in such behavior which should be punished by beating.[10]
Contemporary Jewish traditional responses to lesbianism tend
to be more harsh. Although "traditional Jewish legal texts on
lesbianism lead to the conclusion that the private sexual behavior of women was viewed as trivial . . . now that lesbianism has
become public and challenges heterosexuality, the response
from traditional circles is anger and revulsion" (Albert 33). In
inserting the figure of the lesbian into Jewish folklore, Katz and
Galford explicate a presence long denied and feared.

Tony Kushner's reading of the Ansky play, in which Kushner
discovers a homosexual subtext, indicates a precedent for using
the transgressive figure of the dybbuk as an emblem with which
to interrogate the rabbinic response to homosexuality. "According to Kushner . . . Khonon's father and Leah's father, who
loved each other as young yeshiva students, promised to con-

summate their love in the only way the Jewish community would allow—by marrying their children off"; Kushner sees the traditional figure of the dybbuk, as represented in Ansky's play, as "the ultimate image of gender ambiguity and transgression" (Schifrin 35). It is important to note that such ambiguity is particularly threatening in a culture marked by rigid distinctions of gender. In their representations of lesbian dybbuks, then, Galford and Katz appropriate a figure that has already been used to articulate questions of sexual ambiguity. Through their explication and feminization of the homosexual transgressiveness of Ansky's version, Galford and Katz inject a neglected figure into the tradition, proposing what was unthinkable in shtetl society, and to Ansky, that women, as well as men, can love each other with the intensity experienced by fellow yeshiva students.

Judith Katz's *Running Fiercely Toward a High Thin Sound* is, perhaps, less a revision of the dybbuk folktale than an evocation, less a subversive retelling of the original stories than a subversion reading, revealing meanings that are hidden within the folktales and the play. Katz's dybbuk narrative explicates and expands the critique of the politics and economics of arranged marriage implicit in Ansky's play.

The dybbuk of Katz's novel is figuratively, rather than literally possessed. Nadine is the unhappy, unsocialized, lesbian daughter in a conventional Jewish family. Her mental instability recalls the origin of the original dybbuk folktales as a way to account for uncontrollable madwomen. It is Nadine's mother who recognizes her as a dybbuk. After Nadine sets her wild unruly hair (the Jewish hair which so irritates her perfectionist mother) on fire with the family's Sabbath candles, she is left with a harsh "monster voice." It is on hearing this voice that the mother declares: "There's a dybbuk inside her! Just listen!" (18).

The plot of Katz's narrative centers, as does Ansky's play, on the execution of a marriage: in the case of Katz's novel, the marriage of Electa, the sister of Nadine. The ongoing critique of the economics of the institution of heterosexual marriage by the two lesbian sisters of Electa, and Katz's skeptical presentation of heterosexual marriage as a celebration of materialism, directs the reader's attention to the ambivalent representation of marriage in Ansky's text. The arranged marriage was a universal in Eastern European shtetl life (Zborowski 42). Ansky's play, an outgrowth of his ethnographic study of the disappearing world of the shtetl, charts the disaster that follows when Leah's father disregards his daughter's inclination and the earlier promise he made to the friend of his youth, in favor of another richer suitor. Katz's use of the figure of the dybbuk, within her critique of marriage, reveals the critique implicit in Ansky's dybbuk story.

Katz's radical interpretation of Ansky's play is evident in a central scene of the novel that echoes the action of the play. In Ansky's play, an old woman rushes into the synagogue and runs to the Ark to pray for her dying daughter. As *"she opens the Ark, thrusts her head inside"* and begins to chant, the caretaker of the synagogue *"gently"* asks her if she would like a *minyan* to pray for her daughter (10–11). Kushner's version of this scene explicates the cultural misogyny absent from Ansky's more forgiving text. When the old woman bursts into the synagogue, the caretaker tells her "you're not permitted here!" When she threatens to "shove my head in the Ark!" Kushner's caretaker replies "God forbid" (18).

Katz builds on Kushner's critical interpretation of this scene. In her novel, the scene is translated into the occasion of the interrupted wedding, as Nadine performs the narrative function of the dybbuk in Ansky's play. Nadine sneaks into the synagogue before her sister's wedding and hides in the ark with the Torahs during the ceremony (certainly a transgression on the part of a woman whose access to the Torah is limited by law and practice). The force of her response to this wedding, mostly sorrow at seeing her "sweet sister" going "down the river . . . blows [her] out of the Ark, hair flying every which way, her jeans were covered with mud, her vest was ripped to shreds, she looked really bad, and there she was leaping out of the Ark and running down the aisle" (83, 86). This multilayered image simultaneously evokes the old woman tolerated by Ansky's romanticized characters and scorned by Kushner's more realistically misogynistic characters, represents the dybbuk's interruption of the wedding and literalizes Nadine's coming out of the closet.

Unlike Ansky or Kushner, Katz does, however, posit a positive alternative to the conventional heterosexual marriage. During a dreamlike interlude when Nadine, who has tried to drown herself, resides in a fantastic underworld comprised of Holocaust images juxtaposed with images of a lesbian utopia, she experiences a wedding "where about a hundred people were marrying each other, and we all were women." This wedding takes place in a synagogue, with a balcony, the section traditionally reserved for women in gender-segregated synagogues, "but no women had to go sit in it." Although there is a rabbi, the women "all took turns" sharing the authority (151).

As Rebecca Albert notes, Nadine's representation evokes Moses and Elijah; like them she is a prophet who sees an alternate utopia: "Her prophetic role is to reclaim the Jewish past as a lesbian and to bring lesbian sensibilities to the stories of Eastern European Jewish life" (160). Nadine is an oddly silent prophet; ashamed of her monster voice, she seldom speaks and she shares her vision with no one. Nadine does, however, express herself through the music of the violin she inherits from her great-grandfather. And Nadine also expresses herself through her laughter. When her sister Jane reappears unexpectedly, she narrates Nadine's response to her: "you started laughing your head off. I mean you laughed and laughed and laughed and laughed and then, without saying a word . . . You stop laughing and just walk into the kitchen" (40). This laugh recalls the laugh of the monstrous Medusa of Cixous's essay, the laughter that expresses the *jouissance* of the powerful unconventional woman. In the creation of her monster and her story, Katz follows Cixous's advice that women write female sexed texts for themselves, to find their place and meaning in history and literature, a place "where woman has never had *her* turn to speak" (879). Katz's strategy is, as Cixous advocates, to discover her own beauty within the figure of the monster, to use that figure to reinscribe women like herself into the narratives of her tradition. Although Katz's dybbuk cannot sustain her laughter, she is able to prophesize a time when the lesbian is not, like the dybbuk, a code for transgression, but for community.

In *The Dyke and the Dybbuk*, Ellen Galford also looks at the Medusa and finds her laughing. The monster of Galford's novel is the witty, wisecracking narrator, the dybbuk Kokos. Unlike most dybbuks, she is not the disembodied voice of a dead person but an independently existing demon. Kokos is, as she describes herself, an "unorthodox" demon, using unconventional approaches in dybbukry (88). She is also a rebellious demon, fighting against Mephisto Industries, the demonic conglomerate that has taken over her part of the underworld and that is trying to phase her out of her job. She is in the tradition of Satan, the founder of the underworld from which she works: "I remind myself that this entire industry began with a single act of rebellion against the management Upstairs" (146). Kokos also resists more worldly authority, fighting a dynasty of rabbis over the centuries as they try to free her victims from her possession.

Galford uses the figure of her transgressive narrator to inscribe the figure of the vocal woman into the tradition. Kokos narrates the story of Rainbow Rosenbloom, whom Kokos is assigned to possess as the result of a centuries old curse, and it is through the possessing dybbuk that the alienated Rainbow moves closer to her tradition. Kokos, bequeathed to Rainbow, unknowingly, from her dead mother, as a family curse, tells Rainbow the story of her ancestor, Gittel, and the spurned lover, Anya, who initiates the dybbuk curse (96–97). In addition to restoring Rainbow's ancestral history, Kokos restores her ancestral language. Rainbow's ignorance of the various languages of her tradition—Hebrew, Yiddish, Aramaic—is emblematic of the traditional silence of Jewish women and of her alienation from her tradition, a result of the fact that there is no place in the tradition for an articulate lesbian. Rainbow's Jewish voice is restored to her by Kokos, and at her family *seder*, Rainbow finds herself, to her surprise, singing the concluding song *Chad Gadya* "in word-perfect Aramaic" (33). On an outing with her aunts, Rainbow finds herself regaling them with a Yiddish "rendition of a little amorous [meaning obscene] ditty from a shtetl on the banks of the River Vistula" (162). In these episodes, then, Galford pointedly uses the figure of the dybbuk to restore Rainbow's silent Jewish voice, the emblem of her absence from her tradition.

Yet Rainbow, despite her tentative stabs at reclaiming her Jewish tradition, which are partially motivated by a crush she develops on an Orthodox Jewish woman, is a transgressive character, rejoicing particularly, as Kokos notes, in transgressing central tenets of Judaism: in being a lesbian, she engages in "unspeakable acts that rank right up there with throwing your children into the fire as a sacrifice to Baal" and has "flouted that quintessential obligation upon the female Jew to be fruitful and multiply. . . . As [a] film critic . . . , she's turned her passion for graven images [forbidden by the second commandment] into a vocation" (1–2). On leaving the Passover *seder*, at which she has sung, she meets a friend in a Chinese restaurant, where, to counter the overbearing Jewishness of the family seder, both women order a smorgasbord of non-kosher delicacies. Kokos says; "That's better. Injunctions maternal and commandments Levitical dissolve into the smoke of sacrilegious burnt offerings" (38). The transgressive lesbian, Rainbow, like her haunting rebellious dybbuk, Kokos, displays the *jouissance* advocated by Cixous. In word and deed she blithely interrogates and violates the injunctions of the quintessestially patriarchal texts: the Talmud and the Torah.

Yet, Rainbow, singing in Yiddish and Aramaic, does retain her affinity for the traditions of her culture, emblemized by her attraction to an Orthodox woman; her violations of traditional injunctions do not automatically point to a positive alternative. Galford indicates, in her depiction of an Orthodox Jewish community based on the guidelines of the Torah and Talmud, the enduring power and attraction of the tradition; as Galford recognizes, the texts themselves remain resistant to change. It is in her appropriation of the dybbuk folktale, rather than in her characters' transgressions of the patriarchal texts, that Galford posits a positive solution to the problem of the suppression of women by male texts and their resultant exclusion from the tradition. In her depiction of an Orthodox Jewish community, Galford explicitly locates the place of storytelling as the female domain. While the men study, legalistically interpreting every question three ways, building "theoretical palaces," the women tell stories of poor women and werewolves, of girls who listen to the wind in the trees, of angels and demons (80, 82). Galford presents the richness of female storytelling in opposition to male legalism. It is, then, through storytelling—the place where even the most traditional Jewish women already have a foothold—that Galford suggests women can find a place to get into their tradition. (Kokos, unemployed and dispossessed at the end of the narrative, also opts for storytelling; she decides to go into filmmaking with her demon friends, pooling their advanced technical skills and experience with human plots.)

For Galford, as for Piercy, Ozick, and Katz, the way back to Judaism is not through the rigid male-dominated legalism constructed in the Torah and the Talmud but through the already flexible and accessible tales of the tradition—tales of dybbuks and golems—that are already part of the Jewish woman's heritage. Each of these writers recognizes the absence of women from the tradition. This absence is emblemized in each novel (as in the original golem and dybbuk stories that inspire them) by the absence of mothers:[11] Piercy's Shira's mother is an absent, mysterious figure; Ozick's Puttermesser is distanced from her mother as is Katz's Nadine; Rainbow's mother is dead; yet, each of these writers constructs within her text a female Utopia, a place in which the female tradition is recreated and restored: Piercy's Tikva, Ozick's New York; Katz's New Chelm and the dreamworld utopia, and Galford's underworld. Each of these Utopias is a fantastic place, a place structured by the rules of narrative not law, a place where fantasy counters legalism. In ameliorating their situation through fantastic enactments, in pointing the way toward future possibilities, Jewish women writers are also taking a quintessentially Jewish approach. Jews have long told each other idealized stories of the future, of the promised land, the Messianic times, the world to come. The belief in a perfectible future is a central tenet of Jewish belief; and, in reconstructing Jewish folk tales to represent strong powerful articulate Jewish women, Ozick, Piercy, Galford, and Katz include themselves in this tradition. In opposing the female power of narrative to the patriarchal power of law, they discover and recover their rightful place within their tradition.

NOTES

1. A feminist appropriation by Gilbert and Gubar of the theoretical paradigm posited by Harold Bloom in *The Anxiety of Influence*. It is most telling, in the context of this discussion, that Gilbert and Gubar locate the emblem of this anxiety in monstrous characters created by nineteenth-century English women writers.

2. Adler goes on to argue for an "analogy between their [the rabbi's] own experience of marginality and stigma in an often hostile empire, and women's vulnerability and powerlessness under patriarchal institutions" (103).

3. Piercy is not the first Jewish writer to associate the power of the golem, a technological wonder of its time, with the power of the computer. In "The Golem of Prague and the Golem of Rehovot," a speech dedicating a new computer in Israel in 1964, Gershom Scholem, the scholar of Jewish mysticism and Kabbalah, argued for similarities between the two creations and named the newly built computer Golem Aleph (Golem A).

4. Piercy actually evokes two complementary narratives of male appropriation of creation from two different traditions: Mary Shelley's *Frankenstein* and the golem story that may have influenced Shelley.

5. The mayor's name is an intricate linguistic joke. "Malachy Mavett" is a play on the Hebrew "malach hamavett," the Angel of Death; the nickname Matt Mavett also recalls the Hebrew letters inscribed on the golem's forehead; "met" means dead; "mavet" death.

6. Ozick articulates this stance in "Notes Toward Finding the Right Question."

7. Although Galford lives and writes in England, she is American by birth, training, and sensibility.

8. The dybbuk, like the golem is experiencing a general revival of literary interest. Chayefsky's *The Tenth Man* is a retelling of this folktale; Tony Kushner recently revised Ansky's *The Dybbuk*. Other women writers who revive the dybbuk for their purposes are Francine Prose in *Hungry Hearts* and Eleanor Reissa, who, with Zalman Mlotek, has written "Zise Khaloymes" a recent play in which the dead immigrant mother of an assimilated Jewish woman returns as a dybbuk; despite the daughter's attempt to exorcise her mother's dybbuk, she is influenced by her and returns to her Jewish identity.

9. This text is "a compilation of commentaries on Leviticus from the Roman era, second century C.E." (Albert 29)

10. A more detailed account of the Talmudic response to lesbian activity may be found in Albert, 29–32.

11. In her evocation of female supernatural power and the Goddess, long exiled from Jewish tradition (as noted for example in Rich's essay "The Primacy of the Mother," Kristeva's *Powers of Horror* [100] and the collection of essays, *The Absent Mother: Restoring the Goddess to Judaism and Christianity*), Galford indicates another explanation for the prevalence of the motif of the absent mother in the texts of Jewish women. Within this reading, the absent mother-emblemizes the Goddess, abjected by the male, overwhelmingly patriarchal Jewish God.

WORKS CITED

Adler, Rachel. 1988. The virgin in the brothel and other anomalies: character and context in the legend of Beruriah. *Tikkun* 3:28–32, 102–5.

Albert, Rebecca. 1997. *Like Bread on the Seder Plate: Jewish Lesbians and the Transformation of Tradition*. New York: Columbia University Press.

Ansky, S. 1998. *A Dybbuk and Other Tales of the Supernatural*. Adapted by Tony Kushner, translated by Joachim Neugroschel. New York: Theatre Communications Group.

———. *The Dybbuk and Other Writings*. 1992. Translated by Golda Werman. New York: Schocken.

Biale, Rachel. 1995. *Women and Jewish Law: The Essential Texts, Their History, and Their Relevance for Today*. New York: Schocken.

Bloom, Harold. 1973. *The Anxiety of Influence*. London: Oxford University Press.

Chayefsky, Paddy. 1961. *The Tenth Man*. New York: Random House.

Cixous, Hélène. 1976. "The Laugh of the Medusa." Translated by Keith Cohen and Paula Cohen. *Signs: Journal of Women in Culture and Society* 1:875–93.

Galford, Ellen. 1994. *The Dyke and the Dybbuk*. Seattle: Seal Press.

Gilbert, Sandra and Susan Gubar. 1979. *The Madwoman in the Attic: The Woman Writer and the Nineteenth-Century Literary Imagination*. New Haven: Yale University Press.

Halberstam, Judith. 1995. *Skin Shows: Gothic Horror and the Technology of Monsters*. Durham: Duke University Press.

Hamill, Pete. 1997. *Snow in August*. New York: Warner.

Isler, Alan. 1997. *The Bacon Fancier*. New York: Penguin.

Katz, Judith. 1992. *Running Fiercely Toward a High Thin Sound*. Ithaca, NY: Firebrand Books.

Kristeva, Julia. 1982. *Powers of Horror: An Essay on Abjection*. Translated by Leon S. Roudiez. New York: Columbia University Press.

Minkin, Jacob S. 1941. "Golem." *The Universal Jewish Encyclopedia*. Edited by Isaac Landman. 10 vols. New York: *The Universal Jewish Encyclopedia*.

Moers, Ellen. 1976. *Literary Women: The Great Writers*. New York: Doubleday.

Niditch, Susan. 1983. The cosmic Adam: man as mediator in rabbinic literature. *Journal of Jewish Studies* 34:137–46.

Ozick, Cynthia. 1979. Notes toward finding the right question: fifteen brief meditations. *Lilith* 6:19–29.

———. 1997. *The Puttermesser Papers*. New York: Knopf.

Piercy, Marge. 1991. *He, She and It*. New York: Fawcett.

Pirani, Alix., ed. 1991. *The Absent Mother: Restoring the Goddess to Judaism and Christianity*. London: Mandala.

Rich, Adrienne. 1979. Jane Eyre: the temptations of a motherless woman. In *On Lies, Secrets, and Silence: Selected Prose, 1966–1978*, 89–106. New York: Norton.

———. 1986. The primacy of the mother. In *Of Woman Born: Motherhood as Experience and Institution*, 84–109. New York: Norton.

Schifrin, Daniel R. 1997. A play for all seasons. *Hadassah Magazine* 78:32–35.

Scholem, Gershom. 1995. The Golem of Prague and the Golem of Rehovot. In *The Messianic Idea in Judaism and Other Essays on Jewish Spirituality*, 335–340. New York: Schocken.

Shelley, Mary. 1963. *Frankenstein*. London: Dent.

Showalter, Elaine. 1977. *A Literature of Their Own: British Novelists from Bronte to Lessing*. Princeton: Princeton University Press.

Taitz, Emily. 1986. Kol Ishah—The voice of woman: where was it heard in medieval Europe? *Conservative Judaism* 38:46–61.

Woolf, Virginia. 1929. *A Room of One's Own*. New York: Harcourt Brace Jovanovich.

Zborowski, Mark and Elizabeth Herzog. 1952. *Life Is with People: The Culture of the Shtetl*. New York: Schocken.

The Reclamation of the Feminine Divine: "Walking in My Body Like a Queen" in Lee Smith's *Fair and Tender Ladies*

Linda J. Byrd

IN LEE SMITH'S 1988 EPISTOLARY NOVEL, *FAIR AND TENDER LADIES,* Smith successfully rewrites the male religious text and envisions a feminine alternative to traditionally patriarchal Christian religion. Ivy Rowe, the novel's sacred-sexual-maternal protagonist, is a female character who inspires veneration and religious respect by her association with divinity. Smith's consistent use of goddess imagery in empowering females serves as a direct reflection of the author's personal quarrel with traditional Christianity and her struggle with the absence of the feminine divine.[1] In the novel, Smith challenges a religion that places sacredness solely in the male domain with the Father God and provides an alternative spirituality based upon a female deity.

Ivy Rowe serves as a reunification of the multitudinous qualities of the original Great Mother Goddess who discovers and accepts the divinity within herself. One of the major battles of Ivy's life is an internal one in which she has always sensed a disturbing discrepancy between what she knows in her heart and what traditional Christianity teaches; she fails to find any comfort or strength in conventional patriarchal religion. Lee Smith voiced a similar personal conflict in an interview with Susan Ketchin: "Ivy is like me; she is unable to find a religion that suits her—an organized religion" (51). Ivy's moral and theological struggles begin early as she writes to a Dutch pen-pal (even though Hanneke never responds); feeling angry and alone, Ivy writes: "[God] is not good or bad ether one. I think it is that He does not care" (17). Ivy never sends this letter, but she continues to search for something in which to have faith, something to provide her with the hope that cannot be found in the patriarchal "anti-woman" mountain church to which she is exposed (Ketchin 54). She writes to her teacher, Mrs. Brown, who has consistently suggested that Ivy pray about her hardships, that she cannot pray, so she knows she is evil, but she doesn't feel evil. Ivy writes: "no I do not pray, nor do I think much of God. It is not right what he sends on people. . . . too much to bare" (32).

In *Rebirth of the Goddess: Finding Meaning in Feminist Spirituality*, theological scholar Carol Christ explains her own realization that something was "wrong with the traditional image of God" that insisted on the dominance of a male father and totally obliterated a female mother. Not unlike Ivy, Christ became "increasingly alienated from God" and found herself unable to attend church or pray to this patriarchal God (2). Realizing she would never be "in his image," Christ struck out on a search for a female deity, a search that eventually led her to the Goddess. Likewise, Ivy's search will also lead to feminine divinity.

Ivy never experiences anything she considers spiritual until she attends one of Sam Russell Sage's prayer meetings in Majestic with Miss Gertrude Torrington, a missionary. Ivy calls the sermon "scarry," with people "crying and then yelling out," and Mr. Sage describing death as a hungry animal "licking his chops" right outside the tent. Ivy writes to Beulah: "I could feel the firey hand of God clutching me in the stomach," but she is prevented from professing her faith by Miss Torrington's "sick spell." Only when Ivy and Miss Torrington get away from the tent does Ivy feel "the firey hand of God let go of my stomach," and Ivy hopes she will not die any time soon since she has yet to be saved (93–94).

Ivy's stomach pain may also signify her emerging sexuality. French feminist Luce Irigaray contends that women's somatic pain is a manifestation of their need for identity ("Women-Mothers" 52). This pain also symbolizes their hunger for an image of the ideal, a divine female against which to measure themselves ("Limits" 111). Both Miss Torrington's "sick spell" and Ivy's stomach pain suggest the absence of feminine divinity in their lives, a void that can only be filled by a deity who unites spirituality and female sexuality.

Smith associates sexual passion with religious passion, the "firey hand" indicating both. The symbolic bond between religion and sexuality initially occurs when Ivy discovers Lonnie Rash, a young boarder at Geneva's who is working in the lumber business. Ivy says that Lonnie stares at her all the time "like he is touching me under my cloths," and that when he is in the same room with her, she feels "that firey hand again and cant hardly breth" (97). In fact, both patriarchal religion and her relationship with Lonnie prove to be suffocating experiences for Ivy. To explain, artist Caz Love describes her feelings of anger and sadness at growing up in a society which robs us of the female deity: "Sometimes I feel like the patriarchy is choking me, has been choking me my whole life," a salient expression of Ivy's sense of suffocation and abandonment (qtd. in Christ 6–7). Ivy thinks of Jane Eyre's experience of feeling "a firey hand in her vitals" when Mister Rochester kisses her and says she knows that such a feeling is a warning from God that "you are bad" (98). God prevents Jane from running away with Rochester, but Ivy says she does not have God to turn to since she is not saved.

Ivy continues to rebel against ownership and any person or belief system that attempts to possess/suffocate her. Although Miss Torrington tells Ivy that God has sent her to Majestic to "save" Ivy, that Ivy has been given to her "by God as a sacred responsibility," Ivy sees Miss Torrington as "the Ice Queen." In competition with Lonnie Rash for Ivy's time and attention, Miss Torrington tells Ivy: "I feel it is a *sin*, Ivy, a great sin, if we do not use our tallents that God has given us, if we do not live up to our potenshal," asking Ivy to go to Boston with her to be properly educated. At the thought of such an opportunity, Ivy feels something like an electrical shock as she listens to Miss Torrington's words and "feel[s] her breth soft as a whisper on my neck" (100–102). Because Miss Torrington, a missionary, ostensibly offers Ivy the correct path to fulfill her "potenshal" and perhaps even serves as Ivy's "salvation," and since Ivy, a bright and eager student, feels starved for information and craves a formal education, she agrees to go to Boston. Even at this young age, Ivy perceives the path to freedom and fulfillment as one based on education and betterment of herself, unlike many earlier Smith protagonists who, trapped within patriarchy, focus only on men.

Yet Ivy is thrown into a state of total confusion about love, religion, and her fundamental beliefs when, during a private drawing lesson Miss Torrington, while looking over Ivy's shoulder at her drawing, kisses Ivy on the neck. Ivy writes to Silvaney: "I froze . . . right there with my pencil above the tree. I could not breth, I could not think what to do" (105). Again, as she has felt with Lonnie and at church, Ivy feels choked, robbed of breath. This experience marks and changes the course of

Ivy's life, and, much later, in Ivy's last letter to Silvaney, when Ivy is close to death and describing the shifting images in her mind, she writes that she sees "Miss Torrington so severe her kiss like fire on the back of my neck yet first born of all my kisses all my life" (316). As a nineteen-year-old girl, Ivy is incapable of accepting or understanding this demonstration of physical affection from another woman, but as years pass and Miss Torrington continues to correspond with Ivy, faithfully sending packages every Christmas to Ivy and her children, Ivy comes to understand what Miss Torrington had written to her in a letter not long after her departure from Majestic: "there are kinds and kinds of love and that sometimes we confuse them being only mortal as we are" (114). Irigaray argues that for women to discover and reclaim their sexual identity and desires, they must also embrace their "auto-eroticism," their "narcissism," their "heterosexuality," and their "homosexuality" since women, having first identified with another woman's body (the mother), "always stand in an archaic and primal relationship with what is known as homosexuality" ("Bodily Encounter" 44). Only after Ivy's affair with Honey Breeding and her recognition of the divinity of female flesh is she able to understand the many types of love to which Miss Torrington referred.

Ivy's calling Miss Torrington's kiss the "first born" of all her kisses and comparing the kiss to fire reiterates that Miss Torrington ignites Ivy's passion for knowledge and that her kiss perhaps impels Ivy to have sex with Lonnie Rash to validate her heterosexuality. In Ivy's relationship with Lonnie, as Dorothy Hill points out, "Smith acknowledges the need to address the purely erotic, but she sees it for what it is," for Ivy doesn't love Lonnie; she's simply sexually attracted to him (115–16). Admitting the thrill of Lonnie's hands on her body and the attractiveness of his muscled arms, Ivy is equally disturbed that Lonnie cannot read or write and has no desire to learn. Ivy writes to Silvaney that she has "let him put his tonge way down in my mouth and the firey hand grabbed me then for good," once more associating physical passion with religious passion. Ivy yearns for the sensation of the "firey hand," writing to Silvaney: "I know this is bad but it feels so good" (98). Like Carol Christ, and even Lee Smith herself, Ivy cannot condone a religious system that upholds the "classical dualisms of spirit and nature, mind and body, rational and irrational, male and female" (xiv). Ivy associates physical passion with guilt, but she is a sexual, sensual young woman and chooses to explore her sexuality anyway; however, no "firey hand" is mentioned during Ivy's first sexual intercourse, suggesting the absence of intensity and passion in this sexual union.

The pain Ivy experiences during sexual intercourse for the first time is indicative of the pain she must endure as a result of her decision to have sex with Lonnie, for immediately after their love-making, Ivy is overcome with sadness, writing to Silvaney: "I knew why [I feel sad], because I have lost it now, Majestic Virginia which used to be mine. And this room in Geneva Hunts boardinghouse is not my own either, not any more, I have lost it too because of bringing Lonnie up here" (107). Ivy has lost much more than her virginity since she will soon discover her pregnancy and inability to go to Boston to follow her dream of acquiring a proper education.

Ivy eventually decides to marry Oakley Fox because he seems to offer her an opportunity to redeem herself for her past behavior, a chance for salvation, much as Miss Torrington had done earlier. Ivy seems to be perpetually searching for some type of salvation outside herself. In *Motherself: A Mythic Analysis of Motherhood*, Kathryn Rabuzzi discusses how patriarchal ideology pushes sexual union as "a desirable goal for salvation" and notes that if a woman desires to be saved from herself, "yes, sexual ecstasy may work," and Ivy has indeed searched for salvation, with no success, in her sexual relationships (105). But Ivy must find salvation within herself, in her psyche, a "place in which both divine and demonic elements of a collective nature manifest themselves," not in a relationship with another person (6). Moreover, Oakley's feelings for Ivy have always involved a sense of ownership, hinting at an incipient conflict. Even after their marriage, Oakley tells Ivy: "You are a sassy woman but you are mine" (192). But Ivy, connecting this natural man (appropriately named "Oakley") to her father, responds to Oakley's closeness to nature. Writing to Silvaney about her marriage to Oakley, Ivy explains: "And when Oakley kisses me, it seems like I can hear Daddy saying, *Slow down, slow down now, Ivy. This is the taste of spring*" (175). As Rabuzzi acknowledges, nature often functions as the location for sacredness and Ivy's attraction to Oakley reflects her sense of the divine in nature (6).

The "firey hand of God" no longer clutches Ivy's stomach at church or in the bedroom with her husband as Ivy gradually realizes that neither Oakley nor God will "save" her. In an interview with Nancy Parrish, Smith admitted her lack of faith in the male-imaged God: "I *wish* I could believe in religion as Oakley

Fox did, but I really can't," and neither can Ivy (399). After giving birth to five more children and a sixth pregnancy that doesn't come to full term, all over a period of nine years, a feeling of resignation gradually replaces Ivy's old passion. About going to church, Ivy says: "It don't make· me feel better nor worse" (205). Whereas Oakley continues to derive pleasure from working with the land despite the deterioration of his health, Ivy writes in a letter to Silvaney: "when his work is done of an evening then it is *done*, for he don't have to mend the clothes or can the corn or feed the baby" (200). Here Ivy perfectly articulates the gap between the roles of husband/father and wife/mother; the work never subsides for the female while the male at least can rest at the end of his workday. Ivy begins to fear that she and Oakley are falling into the same trap her own parents did, for work and children are wearing her down, and her image of Oakley has become one of a man constantly working, with his back bent and his face always turned away from her.

At age thirty-seven and the mother of five children, Ivy suffers a metaphorical death as she sinks into what Irigaray explains as a "depressive collapse," the physical expression of years of inaudible pain ("Women-Mothers" 48). For six years, Ivy writes nothing. During this period of not expressing her feelings through letters, Ivy falls into what she calls "a great soft darkness, a blackness so deep and so soft that you can fall in there and get comfortable and never know you are falling in at all" (193). She wonders if this is what happened to her mother, who was never able to climb out. In *The Moon and the Virgin: Reflections on the Archetypal Feminine*, Nor Hall explains the motif of descent as essential in a woman's search for self (206). Ivy's feelings of falling into a dark hole, "going under," represent the intensity of her need to discover her self apart from her children and her husband (24). And, as Katherine Kearns notes, Ivy's silence (the absence of her letters) is like a loss of self for her as writing always was a way of validating her experiences and her life (189).

Ivy ultimately writes to Silvaney that she is "tired unto death," and that when Maudy, her baby, nurses, "it is like she is sucking my life right out of me." Even though she eats, Ivy can't gain any weight, describing herself as "nothing but skin and bones," a "dried-up husk . . . leeched out by hard work and babies." Ivy expresses this loss of self perfectly when she says she feels like "bits and pieces of me have rolled off and been lost along the way," existing in a state of temporary paralysis, as if she's been "flung down into darkness, frozen there" (193–94). Irigaray addresses the problem of the woman-mother torn to pieces, fragmented, "splitting apart," as "volume without contours" unable to articulate her feelings and therefore silent ("Volume" 53–54). Admitting that she never dreams anymore, never goes anywhere, and can not take an interest in reading anymore, Ivy says all she wants to do when she's not working is rest, "lean back and shut my eyes and fall straight as a plum down into that darkness" (194). But Ivy will eventually regain movement through starting to write her letters again and coming to know her inner sacred self.

Ivy's feelings of "wildness" finally resurface after many years of submergence in her subconscious while she lost herself in the role of the domestic wife. Writing to Silvaney, Ivy gives reasons for her re-emerging turbulence that help to explain the conflict she is experiencing between expressing her sexuality and performing the duties motherhood demands:

> And yet you know that I love Oakley. He is my life. I love this farm, and these children, and Oakley, with all my heart. But there is something about a man that is *too good* which will drive you crazy, you can't hardly stand it. It makes you want to run or scream or roll down the hill in the leaves the way we used to do, never checking for rocks, not thinking where we might land. It makes you want to dance in the thunderstorm like we danced up on Pilgrim Knob. (209)

Here Ivy metaphorically describes exactly what is to come with Honey Breeding since Ivy will go away with this man, leaving her husband and family, never "checking for rocks" or thinking of "where she might land" or what she stands to lose. Irigaray argues that paralysis of sexual expression manifests itself in desires to "scream" and engage in destructive behavior ("Women-Mothers" 52). Ivy's wish to dance on the mountaintop powerfully reflects her need to honor and communicate with the Goddess in a ritualistic dance of ecstasy. Anne Baring and Jules Cashford explain one interpretation of the dance is "the soul's wandering . . . where obstacles in the way of reaching the centre symbolize the sacrifices that progressively make possible the way forward, until at the centre the union creates transformation, and . . . allows rebirth" (136–37). Ivy's imagined "rolling down the hill" and over rocks in her path suggests her progress toward integration and regeneration although the sacrifices she makes are great, but necessary, for meeting the Goddess.

It is only when Ivy deserts her husband and children and climbs to the top of Blue Star Mountain with Honey Breeding, the "bee man," that she recognizes and reclaims the divinity within herself. The name "Honey Breeding" clearly suggests the union of male and female ("breeding") and the sweetness ("honey") of such a union. On first meeting him, Ivy describes Honey as "skinny, wiry, with pale thick curly gold hair on his head and thick gold eyebrows that nearabout grow together, and hair all over him like spun gold on his folded forearms," then later notes that he has "golden elf-hair curling in his ears" and "even his back [i]s almost covered with little bitty golden hairs" (213).

In this description two points are worth mentioning in addition to the repetition of the color gold (a color Smith consistently uses to signal feminine divinity): the supernatural connotation of the word "elf," and Honey's connection to nature in resembling a bee himself.[2] Nor Hall notes the liminal nature of bees who, like elves, "move between worlds of dream and waking reality as if there were no boundaries" (232). Ivy even recognizes Honey's similarity to his own bees, going "*from woman to woman like a bee goes from flower to flower*," but she knows that he is "the last thing left to happen to me" (232–33). Honey deposits sweetness into each flower even as he takes nectar for himself. Noted Lithuanian archeologist Marija Gimbutas affirms that the bee was a symbol of regeneration and an epiphany of the Great Mother Goddess in her representation of regeneration (322). J. J. Bachofen concurs that "the bee was rightly looked upon as a symbol of the feminine potency of nature" (295). Furthermore, Honey resides in the woods, where sacred honey was gathered in ancient Minoan rituals. Ivy's memory of her last moments with Honey consists of his whistling and bees buzzing in the weeds and clover by the side of the road, the humming of bees traditionally understood to be "the 'voice' of the goddess" (Baring and Cashford 119). Honey is all mixed up in her mind with nature, sexuality, and divinity.

Ivy's relationship with this man represents what psychologists Eric and Joan Erikson call the wedding of the "two sides of our basic bisexuality which struggle for reconciliation in all of us" (qtd. in Doyle 37). For many centuries, the image of the Great Mother Goddess embodied male as well as female attributes, and many of the composite androgynous figures convey a sense of "the source that continually generates itself" (Baring and Cashford 74). In Ivy's union with Honey, both male and female are given divine qualities as Smith seeks to reunite the masculine and feminine in what Irigaray calls "an alliance between the divine and the mortal," where a sacred sexual encounter is a "celebration . . . not a disguised or polemic form of the master-slave relationship" that is merely a "meeting within the shadow or orbit of a God the Father who alone lays down the law, or the immutable mouthpiece of a single sex" ("Sexual Difference" 174). Dorothy Hill argues that with Honey and Ivy, Smith offers us a new sex god and sex goddess who are alike in size and essence in their reciprocal relationship based on equality (111).

In Smith's portrayal of Ivy and Honey, the writer offers the prototype for what theologian Rosemary Ruether calls "a new concept of relationships between persons" which is "not competitive or hierarchical but mutually enhancing" (26). Ivy acknowledges the communion she feels with Honey the second time he visits, before she actually goes away with him: "It's like he *is* me, some way, or I am him" (217), and in fact, the two will eventually become one in sexual union. In a letter to Silvaney, Ivy says that she is as big and strong as Honey and describes Honey's legs and rear as being stark white, just as Ivy's body is extremely white all over. As she and Honey lie tangled up together "till you couldn't tell who was who," Ivy says: "I think he *is* me and I am him, and it will be so forever and ever" (230). Ivy's union with Honey is necessary for her to animate that part of herself for which she has quested so long. Baring and Cashford call this missing element her "lost counterpart," retrievable only in "the restoration of the image of the goddess" through her connection with Honey and her "return to the divine world" (628). Ivy writes to Silvaney that she perceives she has reclaimed a part of herself that she "had lost without even knowing it was gone. Honey had given me back my very soul," (232).

Honey's close association with nature further links him to the Great Mother Goddess and sacred sexuality. Described as "a woods creature fetched up somehow from the forest," Honey is strongly linked to Silvaney in his mysterious origins and in the necessity of his existence for Ivy to feel fully alive.[3] As Honey approaches the orchard, a place Ivy describes as "a sea of pale pink flowers," he "walk[s] right through them like he owned it," whistling "like a bird." Ivy, "in a fever" after he leaves, thinks she must be going through "the change of life" (213–15). But this feeling of fiery wildness and passion will continue until she goes away with Honey and together they climb to the highest point of Blue Star Mountain to an area "covered with little white flowers like stars" (225). Ivy writes to Silvaney: "it felt natural to me to be here, to have come up this mountain with this man" (237).

With her portraiture of Honey Breeding, Smith offers her most obvious and significant personification of the dichotomized male in her depiction of him as a divinity (Hill 112). From his first appearance in the novel, Honey is powerfully aligned with divinity as he symbolically offers to Ivy the chance for rebirth. Honey is the fictional Lochinvar personified;[4] it is little wonder Ivy doubts his actual existence and thinks she might have "immaginned [him] until he came true" (213). At first glance, Ivy views Honey "outlined against the sun" with "the sun a blaze behind his head . . . sho[oting] out in rays," forming a golden halo (212). Ivy can hardly see him for the dazzling brightness of the light, and after their affair, Ivy will always remember "those moments with Honey as flashes of light" (247). Baring and Cashford trace the image of light as associated with both the goddess and god, "the androgyny of the primal source," to as far back as Sumeria and connect it with "divine unity" (629). Later, when the two are on the top of the mountain lying in the grass, significantly, Honey spreads Ivy's hair out around her head, creating a halo for her too. Further evidence of Honey's divinity appears on his visit when Ivy and Honey climb the mountain together and he tells her that he is the third of three sons (linking himself to the number three) and that he's from "noplace particular" (224). Honey cannot tolerate being in a city or town; he has "to have mountains, and roam." He is a free spirit incapable of containment, much like Silvaney (235). The sacred mountains, which "perhaps more than any other natural objects . . . represented the Great Mother," are Honey's natural habitat (Walker 695).

Smith enacts a healing reversal in this depiction of a male divinity whose presence supplies Ivy with the necessary insight to enable her to recognize the sacredness in herself. Honey's liminal presence allows Ivy to discover the divinity within herself and to accept the existence of the female deity. Ivy describes the days after meeting Honey as seeming to happen "under water," and she feels like she's "swimming through them," associating her experience with water and rebirth (214). In a setting rife with goddess imagery, as Ivy sits on a big warm rock beside a mysterious pool of water she has never seen, and Honey plays with her long red hair, she thinks: "the funny thing is, it was like I had known him. For ever, for always, years and years and years. . . . We were old hat, him and me" (216). And in fact, they are "old hat," as they reunite the masculine and feminine divine principles, what Jung called the androgynous elements *animus* and *anima*, and what the Taoist tradition calls the yang and yin (Hall 31).

Ivy recognizes the timeless divinity in Honey and automatically connects with him, a face she can see and touch, unlike the face of the God that Ivy "couldn't see" but that Oakley senses when he looks out from the mountain (205). The patriarchal God is intangible for Ivy; she must, as Carol Christ notes, discover "a female image of God" in order to experience rebirth (3). And, paradoxically, it is Honey who provides the divine mirrored presence for which Ivy has yearned all of her life. In her letter to Silvaney when she tells about her first sensations of being "on fire," Ivy refers to Honey twice as "Him," with a capital "H" (208). Although Ivy's spelling and grammar are erratic in her early letters, she doesn't often capitalize common nouns or pronouns, especially in letters written during her middle adult years, so one strongly suspects Smith is purposefully linking Honey to Christ in his offering Ivy "salvation" of self.

As Ivy stands naked at the edge of the cliff at the top of the mountain, Honey tells her: "you look like a Queen," and he creates for her "a double starflower crown" and places it on her head, saying: *"Now stand up and walk, you will be a Queen"* (229, 233). In regaining her soul, Ivy has become a queen, the sexual maternal Goddess that mythologist Paul Friedrich calls for to heal the split between sexuality and motherhood. In naming Ivy "queen," Honey compares her to the queen bee, "whom all the others serve during their brief lives" since she is "an epiphany of the goddess herself." Furthermore, Honey, as an image of the "miraculous interconnectedness of life," parallels the "busy bee, following the impulsion of its nature to pollinate the flowers and gather their nectar to be transformed into honey" (Baring and Cashford 73). In elevating Ivy to the level of a queen, a goddess, Smith imagines a mythology that permits female embodiment of the divine. As Carol Christ notes, the Goddess "can only be understood if we question the assumptions that divinity is transcendent of the body [and] nature"; Ivy is finally able to accept her own female body and recognize her physical beauty (78–79). She has arrived at the summit of Blue Star Mountain, where she imagines Silvaney has been quite often, and has reached her highest point sexually and spiritually.

It is only after Ivy's interlude with Honey that she is at all able to love herself, her husband, and her children completely. With Lonnie, Ivy had discovered her sexuality; with Oakley, she had buried the wild side of herself. Finally, with Honey, she integrates these as he feeds her hunger for language, sweetness, wildness, and divinity. A couple of years after the affair and Ivy's return to her family, she realizes that now Oakley is paying attention to her, that his face is no longer turned away. Ivy notes that Oakley is always "circling around" her, a movement linked to divinity like the hawk that circled while she made love with Honey on the mountain top and the hawk that Ivy's mother saw circling the sky the first day she came to Sugar Fork. Gradually, Ivy becomes more attuned to her own sacredness separate from Honey Breeding. She writes to Silvaney about one Sunday morning when her entire family is eating breakfast and "for a minute . . . I *felt* like church" (247).

Ivy's struggle with religion and the idea of salvation is not yet complete, however. When she begins to attend church with Oakley occasionally, she notices that no one even looks at her during the invitational anymore. She decides that people either think she's already saved or are just accustomed to her "sinful" nature. Then, after a painful experience with her brother Garnie, who has taken up with the famous preacher Sam Russell Sage and become a preacher himself, Ivy decides: "I will not go to any Heaven that has got a place in it for Garnie Rowe," writing to Silvaney about the day she "was not saved" (254). Garnie shouts at Ivy, calling her "a whore and an abomination," and chastises her for her sin of pride which is "an abomination to the Lord." Ivy admits to Silvaney that what Garnie is saying has some truth in it, writing: "I *have* been proud Silvaney, in my body and my mind, I am proud still, and if this is sin then I must claim it as my own" (260–61). As Hélène Cixous insists a woman must do, Ivy refuses to "censor the body," which would in effect "censor breath and speech at the same time." Instead, she writes her defiance—"an act which will . . . 'realize' the decensored relation of woman to her sexuality, to her womanly being, giving her access to her native strength; it will give her back her goods, her pleasures, her organs, her immense bodily territories which have been kept under seal" (250). Ivy significantly signs this letter to Silvaney: "Your loving, proud, and hellbent sister" (263). At this point Ivy has determined that salvation through this God is not a viable option for her.

The divinity Ivy has discovered within herself that has caused her to "feel like church" and experience pride in both her mind and her body is the only form of religion to which she will adhere. The cruel and punitive patriarchal God that Garnie advocates offers no model for embodiment of the sacred in female flesh, symbolically reinforced through Garnie's Bible-quoting "sermon" to Ivy in which he consistently uses the masculine pronoun to represent Ivy: "Can a man take fire in his bosom, and his clothes not be burned? Whoso commiteth adultery with a woman lacketh understanding. He that doeth it destroyeth his own soul." Ivy, disturbed by the gendered pronouns, pointedly asks, "What about the woman? . . . For that is all about a man" (261).[5]

Smith's depiction of Ivy seems to usher in what Patricia Doyle calls "a new era await[ing] realization," a woman uniting within herself "the previously warring alternatives of separate male or female consciousness alone" (38). On her deathbed, Ivy reflects on the purpose of her life and reasserts her inner divinity. She ponders having remained on this sacred mountain, one time going "as high as you can go" up the mountain with Honey Breeding, whose "hair shone golden in the morning light," the image of sweet divinity. Before Ivy's spirit peacefully "sails away" from her body, she writes: "there is a time for every purpose under heaven" as the hawk in the bright blue sky flies around in circles, permanently linking Ivy with divinity. Ivy's last thoughts are of "the old bell ringing" like she used to ring it "to call them home," as she has just "called home" all the memories of her rich life. The last line of the letter, which is left unpunctuated and unsigned, emphasizes Ivy's divine nature: "oh I was young then, and I walked in my body like a Queen" (316–17). Leaving her physical body, she has certainly achieved goddess stature, divine in her own right, successfully healing the split between sexuality and motherhood and aligning herself with the first and oldest female deity, the Great Mother Goddess.

In an interview with Susan Ketchin, Smith commented that Ivy dies without finding God in a traditional sense, acknowledging: "And I might too" (51). Smith's depiction of Ivy, however, offers an alternative option for female characters, perhaps the ultimate option in that, given her limitations and choices, internal conflicts and struggles, Ivy discovers and honors the sacredness of her own body and mind, making divine sense of her life and providing much-needed feminine inspiration.

NOTES

Smith, Fair and Tender Ladies, 317. The original quote is: "oh I [Ivy] was young then, and I walked in my body like a Queen."

1. My contention that Smith (in her writing) reaches back to the archetypal image of the Great Mother Goddess to provide a mythological foremother for female characters is strictly my own interpretation of her work. I am in no way suggesting that Smith consciously drew from this prehistoric female deity, but rather arguing that her writing poignantly reflects the collective unconscious and the disturbing lacuna (for women) in traditional patriarchal Christianity.

2. The sweetness of honey, a motif Smith introduces in Ivy's first letter to Hanneke, continues throughout the novel even before Ivy meets Honey Breeding, who serves as the culmination of Ivy's search for the sweet sexuality within herself. Barbara Walker explains the symbolic significance of honey as a "substance of ressurection-magic" since it was one of the few natural preservatives of which ancients were aware. Honey was regarded as the Goddess' "sacred essence" and falling into a jar of honey became a metaphor for death and rebirth (407).

3. The emphasis Ivy places on her symbolic relationship with Silvaney suggests the necessity of merging mind and body, spirituality and sexuality, in order to achieve integration and wholeness. In *Rebirth of the Goddess*, Carol Christ discusses at length these dualisms on which patriarchal religion operates.

4. As a young girl, Ivy loved the poem about gallant young Lochinvar, described as having yellow hair that stood out around his face "like rays of the sun" (51).

5. In his article, "All in the Family," Tom Rash argues that Honey Breeding represents "something dangerous, electric, forbidden" and that once Ivy achieves "the ideal, she now finds her life as wife and mother to be more satisfactory" (134). "The ideal" for Ivy is the discovery and open expression of her sacred sexuality which Honey, in his divine configuration, awakens within her. With past lovers such as Lonnie and Franklin, Ivy discovered nothing within herself, but rather looked to the male partner for meaning and fulfillment. With Honey, she finds completion within herself. If Ivy's life as wife and mother is "more satisfactory" after her affair with Honey, it is because she is brought back to life, or reborn, as a result of her union with Honey whereas before, she was spiritually and sexually dead, resigned to that "great soft darkness."

WORKS CITED

Bachfen, J. J. *Myth, Religion, and Mother Right.* 1926. Translated by Ralph Manheim. Princeton: Princeton University Press.

Baring, Anne, and Jules Cashford. 1991. *The Myth of the Goddess: Evolution of an Image.* New York: Viking.

Christ, Carol P. 1997. *Rebirth of the Goddess: Finding Meaning in Feminist Spirituality.* New York: Addison-Wesley Publishing Co., Inc.

Cixous, Hélène. 1980. The laugh of the Medusa. In *New French Feminisms: An*

Anthology, edited by Elaine Marks and Isabelle de Courtivron, 245–64. Amherst: University of Massachusetts Press.

Doyle, Patricia Martin. 1974. Women and religion: psychological and cultural implications. In *Religion and Sexism: Images of Woman in the Jewish and Christian Traditions,* edited by Rosemary Radford Ruether, 15–39. New York: Simon and Schuster.

Gimbutas, Marija. 1989. *The Language of the Goddess.* San Francisco: Harper & Row.

Hall, Nor. 1980. *The Moon and the Virgin: Reflections on the Archetypal Feminine.* New York: Harper.

Hill, Dorothy Combs. 1992. *Lee Smith.* New York: Twayne.

Irigaray, Luce. 1991. The bodily encounter with the mother. In *The Irigaray Reader,* edited by Margaret Whitford, 34–46. Cambridge: Basil Blackwell.

———. The limits of transference. 1991. In *The Irigaray Reader,* edited by Margaret Whitford, 105–17. Cambridge: Basil Blackwell.

———. Sexual difference. 1991. In *The Irigaray Reader,* edited by Margaret Whitford, 165–77. Cambridge: Basil Blackwell.

———. Volume without contours. 1991. In *The Irigaray Reader,* edited by Margaret Whitford, 53–67. Cambridge: Basil Blackwell.

———. Women-Mothers, the silent substratum of the social order. 1991. In *The Irigaray Reader,* edited by Margaret Whitford, 47–52. Cambridge: Basil Blackwell.

Kearns, Katherine. 1991. From shadow to substance: the empowerment of the artist figure in Lee Smith's fiction. In *Writing the Woman Artist,* edited by Suzanne W. Jones, 175–95. Philadelphia: University of Pennsylvania Press.

Ketchin, Susan. 1994. *The Christ-Haunted Landscape: Faith and Doubt in Southern Fiction.* Jackson: University Press of Mississippi.

Parrish, Nancy. 1992. Interview with Lee Smith. *Appalachian Journal* 19, no. 4: 394–401.

Rabuzzi, Kathryn Allen. 1988. *Motherself: A Mythic Analysis of Motherhood.* Bloomington: Indiana University Press.

Ruether, Rosemary Radford. 1975. *New Woman, New Earth: Sexist Ideologies and Human Liberation.* New York: The Seabury Press.

Smith, Lee. 1989. *Fair and Tender Ladies.* New York: Ballantine Books.

Walker, Barbara G. 1996. *The Women's Encyclopedia of Myths and Secrets.* Edison, N.J.: Castle Books.

The Red Cow Effect: The Metramorphosis of Hallowing the Hollow and Hollowing the Hallow

BRACHA LICHTENBERG ETTINGER

"The register of extimacy is the register of sacrifice."
—J. A. Miller

INTRODUCTION: DEFERENCE OF IM-PURITY WITH-IN-TER HALLOWING AND HOLLOWING

MY MOTHER, THEY TELL—IT WAS BEFORE I WAS BORN—RAN ALONG the paths of the kibbutz one day and into the dining hall and cried out in panic: "A big red cow is chasing me!" The comrades turned around, and something did really come in after her, but it was small—not big, and black—not red, and it was a turkey, not a cow. My mother didn't know Hebrew then, but insisted on speaking it. The language she spoke was a mixture with vacillating doses of Polish and Hebrew, a "wandering" language that changed from day to day and improved with distressing slowness. I could not return her words to her because they were temporary and did not get stabilized in my memory, and also because she would not have recognized them; they were inventions, already forgotten. When I addressed her in Hebrew she would half-understand me, and when she addressed me in Hebrew, it would shame me. But also, she did not speak with me in her own mother-tongue, since in our home Polish was used only among the grown-ups, in order to speak about what had happened *there*. While I was preparing this essay, I asked her: "So, tell me, in what language did you speak with me?" She answered: "There wasn't so much to talk with you; it didn't matter so much, because *you* didn't speak at all." And she added, "I used to cry all nights because I thought you were mentally retarded."

57

I might have concluded from my experience with my wandering *mamalangue* that there is no touching a mother-tongue except through its translation into a father-tongue—but no! If in the phallic arena it represents a "nature" that the father-tongue has to replace in its constituting order; if the archaic mother is a phallic *objet a* (the object having a sense as absent), sacrificed by castration, and if mother-tongue is a metaphor for an archaic feminine foreignness hidden in me and in others, a concealed "origin/source" that is sacrificed by the subject in the passage to culture and is proffered as an offering to "the Other" in art-work—then I would like to suggest that in the matrixial borderspace[1] various tracks are opened toward and from a *mamalangue*, which was never a fixed origin anyway: lanes that are not a translation in terms of separation and substitution into another language but passageways of scattering and transmission-through-transformation. These lanes knit the *mamalangue* into a sub-symbolic, connectionist twilight web whose threads allow us a relative and partial coexistence with a foreign world and channel us toward the beauty and the pain of the different with no illusion of mastering it, banishing it, or assimilating it. The loss involved in this passage is an outcome of transformation and transmission, fragmentation and severalization, dispersal and sharing of the *already* joint and several, and not tearing-splitting, substitution and replacement. The symbol I chose for movement from the archaic uncanny expanse of joining *with-in-ter the Other* between life and death, between hallowing and hollowing and on-to the art-work, and from art to writing—art as *between art and theory,* is what I call the *Red Cow Effect.*

This effect is a metramorphosis composed of a cross-breed of this little story with the biblical ritual of the "Red Cow"—that sin-offering, which, like any sacrifice, serves as a symbol for connection between man and God and, unlike other sacrifices, is female. The biblical command is to dilute its ashes in water and spray it on the defiled for purification. In Judaism, the Red Cow is considered a paradoxical enigma because of its two-faced function: it both profanes or defiles the pure and purifies the defiled.

Judith Butler, commenting on Mary Douglas's *Purity and Danger,* argues that though Douglas shows how social taboos, imposed through binary distinctions like those of within and without, institute and maintain the boundaries of the body in identity as male and female, she can't point toward an alternative configuration of culture beyond the binary frame. "Ideas

about separating, purifying, demarcating and punishing transgressions have as their main function to impose system on an
inherently untidy experience" while "any kind of unregulated
permeability constitutes a site of pollution and endangerment"
(132). With Kristeva's "abject," "the alien is effectively established through (this) expulsion"; consolidation of inner and
outer, pure and defiled both maintain social regulation and control, and it establishes the Other as rejected and repulsive (Butler 133). The problem is not only how to deconstruct prohibition
sanctions that regulate "man" and "woman," "me" and "Other"
and constitute phallic Law and desire, but mainly how to
achieve "an openness to resignification and recontextualization" of sexuality, how to describe/invent another process of the
meaning of donation/revelation/production (Butler 134, 139).[2]
And, the problem is also, as Griselda Pollock puts it, to find a
way to symbolize nonphallic relations between several irreducible different (part) subjects and to generate not an image of the
trauma, but a symbol that allows the forcluded the relief of signification, a pathway into language.[3] Not only Law and Order,
but also Creation is founded in the phallic paradigm that under-
lines social conventions on clefting light and darkness, and on
the marking of a frontier between pure and impure, in order to
overcome the "abyss" that becomes its Other, its repressed side
which flickers from depths no longer accessible after the completion of the act of creation (Smirgel). Castration as a creative
principle institutes the "abyss" as the sacrificed. Yet another
sacrifice is that of the unsignified, the *objet a*—a waste, not just
repressed but forcluded and lost for the sake of culture. J. Chasquet Smirgel presents the castrative separation as a universal
principle of order, and not as related to social conventions or
ideology, and the breach of separation between subject and
object is presented as perversion.[4] Where indeed such a transgression in the phallic paradigm does stand for a collapse of the
difference between desire, phantasm, and event while castration
establishes the difference between event and representation,
my argument is that in the matrixial paradigm, differentiation-
in-transgression stands for a creative principle which does not
correspond to the phallic Law and Order yet does *not* replace
them either.[5] For the Matrix, creation is before-as-beside the
univocal line of birth/Creation-as-castration; it is in the im-pure
zone of *neither* day *nor* night, of *both* light *and* darkness. From
the prism that I have called *matrixial*, a feminine espacement
hollows channels of meaning and sketches an area of difference,

with sublimatory outlets and ethical values that are indeed paradoxical for the phallic paradigm. Matrixial aspects are articulated in/for/from art, *neither* via male castration and paternal prohibition *nor* via female bodily *jouissance*-without-sacrifice.[6] The Red Cow effect is a metramorphosis of *im-purity* as a *wandering between* pure and defiled: it negotiates *both* purity *and* impurity/defilement with no collapsing of each into the other or no separation intended to repress or exclude the darker side, while producing a third stance of im-purity. This metramorphosis vacillates its borderlinks as a requestioning in *deference*[7] of both poles, to be re-negotiated with each new encounter, with no refuge in the Phallus and no pre-arranged resolution.

DIVINE *JOUISSANCE* BY THE SACRIFICE OF THE RED COW

The scene described in the Old Testament sounds quite gender-neutral to speakers of English: You have to bring a "perfect" ["without blemish"] "red heifer," slay it, burn it, prepare what is called a *nida*-water from its ashes mixed with water, and scatter it over the defiled—someone who has touched a dead person—in order to purify him. But, in Hebrew, the episode drips with a femininity that cannot be sensed in the English version: from the "red *cow*" in the original Hebrew expression, which is a maternal symbol deriving from the root "p.r.h,"—meaning "fertility," "fecundity," "productivity," "fruitfulness," "was born"—in the King James Bible—a *"heifer,"* symbol for a young offspring. The term *nida-water* was translated as: "water of separation," in which we may find an "ideological" phallic interpretation of the Hebrew word *nida*. Nida may derive from the roots "n.d.h.," "n.o.d." or "n.d.d." "N.d.d." and "n.o.d." mean "wandering," "migration," "vacillating," "swinging," "shaking," "moving," "shifting," "mobile," "movable," "vagrancy," "fugitive," "nomad" etc.; "n.d.h." means "remove," "expel," "banish" and "excommunicate." Other interpretations of the word *nida* are derived from the root "y.d.a" which means "throw" and "sprinkle," "scattering" and "dispersing." Most meanings designate liquefied, flexible states, mobility and splashing, throwing, swinging and wandering. A common translation of *"nida* water" is indeed "water of sprinkling." The translators' choice of "water of separation" directs us toward the one official purpose of this sacrifice: to detach defilement from purity.

Separating and purifying is explicitly what the Red Cow sacrifice is about. But in Hebrew, a subnarrative is embedded inside the signifiers. We hear the shifting, vacillating, and dispersed vagrancy no less than the split and separation from impurity, and the special function for which the *Red Cow* is known in the Tradition is the two-sided, elastic, and paradoxical one of defiling the pure and purifying the impure. It is therefore well known as an enigma. In fact, a very common and major meaning of the term *nida*-water, often used in literary texts, has been totally eliminated from translation, even though it is emphasized in the classical interpretations of the Hebrew Scriptures: water of *menstrual blood*. Hartoum interprets this "menstrual water" as "woman's defilement/impurity": "Metaphorically, from woman's defilement/impurity to defilement/impurity in general, [and] the reference [here] is to water that removes the defilement" (76). The menstrual water that impurifies women purifies the sin-impurity?—Or else, menstrual water, defiled in one framework may stand for a specific in-between quality in an-other one, where her paradoxicality becomes its creative potentiality!

The Red Cow has additional paradoxical qualities inscribed in signifiers that point to opposite meanings at once. She is a *hatat*, generally translated as "sin-offering" stemming from the word "sin," yet it also means "sacrifice" as well as "holy to the Lord." The *hatat*, as Rashi interprets it, is a sacrifice that is meant only for God's *jouissance* and is forbidden for that of human beings. She is a hallowed, sanctified vow, whose signifier means both sin *and* holiness, sanctity *and* taboo. So much for the orthodox *halachic* interpretations of the text. And Rashi adds a *midrash* which emphasizes even more the motive of her femaleness erased entirely in the translation: the Red Cow is a symbol and an allegory for a *mother* who atones for her son's sin, the Golden Calf's. The Red Cow is not merely a simple offering compared to just any other. In the Epistle to the Hebrews in the *New Testament* she is likened to Jesus; both of them, perfect and without sin, pay with self-sacrifice for the sins of others. Thus, sin and atonement reveal themselves to be trans-subjective and transgressive between individuals and generations.[8]

The text of the Red Cow, like any text translated from Hebrew to English, has been neutered, de-sexuated, de-genderized, and de-eroticized. In the opposite passage from English to Hebrew, every text is gendered, sexuated, and eroticized; the text attests to the impossibility of translation by means of substitution. Almost every element which is in principle neutered in English, institutes masculinity or femininity in Hebrew; the subjects and the objects "belong" to one gender or the other, the verb designates sex, and so on. The subjects in *I-you* relations, neutral in English, address each other as feminine or masculine and speak from a masculine or feminine stance.[9] For English readers of the Red Cow episode it is difficult to sense its distinctive femaleness and maternality, and these readers may be startled to discover that this cow is so much a "woman-sacrifice"; English readers may prefer to turn her into a male, to prove she leans upon a male fantasy, or that menstrual water is no more contaminating or impurifying than any other blood. But for me, rejecting the femininity which is embedded in the signifiers of a text is a double-edged evasive strategy: from such a rejection, the perceived im-purity of the feminine will remain exactly the same in the eye of the phallus, and in the case before us—as a "woman" sacrifice structured on the authority of "castration." Furthermore, I would grieve to give up this particular manner of *divine jouissance* in favor of the phallus! The biblical sacrifice, usually a male symbolic figure, is meant to cause, or even satisfy God's desire and arise God's compassion, grace, and pardon. The eschewal of an-other feminine interpretation leaves us with a feminine *real* created from a phallic perspective only. I therefore suggest to focus upon the femininity of the Red Cow engraved in the Hebrew signifiers while working through to revise its symbolic value, to expose and draw out from its ever-there signifiers a matrixial *she-law* and gaze which indicates *jouissance* and establishes desire that evades the control of the phallic Law and Gaze. A paradox in the eye of the Phallus reveals itself as a metramorphosis in the eyes of the Matrix.

PROCESSES OF SEPARATION AND SUBSTITUTION IN THE EYE OF THE PHALLUS

We will have to make a long detour along the paths of psychoanalytical theory before returning to the Red Cow effect in order to understand it in the light of feminine sex-difference as an aesthetic-poïetic principle that emerges in the matrixial borderswerve without pretensions to exhaust the mystery of that powerful biblical enigma. Poïetic and aesthetic considerations, and artistic creation in general, are linked in psychoanalysis to sexuality, since we arrive at the function of art by way of libido, drives, part-objects (as present), and *objet a* (the object having a sense as absent). Since artistic creation is linked to the *objet a,* if it is entirely phallic, artistic creation from the psychoanalytic angle should be so as well. But, if it has matrixial aspects and we conceive of a matrixial *objet a* that participates in a *larger, not only-phallic-symbolic* Other, in an unconscious and subjectivizing Other that is not designated by the treasure of the signifiers only,[10] we may develop further ideas on art within the psychoanalytic field without them being appropriated by or produced for, the phallic paradigm.

For Freud, male's bodily specificity—the penis—is considered the *only* sex-difference for *both* sexes; the sexuality of girls is fundamentally male in character and the libido has only one essence.[11] "The sexuality of little girls is of a wholly *masculine* character"; "libido is invariably and necessarily of a *masculine* nature" (1905, 219). To that Freud later adds that only the "activity" and "passivity" meanings are *essential* as meanings of masculine and feminine respectively, while the *sociological* and *biological* are secondary (1915). "Little girls" are "little boys," and at the stage of the pregenital sadistic-anal organization, there is as yet no question of male and female; the antithesis between active and passive is the dominant question. At the following stage of infantile genital organization, which we now know about, *maleness* exists, but not femaleness. The antithesis here is between having a male genital and being castrated. It is not until development has reached its completion at puberty that the sexual polarity coincides with *male* and *female*; maleness combines *subject, activity,* and *possession of the penis*; femaleness takes over *object* and *passivity* (Freud 1923, 145).

We may conclude that the libido's status progressively moves from being considered masculine into being phallic-*male,* and its psychic inscriptions correspond to a phallic/castration paradigm which polarizes those who possess the penis and those who don't possess it into subjects and objects: "This phase [the phallic stage of organization] . . . presents a sexual object and some degree of convergence of the sexual impulses upon that object; but it is differentiated from the final organization of sexual maturity in *one essential respect*. For it *knows* only one kind of genital: *the male one*" (Freud 1924, 199–200). For both sexes, only one genital, namely the *male* one, comes into account. What is present, therefore, is not a primacy of the genitals, but a primacy of the *phallus*.[12] Thus, in the passage from the masculine/feminine to the male/female, Freud adds to the side of maleness linked to male bodily specificity a *subject* position: male is masculine (active) plus penis (the *only* organ relevant to sex-difference) plus subject's position, while femaleness is feminine (passive) plus castration (absence of this *only* organ) plus object's position. Accordingly, femininity, in Freud's "case histories," is mainly femininity in men, and also, the feminine for women is expected to be reflected by a man.[13] Freud used the concept of the Phallus, which was fabricated to deal with male sexuality, to speak of female sexuality as well: she doesn't have it and her position is characterized by the *penisneid*.

Lacan's phallic model incorporates Freud's and deviates from it at the same time. Lacan's famous statement that the woman does not exist and does not signify anything echoes Freud's remark on the pre-pubertial, and mainly pre-Oedipal non-existence of femaleness; but a shift in emphasis occurs: her "lack" in the Real inscribes "nothing" in the Symbolic for both males and females. For Lacan, the phallus, still echoing on the penis (organ in the real), mainly stands for a symbolic principle: it is a *signifier*. It is also the only imaginary representation of sex-difference, and "castration" (having/not-having) is the only passageway to significance. For a woman, the question of her sexuality is not only in terms of *not-having* it, but is in terms of her *being* it or not.

Lacan emphasizes the imaginary and symbolic counterparts of the organ: the phallus. The penis, like any other pre-genital organ, is subjugated as a part-object in the Oedipus complex to retroactive applications of symbolic "castration." In that sense, boys suffer the same symbolic castration as girls: both having to renounce the attachment to their own organ as a part-object, to corporeality, in order to attain the specifically human sphere of subjectivity. "Man" confronts the question of having/not having the phallus and "woman" of being it or not, as an object of/for man-subject. This means that boys give up what they had, while girls are supposed to renounce *what they do not have*, and *be* it through masquerade, as well as to construct *their* desire by the same mechanism—holding on to all kinds of "same" or "opposite" faces of it. The woman doesn't exist; her being is questioned; she wants to *be* the phallus. "It is in order to be the phallus, that is, the signifier of the desire of the Other, that the woman will reject an essential part of her femininity, notably all its attributes, through masquerade" (Lacan 1985, 84). For example, a woman takes upon herself a masquerade through which the original threatening object of desire becomes unrecognizable and she—desirable, or else she is a horrible figure of transgression of the paternal taboo, representing the pre-Oedipal mother desired by the son and therefore incarnating the threat of incest, castration, and psychosis, all intended by the expression: "essential part of her femininity"! Thus, woman is the distance opened from femininity described as "essential" and seen as what we may call *psycho*genic by the Phallus conceived as equipped with *all* possible *symbolo*genic qualities: the phallus as The Signifier without signified, the signifier of absence *and* difference, of difference *as* absence. The incest taboo established by the paternal Law separates son and mother and produces "desire" as repressed and infinitely displaced, and "subject" as split. Desire, as well as the subject, both phallic and patterned upon the male repression of the maternal body, are supposed to account for Desire and Subject in general. Thus, for Lacan, woman is a subject as well, by virtue of her participation in what we may call the *inside-the-phallus subjectivizing dimension* at the cost of a forever enigmatic "femininity."

In the phallic psychic arena (and in the psychoanalytic theory in general), feminine sexuality and the pre-Oedipal mother are structured and given meaning by the pair: phallus/castration. From the outset the Phallus appears as an intermediate concept that commands all three domains of the psyche: it is symbolic, it is imaginary, it is also *between* the Symbolic and the Imaginary, and it has also a correlate in the physical masculine Real—the penis. "A single and same marker dominates the whole register concerning the relationship of the sexuated . . . a privileged signifier. . . . All is reduced to this signifier: the phallus, precisely because it is not in the subject's system, since it does not represent the subject but . . . sexual jouissance as outside system, which is to say, absolute; sexual jouissance in so far as it has this privilege over all the others" (Lacan 1969). The *objet a* leans on a phallic Imaginary and Real, for having/not-having the male sex organ is its paradigmatic emblem, retroactively applied to all early separations: for example, the appearance/disappearance of the mother and the weaning from the maternal breast.

The Symbolic that is presented as a universal structure holding *all* significance is phallic.[14] It is structured like language by binary oppositions in which relations of exclusion resonate: "it is either him/her or me" for "speech is already caught-up in a network of symbolic couples and opposites" (Lacan 1981, 107, 126). "Castration" as equivalent to the Oedipus complex is presented as the sole transition-process that separates events from the Real while creating the subject as divided and the *objet a* as phallic. "The *objet a*, if taken only in Lacan's sense, is a container . . . of the effect of castration, containing the signification of castration" (Miller 1983). In the phallic model, part-objects of self and of what I call the *archaic m/Other* (pre-Oedipal bodily "samplings" of my-corpo*reality and* of my-m/Other) are "cut" and repressed through "castration" that turns them into *lacking* objects—into an *objet a* whose symbolic value is that of a *phallus*. The *objet a* is a trace of a trace[17] that remains forever a "cause of the desire"—and shapes it. The *objet a*—the lacking part-object which is analogous to the "woman" as an absent real Other, the *subject*—who emerges in its place (and *in place of* the "woman" that turns into a radical Other), and *sexuality,* are all shaped by this pair: phallus/castration that acts to separate from, and to replace, the feminine. Not only "the jouissance, sexually speaking, is phallic" but desire is also exclusively phallic, for any release of something from the corpo*real* sexual *jouissance* and partial-dimension to the Symbolic occurs by negation, separation, and displacement (Lacan, 1975, 14). "Castration is even the only liberator of desire that may be conceived of" (Miller 1983). "The so-called phallic jouissance is situated there, at the junction of the Symbolic with the Real. That goes for the subject which is sustained by the by-speak-being (*parl'être*) in the sense that *what I designate as being the unconscious* can be found here" (Lacan, "*Le sinthôme,*" 1975). The phallicity of the entire Unconscious is hereby at stake!

Feminine *jouissance* that is enveloped in its continuity aspires to release itself by *an-other objet a* that will shape a feminine dimension of desire and an-other unconscious zone; but any desire is formulated in the phallic model as castration of this continuity and the passability of *an-other desire* onto culture is prevented. In the transformational processes language allows: metaphor and metonymy, "jouissance is reduced to the phallic signifier" where there is no possible sublimation of the "woman" (Miller 1995).

Hidden Supplementary *Jouissance* and No Sexual Rapport

For Lacan, *any* significance kicks out the beyond-the-phallus femininity. And since *sexual rapport* stems from the forcluded feminine side,[16] "there is no sexual rapport" (1975, *Encore*, 17, 35). There is no link and relation to specifically female experiences, no contact/relation-*rapport* with a feminine-Other in sexual relations based on the phallic *jouissance* in both sexes, and mainly, there are no ways to report on a *rapport* that would be feminine-Other if/where it does occur: no inscription of it in the Symbolic; *"there is no sexual rapport* signifies exactly this rapport's *lack of the signifier,"* that is, a "deficit in knowledge" (Miller 1983). Phallic sexual *jouissance*, whose privileged position in the mental structure of both men and women is shown— and may be also perpetuated—by psychoanalytic experience, is "an obstacle to sexual rapport" (Lacan 1974). Symbolic significance "deadens" the libidinal event and therefore it is an obstacle to the inscription of feminine sexuality *qua* rapport. Thus sexuality, based to begin with on the male bodily specificity, on relations to an object-organ and other-as-object, has the value of nonrapport. A woman is *not-All* in the locus of the phallic *jouissance* since "she has, in relation to what the phallic function designates in terms of jouissance, a *supplementary* jouissance" and *if* there is a point from which sexual rapport could be elaborated it is exactly from "the ladies' side" (*Encore* 68). "Jouissance behind castration" on which the symbolic system is incapable of reporting, which is not an obstacle to sexual rapport but its fulfillment, "would be inconceivable without feminine sexuality" (Miller 1983). It is, however, somehow exposed despite the fact that "language in a way sanctions" it, and a different kind of inscription has to be looked for in order to transfer it onto subjectivity and draw a *beside* unconscious zone (Lacan 1974). *Experiencing* feminine *jouissance* is not enough. Conceptualizing a level of *non-equivalence* between the sexes promoted by nonphallic feminine difference is possible only inasmuch as whatever of it that escapes discourse is yet unthoughtly known and *not only exists* in female corpo-reality: if it also can trace itself, be written, become thinkable, have a meaning (Lacan, "Le sinthôme," 1975). Only if we assume a psychic zone where *traces* of the feminine borderspacing and of the *failure* of the Phallus make intelligible sense, then supplementary feminine psychic dimensions can be claimed. It is the paradigm itself that should rotate, we may conclude, if we claim that anything of the feminine swerve, severality and "rapport" can be nonconsciously inscribed and culturally reported.

The more Lacan structured both the *objet a* and the "woman" as phallic, so too in a characteristic, as J. A. Miller puts it,

"Lacan against Lacan" way, a behind-the-phallus feminine borderspace that I have called matrixial is, to my mind, opened, enabling us to suggest a matrixial aspect of the *objet a* that relates
to an-other *jouissance*. In the later years of his teachings, Lacan
tried to touch, by the use of mathems and graphs as well as by
poetic devices, the inverse face of the field of the Real that does
not stem from the Symbolic, and to report on a sense that vibrates and resonates from *jouissance* and not from signification
established by reason deduced from an already-there Symbolic.
The *objet a* is now "extimate": an intimate exteriority, an exteriority that dwells inside the self, a "hole" hidden from the flagel-
late of signification, located in an extimate space in the Real: a
vacuole (conch, cavity). The *objet a* indexes that *something enjoy-
able or painful has happened* in the vacuole and notes the occur-
rence of this event of *jouissance* as extimate to the subject
(Lacan 1969). It incarnates a surplus-of-enjoying/paining—*plus-
de-jouir*—which cannot be quenched in the sphere of the Imaginary nor exhausted by symbolic signification, but is not their
remnant-surplus either.

In the matrixial borderspace behind the phallus, the signifier
loses his crown as the major creator of sense, the "sexual rapport" (i.e., the relations, connections, contacts) with the
"woman" based on the assumption of a "supplementary" feminine jouissance may be exposed and inscribed as some kind of
knowledge that does not depend on the signifier yet can find/
invent symbols in art and via writing-art to enlarge the Symbolic. Something from the *objet a,* that incarnates and assumes
the shape of horror or beauty and is sacrificed to the Other on a
phantasmatic screen that spreads in the artwork, unveils a feminine sphere of *severality*. Its traces are embedded in the art by
nonphallic sublimation and filter on-to writing-art.

The *incestuous* in/out-side interlacing rapport between subject-to-be and archaic m/Other-to-be, connected to female space
of sex-difference where this incest takes place, is the basis in the
Real for a matrixial stratum that can be abstracted to enlarge
the Symbolic.[17] In the Phallus, her "lack" in the Real inscribes
"nothing" in the Symbolic and inspires imaginary horror. In the
Matrix, female bodily specificity and covenantal coemergence in
the Real inscribe a paradoxical sphere on the Symbolic's margins, where feminine sexuality arises anew, in difference. The
trauma and phantasy of before-birth incest arise in connection
with feminine-Other-desire: with the enigma of what I call matrixial *fading-by-transformation* and with *phallic forclusion* of

the archaic incest with-in/out.[18] When female bodily specificity
is taken into account as a *different* sex-difference that in-forms
subjectivity, difference-in-jointness (rather than being/not
being, presence/absence) and conductible borderlinks between
partial subjects, as well as transmissibility and shareability of
assembled, hybridized objects, not only disturb the phallic interior (intra-psychic) and exterior (cultural and social) scene but
also inform a *beside* (not opposed)—inter-subjective to begin
with—alternative scene and enlarge the Symbolic beyond the
phallic scope. Feminine desire touches upon the connection of
this primordial event with questions of *sexual rapport* and *death*
beyond/before the separating line of Oedipal castration, beyond/
before the threshold of language. The loss involved in the metramorphic passage, I repeat, is an outcome of transformation
and transmission, fragmentation and severalization, dispersal
and re-sharing of the *already* joint and several.

The specificity of the matrixial zone, the sources of its awesome uncanniness and of its a-priori im-purity should be further
clarified before returning to the Red Cow effect, but a remark is
now due: I "re-feminize" a signifier that had been neutralized
in our culture and was made to stand for a general neutral origin upon which traces are inscribed, or a cultural general grid:
"Matrix" is a "womb" in Latin. Yet here, the Matrix doesn't echo
on a biological inside, symbolic of an interior or passive receptacle either, but on a dynamic extimate *borderspace* of active/pas-
sive co-emergence *with*-in and *with*-out the uncognized other,
in relation to a feminine-Other-desire. As a concept, it intends
the cultural Symbolic, Imaginary and Real spheres no less than
the Phallus, even though indexing the male penis in the Real
and imaginary "castration" anxiety is fully acknowledged as
mainly a concept with wide cultural implications. The feminine
"archaic origin" of Matrix (and of Metramorphosis) doesn't indicate any limitation on woman's rights; quite the contrary! As a
concept it supports women's full response-ability for any event
occurring with-in their own not-One corpo-reality and accounts
for the difference of this response-ability from the phallic order.

Via the m/Other-to-be, more archaic than the pre-Oedipal
mother, an-other sexuality filters into, and shapes subjectivity
beyond and *beside* the phallus, but in-side the Symbolic. The
intra-uterine phantasy of the subject-to-be is influenced by, and
influencing the m/Other-to-be's phantasy (that is linked to her
early pictograms) for whom the becoming-infant with-in her is
not entirely "me" and not a total stranger, is not rejected yet not

fused with, and, from a certain moment onwards, is no more an object but not yet a subject.[19] I have suggested in *The Matriaxial Gaze* that in Freud's aesthetic experience of the *Unheimlich*, we separate the *Mutterliebsphantasie—maternal womb/intra-uterine phantasy* from the *castration complex*, and that the womb phantasy is not retroactively folded into the "castration" track but is mounted on a matrixial one (Freud 1919, 244, 248–9).[20] In Freud's consideration of the *uncanny* the phantasy of the maternal matrice is included within the castration prototype; in Lacan's considerations of the uncanny it is excluded by this inclusion—and disappears (Lacan 1981).

Freud and Lacan's variations on the Phallus both reject the womb as an issue of sex-difference, and where Freud does recognize the womb through the question of the origin of babies, it is not considered as another sex-difference alongside the penis but as the first sexual question for boys and explicitly *not* for girls. Freud did not develop it in the direction of a feminine sex-difference, what to my mind would have led to theoretically questioning some basic notions in psychoanalysis, starting with narcissism. Freud did not deny the denial of the womb nor its implications either. On the contrary. He insisted on the *necessity* of such a denial, measured by the importance of what is at stake for males. The penis is considered the central support of "the child's" narcissism (what child, we may ask—male or female?) while the enigma of the sphinx: "where do babies come from?" is central for sexual development of the *male* child. It is *maybe* the first sexual question for boys, he says, but "certainly not" for girls ("Some," 1925, 336). The womb is dismissed since "it was only logical that the child should refuse to grant women the painful prerogative of giving birth to children," that is, since the "neutral" child does not have a womb but wouldn't give up on such an important issue, the child's solution is denial and displacement: "If babies are born through the anus, then a man can give birth just as well as a woman" (Freud, 1908, 219–20).

For the "universal" child, recognizing the womb is catastrophic to his necessary narcissism, since the child believes that he owns every possible valuable organ. But why should the theory deny the womb in agreement with the boy's needs and also ignore its value for female difference, development, and narcissism? Freud's infantile theory of childbirth "saves" at the same time, to my mind, both the neutral-but-phallic narcissism and sexuality and the neutral-but-phallic psychoanalytic theory.[21] Freud's late self criticism deserves our attention: "The discoveries touching the infantile sexuality were done on men, and the theory which emerges from them was elaborated for the *male* infant" (61, my italics).

Similar to the concept of the Phallus, it is not the organ which stays the focal point in the Matrix, but the specific unconscious processes it stands for and what it symbolizes. As a symbol at the service of both sexes, its roots in a *jouissance* in the Real with-in the feminine can't be ignored. To this cluster, in the Real between trauma and phantasy, female subjects have a double access: as archaic outside (for both sexes) and as an inside. Post-Oedipal male subjects are more radically split from it, as their contact/rapport with it in the Real stays forever in an archaic *too early*.

The matrixial cluster engenders *bypassing-phallus sub-knowledge*. "This desire with which the child is invested starts off always as the result of subjective interpretation, as a function of the maternal desire alone, of her own phantasy" (Lacan 1962). In the matrixial borderspace, phantasy relates to desire, the phantasy of the subject-to-be aspires toward the *woman-m/ Other-to-be* in whose phantasy and desire the subject was playing a part already before birth. The becoming-subject in the womb is a pre-subject in the discourse, phantasy, trauma, and desire of the mother-to-be as a subject, who takes part in, and in-forms in return *its* phantasy and trauma. The phantasy of the woman as a partial subject in a matrixial covenant relates to *her* archaic-m/Other-to-be's, to female bodily specificity and also to phallic desire. From the matrixial desire, libidinal *jouissance* is not entirely evaporated.

> I stated by putting it in the present tense that there is no sexual rapport. That is the basis of Psychoanalysis . . . There is no *sexual rapport* except for neighboring generations; namely, parents on the one hand, and children on the other. That's what the interdiction of incest wards off. I talk about sexual rapport. (Lacan 1978)

An encounter occurs at the limits of language, where are carved "the question of the mother and the phantasy of the Origin [la Cause]," the being/entity "for death," the "trauma of the subject and the meeting with the Other" and feminine sexual rapport. "The first desire is the desire of the mother whose value is that of a trauma" (Laurent). Incest is "the return to the maternal womb" (Lemoine). The "woman" relates to

> the *between* involved *in sexual rapport*, but displaced, and precisely, *Other-imposed*. To *Other-impose*, and it is curious that in imposing

this Other, what I advanced today *concerns only the woman*. And it is she who, in this figure of the Other, gives us an illustration within our reach, to be, as a poet has written, "between center and absence," between the meaning she takes from what I've called the *at-least-one*, between the center as *pure existence* or *jouis-presence* and absence . . . which I could not write but to define as "Not-all', that which is not included in the phallic function, yet which is not its negation . . . absence which is no less *jouissance* then being *jouis-absence*." (Lacan 1972)

Such *between*-instances that are not *either/or* but *"and-and"* among oppositions are impossible in terms of the phallic dimension. An *"and-and"* is "what happens in any first encounter with *sexual rapport"* which is feminine (Lacan 1974). In the Matrix, something of an originary coemergence within an impossible position of *"and–and"* drips from the Real to the Imaginary and the Symbolic that are plaited together in a knot, and is transmitted in intersubjectivity. Something of it is accessible to refinement and sublimation (which in psychoanalysis has been considered exclusively phallic) toward art and for further conceptualization in writing-art.

If, for Lacan, the woman is *Other* even when she is a *between center and nothing*, in the Matrix she is not the Other but a *border-Other*, a *becoming in-ter-with the Other*, an *im-pure becoming-between in jointness*. "Woman" is not confined to the contours of the one-body with its inside/outside polarity. In the phallic paradigm, the archaic "nothing" is the focus of prohibition on the elusive feminine incestual rapport, a lack based upon the forclusion of intrauterine incest. The archaic "center" is precisely the focus of such an-other feminine rapport, linked to its *jouissance* as *presence*. Beyond the originary feminine/pre-natal real stage, if "man" is *either* at the center of such a rapport—and then also inside psychosis, *or* cut away from it and in the arms of the law that structures *desire* as masculine, for "woman" there are *between*-instants that are not *either/or* between oppositions that the phallus represents (including the pair: repression/forclusion), but *"and-and"* or *neither/nor* among oppositions. The between-instants of the matrixial sphere are paradoxical in terms of the phallic dimension. An *"and-and"* of incompatible elements becomes meaningful, I suggest, in a matrixial covenant of severality created in contingency and dissolved in a relational, relative, and partial way. Its dissolving is not a cutting but a non-symmetrical with-in-ter transformational co-fading, inscribed as metramorphosis.

BECOMING IN-TER-WITH THE OTHER; AN IM-PURE BECOMING-BETWEEN IN JOINTNESS

The *I*'s phantasy of Origin is involved with that of its singular m/Other-to-be linked to her *non-I*(s), hovering in the same matrix. The enigma of the connection between the phantasy of the partial becoming-subject before entering the world, and the phantasy and desire of the *becoming*-m/Other-to-be in coemergence with it, is to be linked not only to the enigma concerning the *trauma of birth*, but also to prenatal *jouissance*, trauma, and phantasy interconnected through female sex-difference. The matrixial stratum is woven, to begin with, in the psychic plane closest to the bodily experience with-in the womb—in ontogenetic traces of inside *or* outside *me* and/or outside *and* inside *us* that are inscribed with-in-dialogue with the desire of an enlarged, composite Other-"woman." The desire of the potential mother-to-be as subject is already a *networked* desire, composited but not mixed with "man's."[22] Her desire is both phallic and matrixial. An exclusively phallic desire in the matrixial covenant would have designated the reduction of the libido-as-male-only to the, to use Lacan's phrase, Name of the Father at the price of the destruction of supplementary feminine eroticism and would have deepened the *misunderstanding* into which each individual is born.

> There is no other traumatism of birth than that of being born desired. Desired, or not—it's all the same since it comes through the speak/through-being. The speak/through-being in question is generally divided into two speakers. Two speakers who do not speak the same language. Two who do not understand each other speaking. (Lacan 1980)

In the matrixial borderspace, it is not *yet* motherhood, or mother/child relations that is at stake, but the feminine bodily specificity as swerve and rapport and the singularity of each *I/non-I* encounter as inscribed in a *beside* nonconscious zone by means other than repression of signifiers.

"We must look from a side in which the father would be left entirely aside" in order to describe a "primary narcissism" of the infant not as a parasite to the mother but in relation to "those *lost envelopes* where the continuity between the interior and the exterior is so easily read" (Lacan 1962). Indeed! Lacan, however, did not look from this side and therefore, "The whole

dialectic of these past few years up to, and including the Klein-
ian dialectic which is yet the closest, remains falsified because
the emphasis has not been placed on the essential deviation"
["mother" distinct from "father" as a deviation and not as an
opposition] (Lacan 1962). It is impossible to deal with the "lost
envelopes" from the Name of the Father's side, but they did not
get processed in psychoanalytic theory from a side from which
the father moves aside either, and not only because the other
side is "nothing," a lack in the Symbolic; but, to my mind, because it is dangerous to male sexuality for whose service the
theory was intended. As we have seen, a "universal and neutral" narcissism is conceptualized by Freud upon the male
organ, even when the subject doesn't have it. When we divert
the spotlight toward the womb, we are touching upon a basic
taboo. Language "takes disciplinary steps" against the femi-
nine/pre-natal *jouissance* and does not transmit it through itself;
human social Law and Order are built upon its banishing, since
the sexual rapport capsuled through it is the forbidden, dangerous—for the male post-Oedipal subject—incestual rapport between partial-subjects, with the archaic m/Other-to-be (and *not*
of the son with the mother). If Freud develops the narrative of
the archaic father and names the taboo of incest that is structured by/for him, there is no similar *structure* concerning the archaic m/Other-to-be, nor a prohibition parallel to that Oedipal
incest taboo. Indeed the matrixial incest can't be forbidden in
the Real—it occurs to give life. Yet, for its highly psychotic potential in the phallic paradigm it could not even be *elaborated*
but was deeply silenced, not even excluded from the Symbolic
(from which it could then return as its repressed and produce
an-other desire) but marginalized as unthought of. Whatever of
it that did get processed was subjugated to the phallic heterosexual model. Evocations and irruptions of the prebirth incest
are not psychotic, provided we conceive of a wider-Symbolic informed by the Matrix. In the Phallus, the feminine/prenatal encounter was sacrificed so as to preserve and protect the phallic
psychic integrity of the subject.

And indeed, the way of the adult nonpsychotic male is forever
muzzled to this feminine rapport in the Real. From the phallic
angle, the matrixial stratum must be forcluded; contacting it is
too deeply regressive as it means psychic annihilation. But,
from the side of female sexuality in the Matrix, it can't mean the
same thing, or else any subject in rapport with feminine sex-difference is crazy. The woman, rather, as an adult human-being

that huddles like the man in the shade of the phallus' wings, and though from the side of the father her way too is muzzled to this rapport, still touches it. A woman's[23] singular rapport to that "feminine" dimension can't be castrated or forcluded, since she continually experiences phantasies related to her own bodily specificity, and those interlink with archaic matrixial phantasies. The matrixial rapport is *both* deeply regressive and archaic *and* reemerging in late experience, and therefore, I suggest, the "lost envelopes" are only *almost*-lost for a woman. Whether "grains" of her archaic m/Other-to-be are realized in corpo-reality or invested in phantasy, whether a future matrixial encounter in the Real is longed for or rejected, she has no refuge from some unpredictable rapport that carries in its very structure traces of archaic encounter with a feminine *non-I* possibly still longed for. This rapport stamps its feminine-beyond-the-phallus mark from the outset as what is excluded from the future Real and forcluded from the Symbolic for "man," always *too* early *or* too late. But for "woman," both the exclusion of the matrixial incestual rapport *and* certain accessibility to the (past and potentially future) rapport itself co-exist. Thus, the matrixial difference is not equal or opposite but bypasses and supplements the Phallus in subjectivity. Thus, as a symbol it draws a space of paradoxical im-purity, for whom the matrixial incest is an emblem.

I suggest that the *jouissance* that emerges in the *vacuole of encounter* on the level of the pre-birth incest—from trauma and phantasy—between the becoming-subject, male or female, in the womb and the "woman" as *becoming archaic m/Other-to-be*, both of them in their status of partial-subjects *and* part-objects for each other—"grains" of *I* and *non-I* and not yet "mother" and "infant"—and the encounter between the phantasy of the emerging *I* (as a pre-subject) and the *phantasy and desire* of the *non-I* (the woman as a subject), constitute a *feminine rapport*. An enjoying/paining rapport inscribes traces of singularization, together but differently, in both. I propose the hypothesis that this *rapport,* which for psychoanalytic theory is *sexual in the partial pre-Oedipal dimension*, which does not wait to receive permission from the Phallus in order to happen and whose accessibility is obstructed by the Phallus no less than it is blocked away from it, is *inscribed* to make sense. Traces are woven into a web where the joint psychic object of subjectivity-as-an-encounter is created as, and remains an incompatible composite which neither fuses its components nor rejects them. A diffracted, transmitted, and redistributed im-pure, hybrid object corresponds to a matrixial impure covenant of severality.

Before further elaborating the value of the feminine rapport, a remark is due: what is dangerously regressive for the phallic Real has different values for a matrixial Real, and what is related in a double manner to a female bodily specificity can be, as a concept and an image, at the service of both sexes, if the Symbolic does not equate with the Phallus. Evocations of the pre-birth trauma and phantasy are not psychotic, if we presume a wider Symbolic, in-formed and trans-formed by the Matrix, that transgresses the boundaries of the phallic Imaginary by way of intrinsic links.

Im-Purity in the Eyes of the Matrix

Inside the Matrix we are dealing with questions on/from the feminine that the subject orients toward an-Other-woman in search for an-Other-desire. I have suggested examining the potentiality of the feminine/prenatal encounter as a measure of difference that is neither opposite nor the same nor symmetrical to the phallic sex-difference. The Matrix stands for *differentiation-in-co-emergence* with the other (contrary to fusion or rejection). Matrixial subjectivity is a covenant, in which a foreign *non-I* co-emerges with me and some of its traces are inscribed in me, while some of mine are gathered in him/her. And this covenant can't guarantee a happy *menage*. It is the transformation of this witnessing-while-sharing and this co-creating for/with-in co-emerging subjectivity of several others that is offered in art via its incarnation as a matrixial object or link, sacrificed, like the Red Cow, to the Other.

The matrix indicates an existential ontogenesis and an unconscious inscription of (male and female) archaic modes of joint existence, a dynamic *borderspace* of active/passive coemergence *with*-in and *with*-out the uncognized other in relation to a feminine-Other desire, and not an interior passive receptacle, a general neutral origin or a cultural general grid. Processes of *connectivity* carry the different inscription of the matrixial borderspace, in which it is not sufficient to describe the surplus of *jouissance*, the *plus de jouir* of libidinal reality as a *lost object* (a phallic *objet a*), but we need to suggest *conductability* and cycle the idea of originary *transgressivity* that explores and retreats, severalizes, fragments, and composites. By transgression, the remnants-traces of rapport-without-relating create heterogene-ity among the grains. These traces are scattered in a nonsym-metrical and non-equivalent way between the participants of a joint borderspace and in-form a covenant-in-difference which is not based on symbolic-phallic cognition but on re-co-birth into a becoming-Symbolic. Metramorphosis is a conductible un-thought sub-knowledge that re(a)sonates heterogeneity on-to the threshold of culture and webs in it a sievelike borderspace of *co-naissance* and co-fading of several elements in originary differentiation. The pre-natal/feminine encounter serves as a base for a stratum of subjectivization in which "grains" of *I* and *non-I* that reciprocally don't recognize each other, sharing hy-bridized objects and transmitting affects and pathic informa-tion, address one another in a rapport-without-relating that takes place in the course of alternations in distance-in-prox-imity.

The matrixial sphere is created both by encounters on the level of trauma and phantasy, by connections shaped into a sub-symbolic web that in-form a *wider Other*, and by encounter with feminine-Other-desire which is already involved in earlier ma-trixial circles and in dialogue with phallic desire. The matrix is a feminine unconscious space of simultaneous co-emergence and co-fading of the I and the stranger that is neither fused nor rejected. Links between several joint partial subjects co-emerg-ing in differentiation in rapport-without-relating, and connec-tions with their hybrid objects, produce/interlace "woman" that is not confined to the contours of the one-body with its inside versus outside polarity, and indicate a sexual difference based on webbing links and not on essence or negation. Traces of the matrixial encounter-events interlace in inter-subjectivity where metramorphic borderlinks report themselves—even if by para-doxical symbols, like that of the Red Cow, implying different ways of reading into narratives of our culture and transform them from with-in.

The *beyond the phallus* domain hinted by Lacan from within the phallic perspective still keeps the woman—as a surplus or residue—on the axis of the *One* and *Infinite*, with its *same* and *oppositions*, *all* and *nothing*. It posits the woman as *either* a sub-ject in the masculine format *or* an object patterned upon mascu-line desire, as *either* a center (presence) *or* a want/lack. The Matrix weaves the woman as *between* subject and object and *be-tween* center and nothingness on the *axis of heterogeneous sev-erality*. The subsymbolic sieve inscribes the *besidedness* and *with-ness* of the matrixial stratum and allows a sublimation of a feminine rapport. It supplies a supplementary perspective on out-inner extimate intrasubjective events and on inter-subjective events which may be called in-outer (interiority which occurs outside the sole self). The matrixial *objet a*, and the matrixial aspect of subjectivity, can never be entirely present, nor entirely absent, can never be pure neither impure, but are always in-between different degrees of im-purity. The feminine *conductible* difference that concerns, to begin with, the womb as "derivation," re(a)sonates in phantasy with inter-subjective experiences of encounters between partial subjects and part-objects of different individuals, and with intra-subjective experiences of encounters between elements of the same individual. It also penetrates into the transsubjective field and transgresses the generations' barrier.

The process of passage of the matrixial *objet a* and borderlink from artwork onto writing-art is analogous, up to a certain limit, to the passage from the field of the Real to the nonsymbolic "side" of the subject—the *I* or the *non-I*—which is suffused with *jouissance*, and from there to its symbolic zone which is voided of *jouissance*. The limits of the analogy are sketched by Lacan in the following enigmatic way: "Sublimation is the virtue of those who know how to conduct the journey around whatever the *subject who is supposed to know* ('*le sujet suppose savoir*') is reduced to" (1969). That is, for example, sublimation is the virtue of one who knows how to conduct the journey around a trace of subjective-object—the surplus created after the exhaustion of the *jouissance* in the Real, when the preexistent world of the Symbolic cannot encompass knowledge embedded in it. "Every art-work is located in the circumscription of what is left as irreducible in this knowledge as distinct from *jouissance*. Something nonetheless comes to designate its action [of the *jouissance*] in the sense that, in the subject, it will forever designate the impossibility of its full realization" (Lacan 1969). If we agree with that idea, as I do, the necessity of *writing from art* the feminine *jouissance*—since in turn it indicates/produces /constitutes an-other subjectivity—becomes clear.

In the passage from the archaic m/Other-to-be's rapport to the *mamalangue* something gets lost, but the passage itself re(a)-sonates and enactivates; a *beyond language* and *beyond appearance* dimension can later partially be accounted for conceptually, and it can be retroactively and partially contained in a matrixial narrative, receiving an approximate symbolic co-meaning. The *mamalangue* is not doomed to fall under the impact of foreclosure, and may open cultural (social, political) spaces. Metramorphosis inscribed in the artwork knits with the convolutions of its accidental paths the art-work's matrixial field itself. Through metramorphosis, the painter and the viewer, the writer and the reader re-co-emerge anew in various unique ways in-to-gether-with the art-work but differently. The matrixial borderlink, which is not reserved to women *alone*, is an almost-missed encounter between the erotic antennae which extend from with-in and with-out our-selves toward an *emerging feminine-Other-desire*. It digs into the phallus from in-out. Entwined in a subsymbolic connectional web, the feminine participates in the in-formation of the subject through passages which are *not* castration but processes of *transformation-through-transgression* towards the *differentiated-in-jointness* matrixial others. Metramorphosis is a creative potentiality that exchanges and transmits traces, phantasies, affects and information within a joint space, where in each exchange an addition is inscribed, which turns reciprocity into a lack of equivalence. Common ontogenetic "memory" is dispersed and traces of the processing of coemergence are scattered and diffused. The results of its unpredictable actions are inscribed in further unique unexpected encounters. On the matrixial plane, there grows a human ethical possibility in the bosom of the Thing, the significance of which is: that I know that I have a covenantal relations with the other, that I am *co-born* (not in the biological sense) *with certain several strangers* who influence me, and whom I influence, while recognizing the impossibility of my fully recognizing the Other, or while recognizing that a certain foreignness in me and in the other—even the one who is known to me—will never yield to the mastery of my phallic symbolic cognition.

In the cracks of the phallic subject, a supplementary subjectivity weaves itself, and *this* one too will never exhaust itself completely and will continue to leave behind mysterious, poetic relics. The journey from the *jouissance* in the field of the Real through the *objet a* to the subject in terms of castration designates a phallic sublimational zone which acts and signifies in a retroactive gear. The wanderings of the feminine uniqueness from the Real to *co-significance* as co-creating are to be a discovered almost-missed covenant after almost-missed covenant. Matrixial writing—art between poetic and theoretical writing re(a)sonates onto and from art all kinds of im-pure coalitions that are paradoxical in the phallic sphere. The Red Cow effect is one such paradoxical metramorphosis, an almost-missed encounter that interlaces the hallowed and the hollowed.

SHE-LAW: SCATTERING AND WANDERING (*NIDA*) PASSAGEWAYS IN MATRIXIAL SACRIFICE

The Red Cow effect is a metramorphosis in the register of sacrifice where, I suggest, the im-pure is exposed as a specific category for hybridized incompatible composites, to be differentiated from the phallic opposition of impure/defiled *versus* pure. The feminine *jouissance* beyond phallic desire and law exposes the matrixial incest that maleness must foreclose, since it is "beyond the pleasure principle" where libido is connected to the "death" drive. Inscribing feminine *jouissance* may lead to psychic catastrophe in the eyes of the phallus as feminine *jouissance*, which means transgressing the Name of the Father might get incarnated in the fascination by the erotization of death. The fascination of the sacrifice lies in its being man's proof of his knowledge of the desire of the Other *qua* God. It testifies to man's belief in his ability to satisfy God by offering Him his most precious objects. Any subject must sacrifice some of its *jouissance* in order to have access to the Symbolic. In the eyes of the phallus, according to Lacan, woman is men's *objet a* and the infant in the womb is the woman's *objet a*. Woman as a man's sacrifice, as its *objet a* is created by "castration"—castration being always, to begin with, castration of the m/Other-to-be. "Man" sacrifices by castration. How does a "woman" sacrifice, if not by castration? I suggest that a woman sacrifices, and is sacrificed by conductible metramorphosis, and the Red Cow can serve as its emblem: no pure presence, no pure absence, no pure schize and their price to pay, but transmissions and transgressions, impurity and hybridization, fragmentation, partialization and pluralization, and their special price to pay.

From contemplating the Red Cow through a matrixial prism, we can now distinguish in this symbol sub-symbolic branches of another kind. The Bible even indicates here what we may call a *she-symbol*, designated by the signifiers of the text as a law in the feminine: a *khukah*, that I will name, after the Hebrew, a *she-law*, and not a *khok*: a law in the masculine. *Khuka* as a divine command in a feminine form "refers particularly to precepts for which no logical reason can be found" (Hartoum 76). Indeed, there is no logic in this Cow. She emerges from a network of paradoxes and sinks back into them without resolving them; she represents an almost-missed impossible encounter in the form of wanderings between contraries that vitiate the split between the saint and the sinner, the pure and the defiled, the holy and the desecrated, the living and the dead, and creates their co-emergence and co-fading. A special kind of im-purity as hybridity of incompatible composites distinguishes itself in the feminine. The sacrifice of the Red Cow is a metramorphosis that emanates from a *khukah*, from a "she-law" of *and-and* by *nida-mediations—nida* as wanderings and not as separation—between hallowing the hollowed and hollowing the hallowed.[24] The Red Cow effect is susceptible to "non-logical" inscription up to the border of the Symbolic "of dictionaries": "The culture ... participates in that something which derives from an economy founded upon the structure of the *objet a*, which is to say that it is as waste, as excrement of the subjective relation as such that the material of dictionaries is constituted" (Lacan 1969).

The *objet a* is designated as a holy, forbidden and lost "sacrifice" proffered as a self-offering to God or to the grand Other, which marks out sublimational processes, indexes aesthetic objects, and arouses the experience of the *uncanny*-as phallic. "The register of extimacy is the register of sacrifice ... the subject is nothing but what s/he gives up or sacrifices" (Miller 1985). The *objet a* in art is proffered to the Other—to God, as an offering that is meant to arouse his desire, says Lacan. And in relations of love, not only the subject sacrifices, but also the Other, embodied in the specific other, to the extent that there is in each of us a foreignness that is not reducible to the cognized. The Other sacrifices too, for he too is not a chain of signifiers only.

> The Other contains in itself ... the *objet (a)* ... In what are these two terms O and (a) compatible and articulable? ... This *objet (a)* is as much extimate to the subject as extimate to the Other, it is included in the Other in a completely different status than the signifier, as a surplus from the *Thing*, as what the chain of the signifier has not succeeded to take control over when it erased the *Thing*. The *objet a* as an element in the Symbolic aggregate is a *negative* phallic entity of lack, while as a grain, it preserves an indestructible conductivity; it is "both the hole and the cap on this hole." (Lacan 1986)

If "love" in the Lacanian lexicon is the offering of our *nothing* to the Other, and if in the process of transference the Other too sacrifices his *nothing* for you, then, I suggest, in the matrixial stratum we share the erotic antennae that register the traces of the almost-missed-encounters which possess an indestructible *positivity* while being elusive, since they are diffracted and dispersed—half lost, faded. We are in a process of *relative* loss of relations together—but not in the same way and not to the same extent, and not to "the end"—for end and beginning are not the borders of the Matrix—and not limitlessly—for the infinite is not the limit of the several. We are less-than-One—partial, yet One-less—not alone *with-in a rapport*, and we are responsible for unknown others.

The location of femininity in psychoanalysis by means of the *objet a* as a foreign body involves us fatally with the question of the place of the migrant and the exile as psychic reality, as social distress, as aesthetic experience and as ethical problem. By means of the extimacy of the *Thing*, the *objet a* and the *vacuole*, the real Other and the reality of the other/foreigner are articulated: "when we speak of extimacy, on the other within, we posit the question of the immigrant" (Miller 1985). In the phallic paradigm which opens from the *One* and *All* and moves between *either* being *or* lack, each imaginary other that the *I* relates to is a parasitic foreign body destined for annihilation by way of assimilation or banishment: "its either me or him" (Lacan, 1981, 107). "The intimate . . . has a character of exteriority . . . the intimate is the Other. I will say it is like a foreign body, a parasite" (Miller 1986). Yet, in the matrixial borderspace, the foreigner *cannot* be articulated as a parasite. Here, the exiled is not clipped-out from the system; here, along the metramorphic borderlinks, the *other* and *I* share connections that when *fading* by way of transformation are leaving traces in both.

In the matrixial model which opens from *severality* and *contingency*, the *I* and the uncognized *non-I* are partners in a temporary, unpredictable and unique covenant, in which each participant—subject and object—is partial and relative in a composited joint space. The *non-I* is *not* Other but, like the *I*, is a *becoming-in-ter-with*, and therefore a clear cut between the living and the dead, the pure and the impure, so basic in the Phallus, is beyond the matrixial scope; a voyage between them, so paradoxical in the Phallus becomes meaningful in the Matrix. The ashes of the Red Cow are dispersed, diffracted, aspired, and sprayed according to a becoming-feminine-Other-desire. The Red Cow sacrificial borderlink, which quivers and glints from *beyond appearance* is not *the* Holy—as Other or God, nor is it *the*

Impure—as yet another Other or the Dead; but it is the *transversion* of the holy with the impure and their co-emergence in impurity without blending and without annihilation with-in a process of a *becoming-woman-between, inter-with the Other*. The Red Cow effect expresses a metramorphosis that does not perish in a split but diminishes to a small or large extent as a consequence of dispersion and stretching among the several. Wandering, scattered, and sprayed, it is impossible to regather the Red Cow's ashes-traces; one can only find some of them in other and additional matrixes, and follow their footsteps to a labyrinth not envisioned in advance, woven in the course of creating its route through strolling along it. My matrixial *objet a* initiates yours to join in; you proffer in it the relation that you lost together with others, you are the witness of your offering and you offer your witnessing on to further assemblages so that not in total perishing a matrixial sacrifice is inscribed in culture. Antigone's desire bears witness to that.

The tragedy of Antigone fascinates us when it raises the question of the place of the feminine beyond-the-phallus in the Other of culture, not the realization of primordial sexual rapport in an archaic *Real* but tragedy as a channel for expressing a desire that is not written in the existing Law and an incarnation of an extimate *Thing-rapport* that is not subjected to the existing, actual *Symbolic* and which through the art-work expands its borders. In the extimate zone of the *vacuole*, in what we may call the *no-place of the exiles*, some kind of "feminine" rapport, not as a traumatic return on-to the corpo-real, not as psychosis, but as a transformation into the art-work by what I see as matrixial sublimation can be revealed.[25] Antigone desires to hallow the hollow and to hollow the hallow: to violate, desecrate, and break the law while redeeming and hallowing the defiled and disgraced, the dead with whom she shared a maternal womb. Her incestual state of inner exile echoes residuals of her mother's. "Antigone is an exile because of the fact of incest . . . which is one and only: the return to the maternal womb" (Lemoine). The Other gnaws at the *Thing* and contains the residues of its gnawing in the form of *objet a* and *a-links*. In *Antigone*, the *Thing-rapport* resists the existing Symbolic order and does not yield itself, while matrixial residues find sublimatory passages into art. This mistress-piece attests that something of the Red Cow metramorphosis infiltrates and vibrates, beyond horror and anxiety, from the poïetic object to the aesthetic object and back, onto *becoming*-art and from it onwards and back, just until drafting contour-lines for questions culture has to grapple with; even just until questions of ethics—and back. Similarly, a matrixial offering in painting by way of the Red Cow effect contains something of the foreignness of the other who is in rapport with it, retroactively or in potential, sooner or later, and in terms of the other's death—and of mine. In the feminine, says Levinas, the death of the other is more important to me than my own death and therefore "the feminine is that difference, the feminine is that incredible thing in the human by which it is affirmed that without me the world has a meaning" (17).

And if the sin-offering that is structured by means of the phallus is holy, we will recall too that the religious category of the Holy, the numinous, classically connects with the aesthetic category of the Sublime. The *Red Cow effect* is a metramorphosis which produces a *different Sublime* that can be described as *with-in-ter the hollowed* and *the hallowed*.[26] It interlaces temporary intermediate im-pure spaces in which, like for my mother, the turkey is also a cow, and black is also red. Where the *nida*-mediations are sprayed, we return anew—not to a past almost-lost *mamalangue* always wandering on elsewhere, but to its self-renewing thresholds that are not yet a translation, a separation and a substitution into a father-tongue and no more the same *mamalangue*. And also, to one of the unanticipated but too-late encounters that happened to me in the in-visible screen shared between phantasy and painting, I gave the name "Halala."[27] There, the horrible multiplicity of some several and the horrible fading-away of other several became unbearable just until beyond my out-in-ter autistic threshold.

NOTES

This essay was presented in parts at the conferences: *Beautiful Translation*, Tate Gallery, 1/V/95; *Feminism & the Aesthetics of Difference*, Institute of Romance Studies, University of London, 8/IX/95; *Modernism, Difference & Place*, Falmouth College of Arts, 9/IX/95, and a version was printed in *Beautiful Translations—Act 2*, London: Pluto, 1996. I would like to thank Richard Flantz for his help with translation of the first two chapters and the last one. Translation of quotes from Jacques Lacan and Jaques-Alain Miller by Joseph Simas and Bracha Lichtenberg Ettinger.

1. Readers who are not acquainted with the concepts "Matrix" and "Metramorphosis" may consult: B. Lichtenberg Ettinger, "Matrix and Metramorphosis," in *Differences* 4:3, Bloomington: Indiana University Press, 1992; "The Almost-Missed Encounters as Eroticized Aerials of the Psyche," in *Third Text*, 28–29, London: Kala, 1994; *The Matrixial Gaze*, Feminist Arts and Histories

Network—Fine Arts, Leeds University 1995; "The With-In-Visible Screen," in *Inside the Visible*, ed. C. de Zegher, Boston: MIT Press, 1996.

4. For Butler, parody is the way to achieve these aims.

5. Pollock argues that the matrixial possibility is something that can be discerned already there in texts, signifiers, legends, painting, ourselves, suggesting that the matrixial paradigm indicates another possible strategy for feminism that has been waging a war on the myths, legends, texts, and canons of what it names patriarchal culture and indeed were caught, by doing so, in the phallic trap of binary oppositions. Griselda Pollock, "After the Reapers" in catalogue: *Bracha Lichtenberg Ettinger: Halala—Autistwork*. The Israel Museum, Jerusalem & Arfiac, 1995. See also Pollock's "Inscriptions in the Feminine" in *Inside the Visible*, ed. C. de Zegher. Boston: MIT Press, 1996.

4. In agreement with Lacan's account on perversion in the 1960s, it is interesting to note that psychoanalytic experience in general shows perversion to be a male "specialty."

5. On the one hand, I try to draw the limits of the phallic Law and Order—as castration-separation and substitution—that pretend to account for just any aesthetic principles of creation, and on the other hand, I raise the possibility that something of the matrixial aesthetics relates to ethics as well. Some aspects of the Matrix come close to the ethics evoked by Levinas with regards to *The Face (le Visage)*. Lacan's ethical considerations in relation to Antigone's tragedy reflects, to my mind, other matrixial possibilities.

6. *"Jouissance"* signifies sensual enjoyment or pain in the Real.

7. Deferent (adj.) stands for transporting and transmitting out, as well as for acting with reverence. Deference also stands for respect, reverence, awe. By using this term here I intend both respect and awe, and transportation and transmission.

8. See also: *Old Testament*, Numbers 14:18; Deuteronomy 5:9; Exodus 34:5–6.

9. In English, for example, when you read "I love you," this can be understood in any one of four ways: between a woman and a man, between a man and a woman, between a woman and a woman and between a man and a man; in Hebrew, the statement is structured as gendered and sexual; it is erotic, and each of these possibilities is said in a different way.

10. The Other is classically defined as "the treasure of the signifiers" in the early Lacanian theory.

11. Since my use of the term "feminine" in the matrixial perspective is in criticism of Freud's "feminine" and "female" and close to Lacan's "supplementary femininity," I'll briefly sketch Freud's phallic paradigm of masculine/feminine and maleness/femaleness.

12. Freud states this even though, he continues, "Unfortunately we can describe this state of things only as it affects the male child; the corresponding processes in the little girl are not known to us" (1923, 142).

13. Thus, for example, "feminine masochism" is the stance of the boy toward his father—a "masculine phantasy" (Lacan, 1981, 192). Little Hans and the Wolf Man search the meaning of the capacity to carry children in the womb, and the hallucination of being a woman in the psychotic takes place in the mind of a male patient. The incarnation of this femininity in hallucinations stands in direct relation to its foreclosure from the symbolic system. As for women patients, according to Freud, they are supposed to seek in a man the answer to their question about the feminine. Analyzing Freud's patient Dora,

I suggest that it is in relation to the matrixial-feminine that girls seek, to begin with, the answer to their question about the feminine—*addressed to a woman.*

14. For a criticism of Lacan's "phallgocentrism" see Luce Irigaray, *Speculum of the Other Woman*, trans. Gillian C. Gill. Ithaca: Cornell University Press, 1985.

15. This trace of a trace is created in the course of a schism through which the subject itself emerges as well, when the signifiers of language blur the individual's archaic modes of experience and nests *in their place,* and when discourse conducted by speech vehicles the principles of language and society (that dwell in the Symbolic) and restructures the archaic processes, modes, and materials as no longer accessible.

16. "Forclusion" is a mechanism of a-priory noninclusion of the signifier, operating in psychosis and analogous to repression in the level of neurosis where a signifier was included and then pushed under to become unconscious. While repression explicitly fits the Oedipal model of castration, forclusion that is supposed to be pre-Oedipal is still structured as some kind of castration, since it indexes a total presence in the Real and a total absence of passage to the Symbolic on the presence/absence axis of the phallic paradigm. Thus, the feminine is either "castrated" in the post-Oedipal era or "forcluded" in the pre-Oedipal one, and is either way excluded from the Symbolic.

17. The archaic, the Real and even the Id are not a question of pure nature in psychoanalysis. See Russell Jacoby, *Social Amnesia: A Critique of Conformist Psychology from Adler to Laing*, Brighton: Harvester 1977.

18. I suggest to differentiate *fading-by-transformation* from both normal/neurotic repression and psychotic forclusion—both corresponding differently to a "castration mechanism." It relates to the phenomenon of *surmounting* discussed by Freud (1919, 249).

19. Toward the end of pregnancy the *post-mature* infant inside the womb can be considered as a partial *subject*, a matrixial *subject* or a *subject-to-be.* At an earlier stage of pregnancy, the fetus is a phallic or matrixial part-*object*, and not yet a partial *subject.*

20. What seems to support my suggestion that the matrixial phantasy can't be subjugated to the castration phantasy is that while a castration phantasy is frightening at the point of its original emergence before its repression, a matrixial phantasy becomes frightening only when it is repressed but is not frightening at the point of its original sprouting.

21. M. C. Hamon defends the idea that "for the two sexes, only one genital organ, the male organ, plays a role" and "there is no other representation of the loss for the Unconscious except this one" (38, 98). She subjugates all other organs, including the uterus (as referred to in the works of Deutch, Horney, Ferenzi, Abraham, Jones, and Klein) to the *phallus.* In my diffracted view, any object, *even the penis,* may be related to, under certain circumstances, by non-phallic processes. For Hamon the phallus/castration position strictly represents Lacan's position; in my view, it represents only the early Lacan.

22. The symbolic phallus, the signifier's chains and the social and cultural principles inscribed in the Symbolic and transmitted by the discourse.

23. Mother *or not.* It is not maternity that is discussed here but a human potentiality related to female bodily specificity.

24. Hollowed, *mehoulelet, halala,* from the root: *h-l-l* in Hebrew means impurified, profaned, and desecrated but also may stand, in my sense, for "spaced," "laid apart," "derivated," and "created." Halal—"space" and "dead"—comes from the same root, and also "creating" and "dancing" (*leholel*).

25. In Hebrew, the words for "exile" and "revelation" stem from the same root: "g.l.h." Lacan refers to James Joyce's Exiles, in: *Le sinthôme*, unedited seminar, 1975–76.

26. In divergence from some feminist tendencies to reject the category of the Sublime altogether (and, in general, to reject categories that are too established within phallocentric discourse), I suggest to divert it from the phallic paradigm and examine it under the matrixial paradigm.

27. *Halala* is a feminization of the Hebrew masculine noun *halal*, which has two distinct meanings—"space" and "dead," but which in the feminine form signifies desecrated, violated, profaned, espaced, hollowed, as well as "her space," and may signify "her espacement," "her derivation," and "her creation." See my: *Matrix • Halal(a)—Lapsus, Notes on Painting 1985–1992*, Oxford: MoMA, 1993.

WORKS CITED

Butler, Judith. 1990. *Gender Trouble*. New York: Routledge.

Freud, Sigmund. 1923. *The Infantile Genital Organization*, S. E. 19. London: Hogarth Press.

———. 1908. *On the Sexual Theories of Children*, S. E. 9. London: Hogarth Press.

———. 1991. *Sigmund Freud presenté par lui-même* (1925). Paris: Gallimard.

———. 1925. *Some Psychical Consequences of the Anatomical Distinction Between the*

Sexes, vol. 7. New York: Penguin Books.

———. 1905. *Three Essays on the Theory of Sexuality*, S. E. 7. London: Hogarth Press.

———. 1919. *The "Uncanny,"* S. E. 17. London: Hogarth Press.

Gouglas, Mary. 1969. *Purity and Danger.* London: Routledge.

Hadarshan, Rabbi Moshe. 1984. *The Bible* with Rashi interpretations, Numbers 19. Paris: Samuel & Odette Levy.

Hamon, M. C. 1992. *Pourqoui les Femmes Aiment-elles les Hommes?* Paris: Seuil.

Hartoum, Prof. 1992. *The Bible with Hartoum Interpretations following Cassouto's Method.* Tel Aviv: Yavne.

Kristeva, Julia. 1980. *Desire in Language, A Semiotic Approach to Literature and Art*. Edited by Leon S. Roudiez, translated by T. Gorz, A. Jardine, and L. S. Roudiez. New York: Columbia University Press.

Lacan, Jacques. 14/5/69. *D'un autre a l'Autre* (From other to Other). Unedited seminar.

———. 1981. *The Four Fundamental Concepts of Psycho-analysis*. Translated by A. Sheridan. New York: Norton.

———. May 1962. *L'identification*. Unedited seminar.

———. 1980. *Le malentendu* (The misunderstanding). *Ornicar?* 22, *Bulletin du Champs Freudien*.

———. 1985. The meaning of the phallus. In *Feminine Sexuality: Jacques*

Lacan and the Ecole Freudienne, edited by Juliette Mitchell and Jacqueline Rose, translated by J. Rose. New York: Norton.

———. 11/4/78. *Le moment de conclure* (Time to conclude). Unedited seminar.

———. 21/5/74. *Les non-dupes errent.* Unedited seminar.

———. 8/3/72. *Ou pire.* Unedited seminar.

———. 1981. *Le séminaire de Jacques Lacan, Livre III: Les psychoses.* Paris: Seuil.

———. 1975. *Le séminaire de Jacques Lacan, Livre XX: Encore.* Paris: Seuil.

———. 12/16/75. *Le sinthôme.* Unedited seminar.

Laurent, E. 2/13/95. *Soiree Paris,* unedited.

Lemoine, E. 1995. *L'Envers de Paris,* unedited.

Levinas, E., in conversation with Bracha Lichtenberg-Ettinger. 1993. *Time is the Breath of the Spirit.* Translated by J. Simas and C. Ducker. Oxford: MoMA.

Miller, J. A. 11/13/85. *Extimité.* Unedited seminar.

———. 1995. *Silet.* Unedited seminar.

———. 4/5/83. *Du symptome au fonction et retour* (from *Symptom to Function and Back*). Unedited seminar.

Smirgel, J. Chasquet. 1985. *Creativity and Perversion.* London: Free Association Books.

Part 2
Sexual Re-Identification

Signifyin(g) Sex: Gloria Naylor's *Bailey's Cafe* and Western Religious Tradition

Lynn Alexander

IN A 1992 INTERVIEW ON NATIONAL PUBLIC RADIO, GLORIA NAYLOR AS-
serted that a driving force behind virtually all of her fiction was
the recovery of things lost, either through the passage of time or
through usurpation by dominant social groups. In the case of
Bailey's Cafe, she further argued that what was lost was language, the way people talk about and identify themselves—in
particular, the way one subgroup of women is identified. At its
core, she asserts, *Bailey's Cafe* is concerned with the recovery
of the term "whore" by the very women against whom it is pejoratively leveled. A year later Naylor reasserted the premise that
Bailey's Cafe is "about sexuality and sexual identity," explaining that "the core of the work is indeed the way in which the
word *whore* has been used against women or to manipulate female sexuality" (Interview 150).

Such recovery necessitates an interrogation of the cultural
conceptions of women and their sexuality. To this end, Naylor
employs the African-American strategy of "Signifyin(g)," characterized by Henry Louis Gates, Jr., as utilizing others' characters and themes as the foundation from which to build one's
own variations and marked by "a rhetorical practice that is not
engaged in the game of information giving . . . [but] turns on the
play of a chain of signifiers, and not on some supposedly tran-
scendental signified" (52). The use of this technique is not surprising since the Signification of Shakespeare and Dante in her
works is well established,[1] and Signifyin(g) is "a principle of language use"(90). Borrowed from Chaucer, Naylor's unnamed
cafe owner[2] links the stories of various women, creating the
framework for the individual tales much as Harry Bailey of the
Tabord Inn does. And much like Chaucer's pilgrims, the characters represent a cross-section of society: each having a tale—
part truth, part fiction—of hopes abandoned and dreams

91

deferred. It is the narrator who provides clues as to relationships among characters and as to how to read their stories:
"Anything really worth hearing in this greasy spoon happens
under the surface. You need to know that if you plan to stick
around here and listen while we play it all out" (35). Such readings are typical of Signification, which builds along the vertical,
paradigmatic axis of language, using what Saussure identifies
as "associative relations." Typically such readings direct or re-
direct the reader's attention from the semantic to the rhetorical
level. And "it is this redirection that allows us to bring the repressed meanings of a word, the meanings that lie in wait on the
paradigmatic axis of discourse, to bear upon the syntagmatic
axis" (Gates 58). It is not surprising then that instead of a shrine,
the refuge sought by the various women is Eve's boarding
house/brothel, a brownstone surrounded by a garden of wild-
flowers.

But Naylor does not restrict her retelling to Chaucer; just as
in her earlier novels, Naylor signifies multiple texts. While
Chaucer informs the structure of *Bailey's Cafe*, much of the
story is a revisioning of biblical literature. And as in previous
novels, she puts into play and tests both positive and negative
attitudes toward the signified texts, dramatizing "the conflict
between established and emergent traditions" (Erickson 233).
Naylor concentrates on five stories, all dealing with female sexuality, all rooted in Judeo-Christian tradition, and all informing
contemporary attitudes toward women and sexuality: Eve, Esther, Mary Magdalene, Jezebel, and the Virgin Mary. Not only
is the cafe visited by five women named for these biblical figures—Eve, Esther, Mary (Peaches), Jesse Bell, and Mariam—
but also their stories revisit and revise biblical tradition.
Traditionally the biblical predecessors are freely associated
with sexuality but it is an association forced on them through
patriarchal tradition: other than nudity and childbirth there is
nothing sexual in Genesis; Esther's beauty gains her the position of queen and the opportunity to save her people from
slaughter; Jezebel's story centers around fear of religious and
cultural differences; Mary Magdalene has been cast as the pro-
totypical reformed prostitute by Church doctrine and tradition;
and Mary is associated with sexuality because of the virgin
birth. Typical of Signification, where "the sign itself appears to
be double, at the very least, and (re)doubled upon ever closer
examination" (Gates 40), Naylor recasts female sexuality as
shaped by Judeo-Christian tradition in which the virgin/whore

dichotomy is inescapable (not least because the issue of feminine sexuality beginning with Eve and ending with Mary becomes circular through the issue of childbirth). She creates a discordant parallel with biblical tradition, which identifies women through implied sexuality rather than actual transgression, in which the movement shifts from women as whores to whores as women, from transgressors to transgressed. What Naylor creates is a gendered context in which to tell stories of neglect, suffering, and abuse, and through these stories she subverts patriarchal authority established through biblical tradition, and constructs a new world order among women marginalized or outcast from traditional society.

Eve was the first customer to arrive at Bailey's Cafe, and her story provides the parameters for those who later come to stay with her (80). Just as the biblical Eve is a cultural and mythical touchstone by which female sexuality is ambiguously defined— temptress and mother—Eve sets the standard that determines which women will be allowed sanctuary in her "whorehouse convent" (116). To stay at Eve's, a woman must "know about delta dust," which not only means an understanding of the mythical, but also possessing the inner strength to escape abuse and redefine herself in the face of rejection (81). According to William Nash, Eve commits herself to empowering those rendered powerless by circumstance and experience, she does so in terms that recognize oppressive social conditions and teach survival rather than pure transcendence. Rather than dreaming of tearing down walls, Eve shows the women within her walls how to articulate their individual positions of power and to claim their right to selfhood by inverting the dreams that once bound them (215). Eve forces her boarders, and through them her readers, to confront the cultural definitions and expectations that have limited their opportunities and compelled them into situations where selfhood is defined by sexuality.

Eve's is not the first story in the text, but it is the first revision. Raised by "Godfather," the strict, dictatorial preacher who "always told me that since I never had a real mother or father and wouldn't be alive if it weren't for him, *he* would decide when I was born," Eve finds herself emotionally abandoned as she begins to mature sexually (82). When he discovers her finding sexual release by lying pressed to the ground while Billy Boy stomps around her, Godfather laughs and then punishes her for her sexual transgression. Stripped of the clothing and purged of the food he has provided, he sends her away naked and hungry.

Eve's name and the story of naive sexuality resulting in exile immediately calls to mind her biblical predecessor. But in telling Eve's story, Naylor reclaims female sexuality from a patriarchal tradition which would condemn it as destructive defiance of divine law. For while Godfather represents, as his name suggests, patriarchal authority, particularly that associated with western religious tradition, Eve's rejection of his authority and her realization that he is constrained by his fear of gossip undermines his authority and reduces him to little more than a petty despot. As Maxine Lavon Montgomery explains: "Perhaps the most definitive change in Eve's evolving consciousness occurs when she comes to recognize his church as a social construct reflecting the hierarchies of a society which relegates women to the undesirable position of subservient 'other' " (28). Such positioning is an integral part of the Signification process, since Signifyin(g) is, in the Lacanian sense, the Other of discourse (Gates 50). Thus Eve's defining moment, and the moment she looks for when deciding which women can stay at her boardinghouse, occurs when she rejects the language, and thus the signification,[3] of the father to embrace that of the Other, the feminine.[4]

Realizing that "to be thrown out of his church was to be thrown out of the world" (85), Eve recreates herself by returning to her most elemental form; after wandering to Arabi, she wanders on toward New Orleans realizing "the only road that lay open to me was the one ahead, and the only way I could walk it was the way I was. I had no choice but to walk into New Orleans neither male nor female—mud" (91). Even when living with Godfather, Eve had identified with the earth, trying "to blend in, with my brown hair, brown skin, and brown sack dress" (86). But it is in her journey that Eve returns to the form which, according to western patriarchal tradition, man was formed: dust. But Eve's story claims a new tradition: it is woman who is born out of the dust:

> The delta dust exists to be wet. And the delta dust exists to grow things, anything, in soil so fertile its tomatoes, beans, and cotton are obscene in their richness. And since that was one of the driest winters in living memory, the dust sought out what wetness it could and clung to the tiny drops of perspiration in my pores. It used that thin film of moisture to creep its way up toward the saliva in my mouth, the mucus in my nose. Mud forming and caking around the tear ducts in my eyes, gluing my lashes together. There was even enough moisture deep within my earwax to draw it; my head becoming

stuffed up and all sounds a deep hum. It found the hidden damp-
ness under my fingernails, between my toes. The moist space between my hips was easy, but then even into the crevices around the
anus, drawing itself up into my menstrual blood. Layers and layers
of it were forming, forming, doing what it existed to do, growing the
only thing it could find in one of the driest winters in living memory.
Godfather always said that he made me, but I was born of the delta.
(90)

In her return to the primordial, Eve also reclaims autonomy
and identity, rejecting the patriarchal claims of Godfather and
western religious tradition to become the very essence of her
name, "the mother of all living things." Rather than being ex-
pelled from a garden paradise to face a harsh world, Naylor's
Eve creates her own private, eternal garden: "Even the stone
wall blooms around Eve's garden. And there's never a single
season without flowers" (91–92). At the center of the yard is "the
stump of her only tree" surrounded by "circles and circles of
lilies" of every kind (92). The allusions are clear, as is much of
the revisioning: the large tree stump, representative of the
knowledge prohibited by patriarchal authority has been cut
down and is now surrounded by flowers, traditional symbols of
feminine beauty and sexuality. Further, the flowers which immediately encircle and overwhelm the phallic tree are lilies, associated with purity and virginal love. Equally significant is the
fact that the garden is part of the litmus test for women who
wish to stay at Eve's: when they ask Bailey for directions, he
tells them, "Go out the door, make a right, and when you see the
garden—if you see the garden—you're there" (92). The flowers
are also linked to the reclaiming of self-worth and identity for
the women staying there. None of the women staying at Eve's
are paid by their "gentleman callers"; instead, each caller must
bring the woman he visits the flower of her choice: "If he can't
do that much for you, he doesn't need to waste your time" (93).
Each woman chooses her flower according to her personality,
her story, or her sense of self-worth: Esther receives white roses
"that show up in the dark" (99); Peaches demands daffodils; and
Jesse Bell insists Eve cultivate dandelions, but refuses callers.
The only flowers in Eve's garden that are not for sale are hers,
the lilies. The flowers become part of the healing process for the
women coming to Eve, blurring the issue of prostitution by removing the cash nexus while nurturing their sense of self-worth
through their association with natural beauty. Eve's refusal to

sell her lilies manifests her reclamation of her sexuality and her sense that her sexuality is hers alone.

Eve's significance, however, extends beyond the reclamation of female sexuality signified through her name, origin, occupation, and garden. In rejecting Godfather's assertion that he "made" her and in recreating herself out of the delta dust, Eve is rejecting the masculine appropriation of generativity, reclaiming it for the feminine. Such a reclaiming of generative power aligns Eve with the earth-mother and fertility goddesses of other traditions rejected and repressed in favor of the patriarchal within western tradition.[5] Further, Eve's refusal to justify her life or her decisions, her statement that "right or wrong, good or bad . . . what I am—I am" (85), echoes God's self-identification to Moses, "I am that 'I Am' " (Exodus 3:14). Finally, in having Eve leave Godfather's by walking from east of the delta, from Pilottown, to Arabi and New Orleans in a journey that takes a thousand years, Naylor creates an allusion linking Eve, and her role among a community of women outcast from society, with the millennial reign of Christ (Montgomery 29). Both the physical journey which reverses the history of patriarchal religion—moving from the allusion to Pilot washing his hands of responsibility, to the flight into Egypt, to the garden—and the time frame encourages the view of Eve as a creative revisioning of feminine salvation. And for the women who live in her house, Eve is a figure of redemption.

If "Eve's Song" debunks the story of original sin in which female sexuality brings about the downfall of man, "Sweet Esther" casts aside the story of sexual power of the enslaved woman. The biblical Esther, one of the captives taken from Jerusalem and brought into the land of Babylon, is raised by her older cousin Mordecai, and selected to join the harem of King Xerxes after he divorced his wife because she would not obey him when he asked her to appear before guests. The king falls in love with Esther and makes her queen. Later, when one of the king's advisors, Haman, plots to kill Mordecai and all the Jews in the kingdom, Esther risks the king's displeasure by approaching him personally and interceding on behalf of her people. Esther is successful and Haman is executed.

Traditionally the biblical story of Esther is viewed as that of a woman singled out by her beauty who manipulates her husband/king in order to save the lives of her people. Naylor reconstructs the story so that the issue of slavery is in the forefront along with the profligate behavior of the men who buy and sell women. Naylor's Esther is a twelve-year-old who has been sold by her brother to the sexually sadistic farmer for whom he works. Surrounded by the relative richness of her new home, Esther imagines herself as being like a "princess" and does not immediately understand her situation (96). Indeed, the expectations of her captor are beyond her experience, and to her distress and confusion she finds "that in the dark, words have a different meaning" (97). Although she "tr[ies] to find a word for what happens . . . in the cellar," it is so far outside her realm of experience it is only through stories of extreme good and evil (*The Shadow*) that she comes to realize that "what we do in the cellar is make evil" (98). She stays with the farmer for twelve years, one for every year her brother, despite his wife's complaints, let her live in his house. But unlike the biblical Esther she does not rescue her brother or those like her. Although she contemplates killing the farmer, "sparing the other twelve-year-olds . . . with brothers," she concludes that "There are too many of them to kill" (99).

Esther's narrative is continuously broken by the voice of patriarchal authority: *"We won't speak about this, Esther."* Centered and italicized, the sentence represents the silencing authority against which the narrative is set. Yet the final voice is Esther's, not just in the telling of her story, but in the closing indictment against her brother. For not only does Esther insist that all her male visitors bring her white roses that "show up in the dark" and which she can see as they "wither and die," but also that the men call her *"little sister,"* her brother's name for her (99). Thus Esther's story breaks the cycle of silence which represses stories of slavery and abuse.

The most playful narrative is that of "Jesse Bell," which builds upon puns and free play with the associations western culture has built around the biblical story of Jezebel. By tradition, "Jezebel" is used to describe someone who is adulterous and seductive, a manipulator of men. Within the Bible her sins seem to center around two issues: first, she is a non-Israelite and priestess of a female deity whose worship includes both homosexual and heterosexual celebrations; second, she subverts patriarchal authority when she influences her husband, King Ahab, and when she takes Naboth's vineyard. Similarly, the main "sins" of Jesse Bell center around issues of sexuality (bisexuality) and cultural difference (class), but throughout the story, Naylor creates what Bakhtin describes as a double-voiced narrative by inserting "a new semantic orientation" into a discourse "that already has, and keeps, its own orientation" (qtd. in Todorov 71). In part, Naylor maintains reader awareness of the multivocality through the use of puns, both verbal and situational: *Jesse Bell* marries into the *King* family, incurring the hatred of *Uncle Eli*; she maintains the integrity of her cultural roots and refuses to adopt the Kings' "religion": "white folks . . . were Uncle Eli's god. And it was a god I wasn't buying" (125). Her husband divorces her, not because she has a lesbian lover (he repeatedly suggests a *ménage à trois*) but because she is arrested in a police raid of a "dyke club" (131); and at Eve's boarding house Jesse is known for her refusal of gentleman callers.

But Jesse's story is more than a comedic revision of indictments against gender and cultural difference; a large part of Jesse's narrative focuses on Jesse's heroin addiction and Eve's role in her recovery. When Jesse Bell's marriage into the wealthy Sugar Hill King family ends in a bitter divorce, and she loses not only her home and her husband but also her children and her reputation because of sensationalized stories printed by her husband's friends in the *Herald Tribune*, she turned to heroin and female lovers. Eve met Jesse in the women's house of detention and gave Jesse her card, telling her "when she was tired of wallowing in her own shit, come and find her" (133). Eve helps Jesse kick her habit, but through unconventional means: after helping her through withdrawal, Eve gives her a gift: a "velvet case . . . lined with sky blue silk. The eyedropper was made of crystal, the teaspoon and syringe pure silver, the book of matches embossed" (139). Jesse also appears to have unlimited access to the enslaving drug. When Jesse succumbs to temptation and must again suffer through withdrawal, Eve again sees her through and then presents her with a gold set of works. When Jesse bitterly asks if the next set would be platinum, Eve tells her, "Remember where we are; that's only the beginning of what's available here" (142). Thus Eve will support Jesse in her struggle, but in the end Jesse must draw upon her own strength of will to renounce the drug. In other words she must save herself in order to recover. According to Bailey, "A woman is either ready for Eve's or she's not. And if she's ready, she'll ask where to find it on her own" (80). Thus, feminine salvation, as embodied through Eve, demands self-knowledge, self-worth, and self-determination, not just a vague desire for redemption.

But such revision is not without ambiguity. During Jesse's recovery, in a moment of frustration and desperation, she tells

Eve to go to hell. Eve's response, "I think you've forgotten that's where we are" (141), ambiguously points to Jesse's immediate situation, the withdrawal from heroin, but also to the ambiguity of Eve's house. Described by Jesse as a "whorehouse convent" and viewed by some as "a house full of nothing but sluts and whores and tramps" (80), it is more than a house of prostitution. Bailey tells readers that "Eve lets out rooms in her house to single women. Sometimes they pay her, sometimes they don't. I don't know how she decides when to charge or not. . . . I do know that charity has nothing to do with it. Eve is not a charitable person" (80). For those making the journey, the first stop is Gabe's pawn shop, on the other side of Bailey's Cafe from Eve's, but they have to

> be smart enough to understand the sign. One side of the cardboard hanging on his front door has a painted clock with movable hands. It reads, Back at —— ——, and each hour he keeps moving the hands one hour forward. And under the clock is a red-and gold arrow pointing down the street to us. After two or three hours, if the person keeps coming back without getting the message, and he thinks they're still worth it, he'll flip the sign over to where it reads, Out of Business, with that same arrow pointing down the street to us. Gabe is never open—we never close. (144–45)

For those who figure out the sign, Bailey's Cafe is "a way station" (159), a place where time is frozen (219); it is mobile so that when people find themselves "hanging on the edge" they can "take a breather for a while" (28); and it can be "the last place before the end of the world" (68), a "limbo" (221) that "sits right on the margin between the edge of the world and infinite possibility" with "the back door open[ing] out to a void" (76). The last stop on the "relay for broken dreams" (144), Eve's brownstone is available only to those who can find it. But for those who can see the garden, Eve's represents an alternative to both the past (Gabe's) and the void (Bailey's); it represents the possibility of a future.

While Eve is on one level a figure of salvation, she does not obviously encompass traditional moral or ethical attributes. Further, admittance to Eve's brownstone does not always signify recovery, as demonstrated in "Mary (Take One)." Within Western tradition the name "Mary" signifies both the Virgin and the Magdalene, and Naylor's revisionist text reveals how the identities of "virgin" and "whore" are social constructs that are at once mutually defining and mutually destructive. When her narrative opens, Mary (Peaches) seems unquestionably aligned with the image of Mary Magdalene: when she first appears at Bailey's Cafe, Sugar Man, a local pimp, "whisper[s] what every man [there] was thinking: Born to be fucked" (102). More subtly, her father comes looking for her but "no one knows her by that name," echoing the compressing of several biblical women into a single figure better known by her title, the Magdalene, than her name (100). Naylor's recontextualization, however, focuses on the cultural expectations and contradictions surrounding female beauty and sexuality.

Desired by men and envied and feared by women because of her physical beauty, Peaches is a young woman viewed by society as a sexual object, while viewing herself as an innocent child. When she was a child her father attempted to maintain her virginal status by building walls, literal and figurative, around her. But he cannot isolate her from the cultural expectations: when she is a child he shows her off to her friends who set her on their laps, say she "has promise," and secretly fondle her; when she is a teenager he enjoys the fact that boys come calling, and he tries to make the young men voice their sexual desires (104). For Peaches these expectations are revealed through the "gaze." Every holiday her father gives her expensive, elegant mirrors to be placed in her bedroom, and she begins to search in these mirrors for the image that others see so that she might reconcile their reactions with her sense of self. Instead, compelled by the need to believe in her own worth apart from the sexual desire she sees in the eyes of those around her, she internalizes the whore/virgin dichotomy, compartmentalizing her behavior and divorcing her reflected self from her body: "everywhere I turned, I could see her. But what was she doing in my room? She was a whore and I was Daddy's baby" (104). As she grows up, Peaches endeavors to overcome the threat posed by outer beauty by establishing an inner worth through intellectual achievement, good deeds, and hard works. But repeatedly she is judged by outward appearance until she finally surrenders to society's judgment. But with the loss of her ability to separate her inner- and outer-self, Peaches loses all sense of self-worth except as a sexual object and begins to despise herself: "Before, I had only hated her. Now I wanted to hate myself" (107). Finally, in the belief that her outer self should reflect the distorted inner image, she goes to the mirror, the symbol of her external beauty, and uses a beer opener to rip open her cheek.

Both Freudian and Lacanian theories argue that the gaze is not simply an act of vision, but rather an ideological arena enclosing and dramatizing power relationships. And here as elsewhere, cultural dynamics inevitably invoke a series of binaries—active/passive, object/subject, male/female—with the male designated as spectator and the female as spectacle. According to Lacanian theory, when Peaches gazes at herself in the mirror and sees herself seeing herself, she sees the "*outside*," not a perception of the inner being, but rather "the objects that it apprehends" (80). Further, the direct gaze caries with it a proprietary aspect, a "*belong to me* aspect," that "annihilates" the subject (81). Thus when she looks in the mirror, her gaze reflects the masculine, which reduces her image to that of an object of desire and destroys the inner self: "For as long as I could remember, I could see her in their eyes. But now as I looked in the mirror . . . I could see her in mine" (107). The resulting self-hatred eventually demands that she destroy the object, just as it has destroyed the subject. "Mary (Take One)" presents readers with one of the most powerful fictional depictions of the "devastation caused by patriarchal reduction of women to their physical appearance" (Fowler 132), yet it is clear within the context of Naylor's novel that it is not only the extraordinarily beautiful women who are subject to reduction to sexual object. At one point Nadine, Bailey's wife, tells him "I am more than my body"; and while her insistence that he recognize the inner—as well as the outer—self "crushes" him at the time, he develops "a whole different way of looking at her—and at women" (18–19). Being defined in terms of the physical, in terms of their sexuality, is a common bond among the women in the novel, and the women of Eve's boarding house each reflect the destructive force of such objectification in different ways.

At Eve's, Peaches tries to transform the damaged self-image and the damaged self into a unified, beautiful whole. But the ambiguity occurs when Peaches's father comes to take back his daughter, and Eve urges him to trust her power to heal: "— Leave your daughter here . . . I'll return her to you whole," reassuring him that "whatever she's doing up in that room, she's doing it feeling beautiful" (113–14). Nevertheless, the vignette ends in ambiguity despite the decreased number of visitors and increased length of the visits, both presented as signs that eventually one man will realize her true worth and there will be no one else waiting. Twice more Eve tells Peaches' father to "go home," reassuring him that she will return his daughter "whole." But the last time he is standing in front of Eve's crying, calling for his daughter. And not only does Peaches refuse to answer, but also, before he hears Eve's assurance of healing, "he hears the bolt slide shut as the autumn winds blow cold," suggesting that he is shut out of Peaches's life and that "whole" will not encompass a return to him on an emotional level (114).

The final person to arrive at Bailey's Cafe is Mariam, "Mary (Take Two)," and her story finalizes Naylor's reconstruction. In many ways Mariam represents the epitome of the virgin/whore dichotomy. As the subject of female circumcision in her homeland, she is demonstrably virginal—any penetration would be obvious. Nevertheless, she has been impregnated, and as a result cast out from her community for violating sexual mores. The presentation of Mariam as a simplistic young woman who does not comprehend her situation makes her a victim at both ends of the spectrum: she is at once virgin/not virgin, whore/not whore. Thus, through Mariam's duality Naylor deconstructs the patriarchal concept of female sexuality.

As with the other stories, Naylor establishes a number of parallels between her character, an Ethiopian Jew, and her biblical predecessor: Mariam is fourteen; her people are ex-slaves, dispossessed "outcasts in their own nation"; much as the biblical Mary was turned away at the inn, Mariam is turned away from Israel because she "has no knowledge of the Talmud"; and she is brought to Eve's by Gabe, named for the archangel of the Annunciation (143, 146, 221). And just as the biblical stories of Eve and Mary set up as dynamic parallels, Mariam's story in many ways balances Eve's: sometimes analogous, sometimes opposite. Echoing Eve's thousand-year journey from Pilottown, through Arabi, to New Orleans, Mariam is mystically spirited from her village in the mountains of Ethiopia, five hundred miles south to Addis Ababa, to Gabe's pawn shop. But while Eve is assertive and knowing, Mariam is passive and simple. And if Eve's story is a rejection of the *logos*, the word of the father, Mariam's is a rejection of the cultural rituals performed in the name of the father. As Eve tells Nadine, "I know my bible well, . . . this *isn't* in the Law of Moses" (150). And although Naylor presents us with the biblical passages and ceremonial chants used to support female circumcision, Eve's graphic demonstration with the plum encapsulated within the recounting of Mariam's circumcision reveals the pain and physical suffering

inflicted on women by patriarchal religion in the name of preserving purity and repressing sexuality.

Naylor links Mariam's story with earlier narratives as well,
particularly Esther's. Just as Esther's narrative was broken with
the repeated, centered, and italicized, *"We won't speak of this,
Esther,"* the first few pages of Mariam's story are broken by the
repeated, centered, and italicized, *"No man has ever touched
me."* But while the voice in Esther's narrative is an intrusion of
the patriarchal into her recounting, the voice in Mariam's story
is her own. In fact, unlike the other boarders, Mariam does not
narrate her own story; rather, it is presented by Nadine, Eve,
and a third-person omniscient narrator who assumes various
points of view (Mariam's mother, the high priest's wife, and,
briefly and impressionistically describing the circumcision, Mariam). The italicized phrase is the only thing we hear Mariam
say; thus, Mariam's denial becomes the enforced silence com-
manded by the patriarchal authority of the earlier narrative.

The most overt (re)doubling, however, is signified by the
plum Mariam gives Eve when Gabe first brings her to Eve's.
Through western tradition, Eve and her expulsion from the
Garden has been linked with "the fruit of the tree," the apple,
while the Virgin Mary is associated with flowers, specifically the
lily. Within *Bailey's Cafe*, Naylor reverses these associations:
while Eve has been strongly linked to the Genesis story through
references to her garden, she is signified through flowers, specifically the lily, and is never associated with images of fruit. But
when presenting the figure traditionally seen as Eve's converse,
the female figure whose actions ameliorate Eve's sin, Naylor
links her with the biblical Eve by having Mariam hand Eve the
plum. It is with the plum that Eve explains, and graphically
demonstrates, to Nadine and to the reader, the horror of female
circumcision. But more importantly, the plum encapsulates the
consequences societal acceptance of the virgin/whore dichotomy: the essentialist assumptions which allow society to blame
the victim and mandate extreme measures to guard against
physical violation. Eve's dissection of a plum is a conscious, ritualized reversing of Mariam's circumcision, a rejection of patriarchal law and tradition in its oldest and most physical form. And
in the end, Eve assumes the role of midwife as Mariam, a refig-
ured Madonna, gives birth to the hope of the future, a son
named George. Thus as Nadine and Eve tell Mariam's story,
Naylor brings together issues of race, religion, and gender, all

revolving around the circumcision, pregnancy, and exile of this woman.

Finally, Naylor's reconceptualization of female sexuality within western religious tradition also alludes to Jesus's interrogations by the Pharisees when Eve confronts Sister Carrie of the Temple of Perpetual Redemption. Carrie continually confronts Eve and her boarders with "whore Scriptures," forgetting that, raised by a preacher, Eve can reply in kind. In fact, while Carrie has to hurriedly thumb through her bible to locate relevant scripture, Eve can not only identify the source, she can reply from the same book. When Sister Carrie quotes from Ezekiel condemning Eve for having "multiplied thy whoredoms" and doing "the work of an imperious whorish woman," Eve not only identifies the chapter and verses but also answers with a quotation from the same book a few verses later: "—Thou also, which hast judged thy sisters, bear thine own shame for thy sins that thou hast committed more abominable than they: they are more righteous than thou: yea, be thou confounded also, and bear thy shame, in that thou hast justified thy sisters" (134–35). Eve's answer emphasizes the theme of female community and of self-reliance. As interpreted through Bailey, Eve's reply reverses Sister Carrie's narrow-minded, misogynistic stance by stressing the basic connections between Jews and Christians and presenting within divine law an apparent advocation of a nonjudgmental stance toward feminine moral issues (136). Further, the heavy reliance on scripture from the Old Testament relevant to female sexuality points to a reclamation of status and dignity denied in the accepted patriarchal tradition.

In a novel consisting of narratively disconnected stories of individual women, Naylor presents a "double-voiced representation in art [utilizing] . . . [r]epetition, with a signal difference" (Gates 51). The discourse functions as a womanist reconceptualization of female sexuality, shifting the stigma of prostitution from the illicit sexuality of women to the illicit complicity of family, lovers, and society. And in so doing, Naylor revises the codes of power and dominance handed down through male-authored texts and reclaims women's histories of abuse and oppression, rescuing them from silence.

Notes

1. Peter Erickson has identified the Shakespearean motif, *A Midsummer Night's Dream*, in *The Women of Brewster Place*, while Jewelle Gomez notes

the adaptation of Dante's *Inferno* in *Linden Hills*, and Bharati Mukherjee has identified *The Tempest, Romeo and Juliet*, and *The Taming of the Shrew* as literary referents for *Mama Day*.

2. He adopts the name of the cafe and, through usage, the name of its previous owner when he buys the cafe.

3. Here I am using the term "signification" in the Saussurean sense which builds along the horizontal, syntagmatic axis, as compared to the African-American usage which builds upon the vertical, paradigmatic axis.

4. The recasting of authority is significant in terms of both form and content. For as Bakhtin asserts, the word of the father, authoritative discourse, permits no play and thus cannot enter into hybrid constructions such as Signification (342–44).

5. See Alicia Ostriker's *Feminist Revision and the Bible* (Cambridge: Blackwell Press, 1993) for a further discussion of the idea that the repressed of biblical narrative is evidently not the slain Father but the slain (and immortal) Mother.

WORKS CITED

Bakhtin, M. M. 1981. *The Dialogic Imagination*. Translated by Caryl Emerson and Michael Holquist. Austin: University of Texas Press.

Erickson, Peter. 1991. *Rewriting Shakespeare, Rewriting Ourselves*. Berkeley: University of California Press.

Fowler, Virginia C. 1996. *Gloria Naylor: In Search of Sanctuary*. New York: Twayne Publishers.

Gates, Henry Louis, Jr. 1988. *The Signifying Monkey: A Theory of African-American Literary Criticism*. New York: Oxford University Press.

Gomez, Jewelle. 1985. Naylor's inferno. Review of *Linden Hills*, by Gloria Naylor. *Women's Review of Books*: 7–8.

Lacan, Jacques. 1981. *The Four Fundamental Concepts of Psycho-Analysis*. Translated by Alan Sheridan, edited by Jacques-Alain Miller. New York: Norton.

Montgomery, Maxine Lavon. 1995. Authority, multivocality, and the new world order in Gloria Naylor's *Bailey's Café*. *African American Review* 29, no. 1:27–41.

Mukherjee, Bharati. 1988. There are four sides to everything. Review of *Mama Day*, by Gloria Naylor. *New York Times Book Review* 21:7.

Nash, William R. 1997. The dream defined: *Bailey's Cafe* and the reconstruction of American cultural identities. In *The Cultural Response to Gloria Naylor*, edited by Sharon Felton and Michelle C. Loris, 211–25. Westport, CT: Greenwood Press.

Naylor, Gloria. 1992. *Bailey's Cafe*. New York: Random House.

———. Interview. In *Gloria Naylor: In Search of Sanctuary*, by Virginia C. Fowler, 143–57. New York: Twayne.

Todorov, Tzvetan. 1984. *Mikhail Bakhtin: The Dialogical Principle*. Translated by Wlad Godzich. Minneapolis: University of Minnesota Press.

Taking America as a Lover: Contemporary Women "Engage" the American

MERRI LISA JOHNSON

"The answers are getting harder."
—*Blues Traveler, "Stand"*

WHAT WOULD HENRY DAVID THOREAU HAVE BEEN LIKE IN BED? Would he speak a word for nature in my ear? Would he fuck me like he walked westward, seeing in my face an ethereal sky, my body a meandering river? Would his rhythm be as slow and restrained as his prose? I'd like to know if Thoreau's mallard thought would have had to do with grabbing my hair in the same vehement manner with which he rips words from the soil around him, "transplant[ing] them to his page with earth adhering to their roots" (616). If Thoreau were my lover (David, I would have called him), would he have entered my body like he entered the woods—compulsively, spiritually, imperially? Finally, the most important question: *would I have liked it?*

As fun as it is to imagine "doing" the great literary icons of American literature (would Hawthorne have draped his hair about my face, stared with brooding eyes into mine? would Melville have romped on me like a violent sea? speared me like a whale?), the questions I raise serve as more than merely "literate smut."[1] Considering these aesthetic masters as my lovers is my way of reopening the discussion surrounding the relationship between contemporary American women writers, American literature, and the values it imparts. In this article, I will consider how women engage the male (read: traditional or dominant ideological) text of America as idea and reality through an examination of two contemporary authors representing very different feminist approaches to this patriarchal culture, demonstrating that the ways rock music critic and 'zine writer Lisa Carver and feminist anthropologist Ruth Behar "do" America

106

can be elucidated by contemporary psychological approaches to heterosexual love relationships. Based on their romances (one rocketing, one rocky), I conclude by proposing a third option for relationships between men and women on personal and textual levels.

Sandra Gilbert and Susan Gubar are well-known for their analyses of literary relationships between women writers and tradition as ones fraught with anxiety and absurdity. Volumes of feminist literary criticism reiterate the trope of revision, constructing oppositional relationships between contemporary women writers and tradition, suggesting not only that women fill in the absence of women's experience in literature, but that they replace the evils of patriarchy—imperialism and its undergirding hierarchies of culture over nature, men over women, the West over the rest, and so on—with a moral superiority inherent in the female perspective, reversing the hierarchical arrangement they seek to subvert. In order to get away from this combative dynamic among men and women, we need to create a more nuanced description of the relationship between our literatures; we need to imagine this dynamic differently.[2]

One way of doing this is by dwelling on the contradictions, complications, compulsions, and collaborations that characterize this relationship as one conducted between metaphorical lovers. What arises between men and women—the many ways we negotiate our personal daily interactions—resembles and provides insights into the literary lineage inherited and interrogated by women writers in the American tradition. There is more to this relationship than an unremitting turning away. Indeed, the line between love and hate, fucking and fighting, is a thin and fascinating space in which women write something much more complicated than a "revision" of male texts; they write the long, convoluted, sexy scripts of desire that pass between men and women on personal and social levels throughout time. We write the world together on bed-sheets and paper—tossing, turning, tearing—coming, parting, returning and more—always more.

Although Gilbert and Gubar are most often cited for their revision of Bloom's theory of "anxiety of influence" into an "anxiety of authorship" experienced by women who recognize the absence of female writerly role models, a position articulated in *The Madwoman in the Attic*, their sequel, *No Man's Land*, asserts that in place of anxiety, there exists "a paradigm of ambivalent affiliation, a construct which dramatizes women's intertwined attitudes of anxiety and exuberance about creativity" (170). Less well-known than "anxiety of authorship," the paradigm of "ambivalent affiliation" marks the center of my argument regarding the relationship between contemporary American women writers and tradition. Contemporary women writers exist *within* the tradition of American literature and culture; and even as we rework its elements, we continue to find pieces that we love, pieces we desire, pieces we play with—anxiously, exuberantly. Gilbert and Gubar's theory creates a sense of agency in the work of women writers:

> The idea of affiliation, as we propose to use it, suggests an evasion of the inexorable lineage of the biological family even while it also implies a power of decision in two historical directions. One may imagine oneself as having been adopted, and thus legitimized, as a literary heiress, but one may also adopt, and thus sanction, others to carry on the tradition one has established. Unlike 'influence,' then, which connotes an influx or pouring-in of external power, and 'authorship,' which stands for an originatory primacy, the concept of affiliation carries with it possibilities of both choice and continuity. Choice: one may consciously or not decide with whom to affiliate— align or join—oneself. Continuity: one is thereby linked into a constructed genealogical order which has its own quasi-familial inevitability. (171)

Choice and continuity diverge from more one-dimensional analyses of women writers as maids and seamstresses who repair the rips and messes of male canonical authors.

When conceived as lovers (rather than service people), women writers may be seen to struggle toward equitable conversation, personal pleasure, and extrication from oppressive gender structures of thought, engaging in the same struggles as women in love relationships. Ambivalent affiliation leaves space for women to choose America, to love it, and at the same time to influence its definitions and national mythologies.[3] Just like men and women who approach marriage as an opportunity to continue to learn how to love each other better, writers can cross gender lines to negotiate the text of America from various perspectives, to see what is good in each vision, to mirror and struggle over what seems bad. Ambivalent affiliation intervenes in the either-or thinking that dominates feminist literary criticism of contemporary women's texts as passive reiterations of America or active rejections and revisions.

Contemporary texts on heterosexual love relationships contribute useful concepts to the discussion of contemporary women writers and the masculine American literary and cultural tradition. The most useful concepts balance attention to patriarchal domination with a recognition of women's various forms of agency within that framework. In *My Enemy, My Love: Manhating and Ambivalence in Women's Lives*, Judith Levine complicates the antimale sentiment in feminism by revealing the negotiations by women within their love relationships with men. Levine pinpoints her subject as the "powerful unspoken theme of post-World War II feminism," that is, "the struggle with the enormously disquieting ambivalence accompanying the fury of recognized oppression," a complex circumstance she traces through the lives of several representative women (4).

In contrast to radically antimale groups like Women Against Sex who believe that men's sexuality is "violent," making "men so powerful that they can 'reach *within* women to fuck/construct us from the inside out,' " Levine examines the more common female position toward men and heterosexuality: an ambivalence marking the complicated terrain of recognizing the features of patriarchy in the face of a loved one, and vice versa (1). "Once you know something [i.e., develop a feminist consciousness]," Levine explains, "you cannot unknow it . . . but neither does the new knowledge erase the feelings that preceded it" (4). Levine's discussion of women's complicated feelings toward men echoes Gilbert and Gubar's descriptions of women writers and tradition, creating a continuity among narratives of lovers and writers. We affiliate ambivalently with the masculine part of our culture (in the form of boyfriends, fathers, canonized texts, and traditional values), learning to live in the unreconciled space between love and patriarchy. The ability to think outside of systems and relationships of domination characterizes the women Levine writes about, and it characterizes as well the most effective engagements of women writers with the male cultural text of America.

Taking America as a lover, then, functions for me as a paradigm through which to understand women who wrestle with the cultural values and literary texts of this nation in ways that nourish both, looking at America with a loving eye, but not depending on it to fulfill all of one's desires. This theme also appears in the pop psychology book by Judith Sills, *Loving Men More, Needing Men Less*, in which Sills advocates that women read men differently, in less antagonistic terms: "Love him more—because that is the source of the joy. But need him less—

because that will keep you strong" (36). She encourages women to "refocus," a process she defines as "looking inside ourselves for powerful solutions" and "[c]hoosing to see with a loving eye, not to blind yourself to exploitation, but simply so you yourself can enjoy a better view" (56, 60). Her effort to divert women's energy from "fixing him and fixing relationships"—a process she perceives as "inescapably demeaning"—aims at "a fundamental shift of attitude, from woman as reactor to woman as actor" (24, 67).

While I am indeed *ambivalent* toward the self-help industry because of its consistent targeting of female audiences—a perpetuation of sexist divisions among those who act in the world [men] and those who care for others [women] that gives women full responsibility for the nature and success of love relationships in our society, [4] nevertheless Sills' perspective on the fallout of the sexual revolution bears productively on the issue of contemporary women writers and the (male) American tradition. Her ideas place women in the powerful position of deciding how to view this text, whether to experience it as a force of domination or a reservoir of salvageable ideals. First, Sills outlines the reversal of gender roles that once positioned women as dependent and secondary in love relationships:

> If you think of the traditional model's themes of 'live to give' and 'give to get' as a thesis, the Women's Revision, 'give less, take more,' is its antithesis. It is a relationship paradigm born of outrage at the inequities of the traditional deal. It says, in effect, that women are only needier than men because men set it up that way. (28)

The second half of her point is that this reversal left something to be desired: a way to coexist with men; she writes, "The great reward of the Women's Revision was that we like ourselves a lot more. But we liked men a lot less" (29). Finally, she concludes that "an awful lot of us see the Women's Revision as a mixed blessing, because we sense that all this self-focus has pushed us further away from heterosexual love" (31). Levine and Sills present a salient issue for the present generation of feminists as lovers and literary critics dealing with the "mixed blessing" of men and their texts: what to do with the men in our lives who bear simultaneously the features we most appreciate in humanity *and* the visage of oppressors from time immemorial? How can we get in bed with these men and their values, as girlfriends and as writers, without getting wrecked, without simply complying with the forces of female subordination? What would constitute a "safe sex" approach to engaging masculinist texts of America?

This difficult balancing act perhaps gave rise to the separatist impulse of feminist revisionism, but as third wave feminists make clear, the current generation in no way wishes to live apart from men; neither do we succumb to traditional relationship configurations.[5] While separatist feminism presents its occasional thrills—for instance, Inga Muscio's recent monograph, *Cunt: A Declaration of Independence*, which advocates the reclamation of the word "cunt" into a "woman-centered, cuntlovin" perspective on social issues ranging from birth control to masturbation to the support of "cuntlovin' " businesses and political events, it ultimately alienates and divides—"What it boils down to is this: If it didn't *originate* with women or the Goddess, if it does not *spiritually, emotionally, physically, psychologically and financially benefit* women, it does not serve women. So fucken chuck it" (Muscio 76). The spirit of self-recovery and brazen effrontery invoked by Muscio suggests some seductive and transgressive elements worth examining, but these qualities do not require separatism; in fact, they provide driving elements in various nonseparatist feminist negotiations with male texts.

Lisa Carver is equally loud, visceral, and thrilling in *Dancing Queen: A Lusty Look at the American Dream*, a slim pink book that strikes me as at once a reiteration of traditional American characteristics such as exuberance *and* a saucy transgression of American mores. The self-appointed "Adamic namer" enacts this exuberance and transgression through her female aggressiveness and threats to compulsory heterosexuality; Carver's opening lines capture this combination well:

> I'm American. Always have been and I always will be. I'm zesty and smart and cute and sleazy and direct and confrontational. I'll never be elegant and I'll never have a long attention span. I eat Cheerios for breakfast and hot fudge sundaes for dessert. I yell at my TV. I'm enthusiastic, abrupt, self-obsessed, and I love boobs. (xi)

Carver consistently aligns herself with traditional American values, for better and worse; for instance, she writes, "I imagined how I would have an island where loaves of Wonder bread grew on bushes and I could decide who would live and who would die and what jobs everyone would have. . . . Or how I was going to run away as soon as I turned thirteen and be a prostitute and take drugs" (xii). Carver takes on the American identity with all its creativity, capitalist consumption, inherent imperialism, and, especially, its mobility—"The American is wild and free, and her country is big, so she must roam" (xiii)—a freedom traditionally withheld from the lives of women.[6]

Forestalling feminist and otherwise academic tsk-tsking at her book, Carver yells at her readers:

> People are so sensitive these days! They think they're French or something. Americans have forgotten what's great about being American. It's not our sensitivity. It's our impatience, our changeability, our excitement, our openness, our cheer, our sexuality, our very crassness. . . . Let other countries be patient. Let other countries be refined. Let other countries think all the time. They do it better anyway. I'd rather have a peanut butter sundae and do a little dance. (xv)

Peace Corps material she is not; however, her reading of America is a reading of the *dream*, not the *reality*.[7] Though her assertions at times come across as naive—

> What being American meant in the pioneer days, and what it still means today for those with a little bravery, is to create one's own world. If you can't vacuum so great, just write a book about all the things you were dreaming of that were distracting you from noticing those specks in the corner. And everything will be wonderful in the end. (xvi)

—her commitment to American ideals and her appropriation of them into the lives of women are acts that play with and reinvigorate the traditionally masculine text of America that has come under such vigilant attacks from other feminist corners. She makes the idea of America exciting again, and her excitement comes from the feminist appropriation of male privileges and desires for herself, enacting what Naomi Wolf calls "Nike feminism," drawing on the contemporary ad campaign of tennis shoes and sportswear that encourages women to "Just do it." Lisa Carver kicks her heels in the air and "does America" to the hilt.

She takes all the joy men have felt in being American and directs it toward her own life, even though the original male script categorically precluded women from manifesting the traits of the American—freedom, mobility, self-definition, and economic promise. Her sense of entitlement to these traits is absolute, revealing no fear of reprimand, no feeling of inadequacy or anxiety regarding the historical position of women in America. She straps it on like a natural. Yet even as she appropriates these typically male characteristics, Carver resists the rigid gender roles in which they are encrypted; rather than cross-dressing (or donning American-ness like a strap-on), she actually regenders the American from the inside. Instead of describing this process as a feminization of America,[8] I will call it the Americanization of the feminine, a process by which women graft American freedoms on to the female body.

By way of explaining the ingenuity of Carver's gender transfusion in the body of the American, I turn to Patrocinio Schweickart's article on feminist reader-response theory, "Reading Ourselves: Toward a Feminist Theory of Reading." Her negotiation of women's ambiguous reactions to masculinist canonical literature explains how feminist writers can interact positively with male texts, moving beyond the oversimplifying format of the "resisting reader" advocated by Judith Fetterley (and the corresponding war on visual pleasure enacted by Laura Mulvey):

> Feminist critics of male texts, from Kate Millett to Judith Fetterley, have worked under the sign of the "Resisting Reader." Their goal is to disrupt the process of immasculation by exposing it to consciousness, by disclosing the androcentricity of what has customarily passed for the universal. However, feminist criticism written under aegis of the resisting reader leaves certain questions unanswered, questions that are becoming ripe for feminist analysis: Where does the text get its power to draw us into its designs? Why do some (not all) demonstrably sexist texts remain appealing even after they have been subjected to thorough feminist critique? The usual answer—that the power of male texts is the power of the false consciousness into which women as well as men have been socialized—oversimplifies the problem and prevents us from comprehending both the force of literature and the complexity of our responses to it. (618)[9]

Schweickart's answer is "that the male text draws its power over the female reader from authentic desires, which it rouses and then harnesses to the process of immasculation [learning to think like men, to identify with a male point of view, and to accept as normal and legitimate a male system of values, one of whose central principles is misogyny]" (618). In other words, male texts such as that of the American identity contain liberatory kernels which are worthwhile, even empowering, for women to excavate and indulge. The trick to recuperating the liberatory kernel of desire without perpetuating the system of gender domination in which it is enmeshed is to harness that desire to a feminist, rather than masculinist, social vision. Lisa Carver turns this trick.

This double vision of male texts which Schweickart calls "a negative hermeneutic that discloses their complicity with patriarchal ideology, and a positive hermeneutic that recuperates the utopian moment—the authentic kernel—from which they draw a significant portion of their emotional power" appears in *Dancing Queen* in the form of Carver's *jouissant* American dream, a dream defined by traditional American values impressed in service to her *femme* desires, pleasures, fantasies, and life (619). Although she claims that "[l]ike most Americans, [she] know[s] very little about what's going on in the world" and that she "can't seem to figure out politics of the masses of anything of that nature," Carver is clearly aware of the political impact of her voice, addressing a variety of social issues in every chapter and speaking out notably in defense of "white trash" culture as "the fun class" as well as a voracious female libido directed at everything from Russian leaders to Olivia Newton-John (97, 10).

Indeed, the sexuality of contemporary women marks one very important axis along which the Americanization of the feminine occurs.[10] Lisa Carver indulges her female sexuality in ways that position it as a strength in her interaction with the world, an affront and a pleasure, and an attitude that derives directly from her perception of herself as an American. Her revaluation of such female spaces as the gynecologist and the hairdresser demonstrate this willful reconception of female sexuality against the dictates of conventional decorum as she describes the excitement aroused in her by being touched in erotic ways in situations that require the repression of erotic responses; this view is in stark and relieving opposition to the more conventional reading of these spaces as utilitarian at best, violation at worst. Although many women would flinch at Carver's assertion "that every woman, despite her own unique personality, is part submissive masochistic exhibitionist," her position is decidedly constructive, as demonstrated in her chapter on "Other Women's Bodies" in which she eroticizes the non-flat stomach, as opposed to "the Jamie Lee Curtis stomach," about which she says: "It looks miserly. Seeing someone fight nature so hard makes me nervous. Nature wants you to have a belly" (69, 77). Through humor, off-color personal observations, and flagrant admissions of "problem" desires, the exuberance of the American is rewritten in Carver's book as American female *jouissance* by linking freedom and vulgarity with sexual adventurousness and femininity.

I take Carver's effrontery as a model or permission slip to be bad—sexual, explicit. My approach stirs up a number of issues that I discover tangled inside the texts and bodies of women who engage the American (figure, canon, man). I imagine my words and fantasy images raise red flags for feminists because like Carver with her fetish for Russian leaders, I too host "problem" desires.[11] It is through this part of my experience that I rethink the relationship between women writers and male (literary, social, and bodily) texts. Thinking of Schweickart's hesitation about the over-simplication in Fetterley's resisting reader—a position that reduces the complexity of male-female relationships by suppressing the empowering ways women move in and out of "male" roles and texts and ignoring the liberatory kernels men drop here and there in their texts—I see more complicated possibilities for the feminist body in bed (literally and figuratively) with men. The same fluidity of roles occurs in the nonfeminist-looking sex scene: men and women move in and out of positions of author-ity over the texts of sex, love, desire, and relationships. Recognizing this fluidity frees women (and women writers) from feeling nonfeminist when fucking with men and their texts (with all the connotations of playfulness, pleasure, and resistance that phrase evokes).[12]

Lisa Carver consistently engages in this sort of complicated, sexy playfulness. One final example is the closing chapter of *Dancing Queen*—"The Manifest Destiny of Anna Nicole Smith"—in which she "plays" with Anna Nicole's breasts. Regretting the increasing timidity of the American people, Carver reflects on the "born risk takers" by which "[o]ur country was made great" who now "just see[m] to make people mad" (133). As a way of intervening in the dichotomy of today's American "into offended citizens and citizens paralyzed with the fear of offending," Carver introduces, with her compelling combination of seriousness and farce, a fresh view of Anna Nicole Smith's breasts that seems neither traditionally male nor traditionally feminist (133). These surgically assisted monstrosities emblematize for Carver what I am calling American feminist *jouissance*:

I admire Anna Nicole because she is living out the American dream: making the most of her God-given talents without a shred of guilt! . . . To be truly American, one must have lots of personality. It doesn't have to be a good personality; there just needs to be a lot of it. Cordelia Teatherly [local legend of long-lasting female anger], Anna Nicole and Jessica Dubrof [who died at age seven trying to be the youngest pilot to fly across the country] each embody, in their own way, the quality that made America, for better and for worse, what it is. None of the three were proper. All of them went beyond the boundaries. They had that most American of qualities: excess. (137)

The element of excess marks a consistent feminist strategy for overflowing the boundaries of polite discourse and gender roles; in this quality, Carver's feminism strikes me as particularly American. Carver ends on a note of delirium as her pleasure in embracing America mounts: "Long live the fiery, the unguilty, the unhumble, the dazzling, the cheerful and the brave. Even if they don't live long, even if they look obnoxious or even stupid in a certain light, they're still wonderful and magnificent to me, and they're free, free, free" (138). These, the final words to *Dancing Queen*, reiterate Carver's unrelenting and total acceptance of America-the-idea. Bootstraps and pleasure may not be all we need to make it in this world, even less so for some than others, but as gifts to herself and her (white American) readers, they are exciting and valuable booty from the male American text.

While Carver executes a *coup d'etat* toward a feminist America, she leaves crucial elements of her position—purposely, but questionably—unexamined. She fits within Ruth Sidel's category of "New American Dreamers"—young women who appropriate the American dream and neither interrogate its qualities nor recognize its limits, enacting an incomplete feminist ethics.[13] Her unwillingness to critically interrogate the undersides and international implications of American values puts her in the (inadvertant?) position of imperial feminism, flaunting a devil-may-care attitude arising from her working class, bisexual, white American identity, a combination of resistant and complicit subject positions in American culture. At once transgressive and traditional, Carver leaves herself open to accusations of solipsism, isolationism, and exclusionary naming practices. When she cries out, "I'm American," she claims ground for some women and turns a blind eye on the parceling out and policing of entitlement to American freedoms, mobility, and consumption. *Dancing Queen's* merits and faults are one and the same; Carver's American female *jouissance* is both revolutionary and retrograde, depending on which front you're watching. For a more self-conscious and internationally contextualized engagement with the male text of America, it is necessary to turn to the writings of women of color and to postcolonialism. "Woman of color," however, is one among a number of identity labels criticized for its ambiguity and arbitrary usage, its political cachet and artificiality, by feminist anthropologist Ruth Behar, in whose work I discover another version of feminist America, influenced by her position as always *en otro lado*.

Through postcolonial theory and autobiographical scholarship, Behar assesses the limitations and realities of the American dream.[14] Two of her major publications, *Translated Woman: Crossing the Border with Esperanza's Story* and *The Vulnerable Observer: Anthropology that Breaks Your Heart*, include sections that reflect on the author's position as a Cuban-American academic: "Latina" for the purposes of hiring statistics at the University of Michigan, "*gringa*" in Mexico, and "white" by virtue of intellectual achievement according to her family and colleagues. In her stories of border-crossing and immobility, Behar reveals a deep ambivalence about her allegiances: "Trying to figure out where I stood on the border between the United States and Mexico, I felt as though the fault lines of the divided America were quaking within me. Which America was my America? To which of the Americas did I owe my allegiance?" (322). In *Translated Woman*, Behar considers the colonial relationship between the United States and Mexico, a relationship perceived even by the street peddler whose *historias* she translates and transcribes: "Esperanza's keen awareness that Mexicans have been sold to the United States by their government suggests that she is awake to her status as a colonized person" (319). Behar extends her analysis of colonialism to gender issues as well, examining the enclosures of capitalism and patriarchy: "Patriarchal law exists within a framework of ownership and possession, in which women are objects of exchange. But what has not always been seen is that women are also subjects who are conscious of themselves as the things being exchanged" (282–83). Although the view from postcolonial feminism attends more to ambivalence than to allegiance, and is more cautious than exuberant, Behar nevertheless acknowledges the slippery strategies of agency developed by women within hierarchical relationships to male cultural and literary texts.

The appropriation of Pancho Villa as an icon in Mexican women's "no-name feminism" demonstrates one method of "loving men more and needing men less" as a method of interacting with masculinist images and mythologies (276). After seeing the women of Mexquitic invoke Pancho Villa in their sacred communal healing rites, Behar poses the crucial question:

> If national identity, in its heroic mode, was figured as male, how then could Mexican women "plot themselves into a narrative without becoming masculine or attempting to speak from the devalued position?" Under these circumstances, is there a place for women in the narrative of national history, or is the only narrative open to them that of a romance outside history and the nation? (315)

Her reflections on the problem of women and (masculine) nationalism underscore the strategy of gender-bending and ambivalent affiliation:

> Esperanza . . . seems to me to be seeking an answer to this question by turning to Pancho Villa as a "metaphor of historical imagination." Plotting herself, with a vengeance, into a national narrative of male heroism, dominance, violence, and coercion, she is writing herself out of the masochistic marianismo narratives of the suffering Virgin and the treacherous woman archetype. And she is writing herself back into national epic history by reenacting that history and appropriating that history as performance and as healing. Refusing to be seduced into femininity, she is cutting out a new window from which to view, and enter, a male narrative that seems to be sealed off to her gaze. (315)

Behar's reading of Esperanza creates a pattern of continuity with Lisa Carver, rejecting traditional femininity in favor of a femme or performative national identity. Behar sees Esperanza as recuperating the liberatory kernel of a masculinist cultural history: "Resurrecting the image of Pancho Villa evokes, among many other contradictory meanings, the promise of social reform symbolized by the Mexican Revolution begun in 1910, in which one million people lost their lives" (307). Esperanza figuratively takes Pancho as a lover, negotiating with his image to emphasize what she can use (the vision of social change) and suppress what would subordinate her (male superiority). She sees in him what is useful and nourishing, excising the rest from her transformative reproduction of his meaning in her life.[15]

Esperanza's *historias* are punctuated with the word, *"coraje,"* which means a rage that makes a person physically sick. This rage is one form of feminist response to masculinist cultural texts through which women appropriate the male text as a tool and reject it as a system of domination:

> [I]n her narrative, coraje is more than an illness state; it becomes a central metaphor for reflecting upon her condition as a woman under patriarchy. Coraje expresses Esperanza's sense of the wrongness of the violence inscribed on her body in the name of patriarchal law. It is her own body that has been history to her, and it is this body that must be healed by being rehistoricized in the magical space of the Pancho Villa cult. (284)

Given this dimension of her story, it is clear that Esperanza's engagement with Pancho is not a simple text of feminine self-subordination. Using her body as a stage upon which to perform rage, masculinity, and liberation, Esperanza undermines the oppositions of male/female in her *historias* of colonization and resistance. *Coraje*, like Lisa Carver's femme American identity, combines male and female desires and actions in Esperanza's body, a force by which these women break free of the confines of preexisting scripts of national and gender identity. By loving male texts more (taking from them what is good) and needing them less (excising or engaging differently what is bad and imperial), contemporary women writers can form an allegiance to America (or other male texts and people) that does not require self-subordination.

Esperanza, more than Behar, demonstrates the "love more, need less" paradigm. Behar does not create a vision of recuperating American values, weighting her argument more on the side of critique than embrace. In *The Vulnerable Observer*, Behar includes an essay titled "The Girl in the Cast" in which she discusses the problem of the "prisoner syndrome" experienced by patients who are immobilized by illness or accident, a syndrome she knows first-hand from her childhood experience in a full-body cast after a car wreck with her family. In this essay, the female body appears as a prisoner and a prison; and in order to revise this association, Behar explores the idea of the body as homeland. She learns to tend to her body as a space in which she lives. Although she does not fully pursue the parallel, her article implies the need to reconsider one's nation as a homeland which must be tended well in order to remain or become inhabitable. As a Cuban-American, it is important for Behar to discover strategies for making that national identity an inhabitable space. Her self-images as a "guilty *gringa*" and a "woman in a cast" do not, however, chart a recuperable feminist postcolonial American space in which to live. When she "does" America—in her desires for the things of capitalism like Persian rugs and ceramic tiles—she feels shame as a collaborator in contemporary colonialism; nowhere in her texts does she determine a way of being American or rethinking America that would nourish both partners in the relationship (1993, 336). Perhaps such an engagement is more and less possible depending on race, class, and ethnicity.

Hochschild asserts that race and class affect one's ability to believe in the dream; specifically, she documents the ways reality undermines the dream in the lives of poor African-Americans. Further, she notes the increasingly shared disaffection across racial lines with the American Dream, a phenomenon she considers dire for the future of this nation. Lisa Carver's playfulness ought to be read here as distinctly white and privileged in ways that create in me (another white American woman) a wariness about the ethics of such an exuberant embrace of the world, even as I recognize how good it is for women to finally feel entitled to that world. Linda Bell, in *Rethinking Ethics in the Midst of Violence*, writes, "A spirit of play, coupled with a critical and political awareness, can be used by those who are oppressed to expunge from themselves internalized aspects of oppression and to open a space in which they may begin to relate nonoppressively to themselves and to one another" (qtd. in Landay 208). Carver plays her way clear of oppression, but her critical and political awareness remain questionable. *Dancing Queen* (like Wolf's *Fire with Fire*) elides the problem of social inequality in America. The American as playful can be read, therefore, in variously positive and negative lights. First, I relate it to Maria Lugones' essay on "Playfulness, 'World'-Travelling, and Loving Perception," in which a form of responsible play appears as a theoretical concept by which to engage in cross-cultural loving in personal relationships and reading strategies. This behavior, in Lugones' vision, allows people to bridge the differences that make knowing and reading each other difficult. In particular, Lugones emphasizes the need to shift from "arrogant" to "loving" perceptions of otherness. If the American were playful in this way, our position in an international human community would be one of caring, understanding, and mutual respect. However, these words hardly describe the relationship of America to the rest of the world. Regarding Lugones' essay, Carole Boyce Davies writes:

> even as I understand her arguments, even as I accept the necessity of engaging other cultures, I still find the language 'playful world travelling' troubling. The Caribbean child that I was witnessed many tourists who seemed to be "playful world travellers" in my Caribbean city. We became the backdrop for their encounters. We were never fully thinking, acting beings. The Caribbean is too easily identified as the place of playful world travelling for us to engage that formulation without caution. (23)

Boyce Davies doubts seriously the presence of "mutual respect" between America and the worlds with which it plays; recalling a meeting between George Bush and his ally Mitterrand after the Gulf War, she suggests that "[t]he symbolic meeting of these two on Caribbean shores highlighted the implications of tourist ideology in the perception of the Caribbean as 'prostitute,' as a source of pleasure and relaxation, and the link to economic and political domination and exploitation" (25). Her argument for "moving beyond the limited definition of what is American" attends to the way "the term 'American' has become synonymous with the United States imperialistic identity," an indication of the degree to which "the 'other Americas' [are] being colonized (both internally and externally) by the United States of America" (9). Lisa Carver's decision to let other countries think about "different races . . . war, business, love and betrayal" produces a sense of pleasure around what is actually a clear shirking of responsibility for the ethics embedded in the identity one chooses. The Caribbean as whore is an image that puts the brakes on any flippant reading of sexual indulgence as equal to social revolution, cautioning me to take care in my reading of women writers engaging the male American text because dynamics of inequality remain in play.

While Lisa Carver's American feminist *jouissance* appeals to me with its seductive excesses and the centrality of pleasure, and Ruth Behar's postcolonial feminist self-consciousness appeals as well with its incisive evaluation of inequality in the forms of racism, sexism, classism, and nationalism, I still long for something else: a combination of the two. I desire a literature produced by contemporary American women writers that rejoices in an Americanized female script—female Adams, girls on the road—and also recognizes the limitations of these ideals, their negative implications for the unprivileged, and the failures of these ideals in the realities of many Americans (North, Central, and South). I want a combination of Lisa Carver, who would wholeheartedly support my fantasies of fucking Thoreau and being "man-handled" by him and his ideas for fun, and of Ruth Behar, who would caution me to critically engage the multiple systems of domination dramatized by such a scene. The framework I desire for understanding women's (my own and others') relationship to male texts such as America and American literary tradition needs to accommodate in its theories the nuances of ambivalence, the simultaneity of pleasure in existing systems and the urge toward social change: an erotico-political American feminism.

I find an ally in Laura Kipnis who declares, "I don't particularly want to be part of a movement that sees its task as crushing fantasy and patrolling desire"; her criticism of American feminism in *Ecstasy Unlimited* addresses the inattention of this movement to mobilizing fantasy in the service of political ends (7). American feminism, from this point of view, needs to move away from attempts to eradicate and sterilize traditional American values from contemporary women's writing and thoughts. Some women still fantasize about individualism, mobility, the acquisition of Persian rugs, playing "bottom" to Thoreau's "top," and other complex freedoms; we need a way of enacting these fantasies in our writing and our lives that nourishes each party. Is there a way to understand Thoreau (David) holding me by the hair while we thrash about on the small bed in his cottage (or less figuratively, that understands a contemporary woman writer writing in the Thoreauvian tradition) that neither downplays my pleasure as an American woman nor oversimplifies the dynamics of power relations within America? Can I fuck (with) Thoreau (his texts, America, or my cowboy boyfriend) like I walk—balancing ethics and joy in the space between love and patriarchy?

NOTES

1. I take this phrase from the subtitle of a recent collection of literary sex-writing, *Nerve: Literate Smut*, edited by Genevieve Field and Rufus Griscom.

2. I agree with "fem*e*nist" John Hampsey when he writes,

The fundamental truth behind any feminism/masculinism debate is that men and women need to behave differently to each other than they have in the past. As William Blake argued in his poetic chastisement of Milton (for Milton's misunderstanding of women), the key is imagination. We have to imagine other possibilities for the opposite gender, as well as for our own. (215)

Part of my impetus for writing this essay is to pick up where existing feminisms leave off, to work inside the gap left by feminisms and by American literary criticisms that have not yet effectively theorized a heterosexuality we can live with. Nina Baym is a good source on both these points in her essays, "The Madwoman and Her Languages: Why I Don't Do Feminist Literary Theory" and "Melodramas of Beset Manhood," respectively.

3. Like Louise Yelin in her postcolonial feminist study of South African novelists, *From the Margins of Empire*, I am interested in exploring how the texts of contemporary women "invite us to explore what it means to *choose* a national identity . . . In addressing issues of national affiliation, I examine the ways that [texts] represent their writers' relationship to dominant and oppositional (residual and emergent) national cultures and transnational political entities" (5).

4. bell hooks repeatedly addresses this inequality, addressing in particular the self-help book *Women Who Love Too Much*, about which she writes:

This book . . . like many other self-help books for women, disturbed me because it denied that patriarchy is institutionalized. It made it seem that women could change everything in our lives by sheer acts of personal will. It did not even suggest that we would need to organize politically to change society in conjunction with our efforts to transform ourselves. (4)

Sills' title sounds more one-sided than her content turns out to be, although her thesis places her on thin ice, a condition she recognizes and navigates carefully throughout the book. Her definition of one half of her title serves well to exemplify this navigation: " 'Need him less' is not an indirect criticism of women as 'needy.' Nor does it mean that our own needs must come second. . . . 'Need him less' assumes that women's needs are human and reasonable, but that, to realize our vision of love, we must look beyond men to satisfy any of them" (19).

5. Heywood and Drake describe the position of this movement as non-separatist in the introduction to *Third Wave Agenda*:

[F]or most women who are generationally third wave, the feminist -separatist, pro-woman "gynocriticism" and "goddess worship" of some feminisms, although they sometimes sounded nice, seemed all too wishful and frilly and arcane to make sense in any of our lives. . . . [I]t was U.S. third world feminism that modeled a language and a politics of hybridity that can account for our lives at the century's turn." (13).

In their collaborative article in the same volume, "We Learn American Like a Script," they apply this politics of hybridity directly to the question of America as a patriarchal text that women both love and interrogate: "It is this edge, where critique and participation meet, that third wave activists most (must?) work to further contentious public dialogue in and about the multicultural United States" (52). Further, Rebecca Walker articulates this language of hybridity as a feminist of color in *To Be Real*, characterizing this generation as one "that has grown up transgender, bisexual, interracial, and knowing and loving people who are racist, sexist, and otherwise afflicted" and asserting that "[f]or us the lines between Us and Them are often blurred, and as a result we find ourselves seeking to create identities that accommodate ambiguity and our multiple perspectives: including more than excluding, exploring more than defining, searching more than arriving" (xxxii).

6. See: Iris Marion Young's "Throwing Like a Girl: A Phenomenology of Feminine Body Comportment, Motility and Spatiality."

7. One of the most useful sources on analyzing the American Dream for its noble possibilities as well as its inherent flaws and prejudices is political scientist Jennifer Hochschild's *Facing Up to the American Dream: Race, Class, and the Soul of the Nation.*

8. Ann Douglas' text of the same name perpetuates the negative connotations of femininity through this phrase, an inappropriate critical move for my reading of femininity in *Dancing Queen* as a positive force and identity.

9. It is noteworthy that the same debate appears in the world of music criticism, the world from which Lisa Carver hails. Terri Sutton, another feminist rock critic, works through a similar critique of why some young girls "love Metallica *despite* (and it's not because of it; I reject that) the fact that Metallica called them sluts," pointing out the "crushing roller coaster of sound" and the fact that it is possible to "enjoy Aerosmith and find their music funky and slippery and sexy . . . and also find their attitude toward women appalling" (380). Sutton's conclusion that "the way women will overcome being ghettoized or ignored is to pick up the instruments and share what's in our hearts (and in our groins)" mirrors my own perspective on Lisa Carver's relationship to American literature; she picks up the (masculinist) instrument and gives us her version of its music (381).

10. The connection between sexual liberation and social revolution has a long history in psychology—see Hal Cohen for an overview with special attention to Wilhelm Reich and passing mention of Herbert Marcuse—and in feminism: Audre Lorde and bell hooks both offer important treatments of the erotico-political dimension of liberatory movements.

11. bell hooks' position in *Outlaw Culture* represents the "sexually correct" feminism that I am here, in part, rejecting: "one major obstacle preventing us from transforming rape culture is that heterosexual women have not unlearned a heterosexist-based 'eroticism' that constructs desire in such a way that many of us can only respond erotically to male behavior that has already been coded as masculine within the sexist framework" (111). She continues:

> Critically interrogating my responses, I confronted the reality that despite all my years of opposing patriarchy, I had not fully questioned or transformed the structure of my desire. By allowing my erotic desire to still be determined to any extent by conventional sexist constructions, I was acting in complicity with patriarchal thinking. Resisting patriarchy ultimately meant that I had to reconstruct myself as a heterosexual, desiring subject in a manner that would make is possible for me to be fully aroused by male behavior that was not phallocentric. In basic terms, I had to learn how to be sexual with a man in a context where his pleasure and his hard-on is decentered and mutual pleasure is centered instead (112).

I'm all for mutual pleasure, but her interrogation of her eroticism seems to me like a rejection of her own desires—a position encouraged by other feminists as well who consider heterosexuality as *a priori* a form of rape and/or patriarchal domination. I am more interested in complicating the lexicon surrounding sexuality in feminism than in rejecting my "problem" desires. In this desire I take as guides the essay by Jean Grimshaw, "Ethics, Fantasy and Self-Transformation," and Lynne Segal's book, *Straight Sex: Rethinking the Politics of Pleasure*.

12. A small handful of feminists already articulate this stance in which complicated sexual desires are reconciled with feminist commitments. A recent roundtable discussion on the nerve.com webzine between Nancy Friday, Betty Dodson, Sallie Tisdale, Susie Bright, and Daphne Merkin addresses this question and suggests reconciliation is an outmoded problem (listed as "Roundtable" in works cited).

13. As a 'zine writer (currently a columnist for the webzine nerve.com), Carver's tone and content are certainly affected by the fact that she's writing for a general audience and for her own fun, rather than from within the academic community where issues of situated critiques and critical identity politics are required theoretical tools and a necessary prerequisite to entering ongoing conversations about nationalism and female subjectivity. For this reason, as well as the fact that pleasure has a definite value in my version of American feminism, I want to handle her textual body carefully, so as not simply to police and delegitimate her desires.

14. Postcolonial critic Gayatri Spivak urges literary scholars to engage in this sort of interrogation, asserting that "humanities teachers on the tertiary level ought perhaps to ask what the cultural politics of the production of the 'American Way' might be" (782). Further, she believes that "United States women, if they are attentive to the importance of frame narratives, are in a unique and privileged position to continue a *persistent* critique of mere apologists for the Constitution, even as they use its instruments to secure entry into its liberating purview. Persistently to critique a structure that one cannot not (wish to) inhabit is the deconstructive stance" (795). Spivak here defines what I consider the postcolonial feminist stance toward America represented by Ruth Behar.

15. Shu-Mei Shih writes in similar terms of Korean American women's writing, asserting that "one may be able to rethink the reified oppositional relationship between claiming and transcending America and instead see how these opposed agenda might be speaking to each other in dialogic, though paradoxical, ways" (145). Shih is one of the few authors I have encountered who discusses in such effective negotiating terms the problem of nationalism and women's writing in America (feminism and nationalism receives more attention in other cultural settings such as the third world, Ireland, and Africa). Another important author on this subject is Lauren Berlant, whose book, *The Anatomy of National Fantasy*, interrogates the relationship between women's bodies and American nationalism.

WORKS CITED

Baym, Nina. 1985. Melodramas of beset manhood: how theories of American fiction exclude women authors. In *The New Feminist Criticism: Essays on Women, Literature, and Theory*, edited by Elaine Showalter, 63–80. New York: Pantheon.

———. 1997. The madwoman and her languages: why I don't do feminist literary theory. In *Feminisms: An Anthology of Literary Theory and Criticism*, edited by Robyn R. Warhol and Diane Price Herndl, 279–92. New Brunswick, NJ: Rutgers University Press.

Behar, Ruth. 1993. *Translated Woman: Crossing the Border with Esperanza's Story*. Boston: Beacon.

———. 1996. *The Vulnerable Observer: Anthropology that Breaks Your Heart*. Boston: Beacon.

Carver, Lisa. 1996. *Dancing Queen: A Lusty Look at the American Dream*. New York: Owl.

Cohen, Hal. 1999. A secret history of the sexual revolution. *Linguafranca: The Review of Academic Life*: 24–33.

Field, Genevieve and Rufus Griscom, eds. 1998. *Nerve: Literate Smut*. New York: Broadway.

Gilbert, Sandra and Susan Gubar. 1979. *The Madwoman in the Attic: The Woman Writer and the Nineteenth-Century Literary Imagination*. New Haven, CT: Yale University Press.

———. 1988. *No Man's Land: The Place of the Woman Writer in the Twentieth Century*. Vol. 1. The War of the Words. New Haven, CT: Yale University Press.

Grimshaw, Jean. 1997. Ethics, fantasy and self-transformation. In *The Philosophy of Sex: Contemporary Readings*, 3rd ed., edited by Alan Soble, 175–188. Lanham, MD: Rowman and Littlefield.

Heywood, Leslie and Jennifer Drake. 1997. *Third Wave Agenda: Being Feminist, Doing Feminism*. Minneapolis: University of Minnesota Press.

Hochschild, Jennifer. 1995. *Facing Up to the American Dream: Race, Class, and the Soul of the Nation*. Princeton: Princeton University Press.

hooks, bell. 1993. *Sisters of the Yam: Black Women and Self-Recovery*. Boston: South End.

———. 1994. *Outlaw Culture: Resisting Representations*. New York: Routledge.

Muscio, Inga. 1998. *Cunt: A Declaration of Independence*. Toronto: Seal.

Levine, Judith. 1992. *My Enemy, My Love: Man-hating and Ambivalence in Women's Lives*. New York: Doubleday.

Lorde, Audre. 1984. *Sister Outsider: Essays and Speeches*. Trumansburg, NY: Crossing.

Roundtable: Nancy Friday, Betty Dodson, Susie Bright, Sallie Tisdale, and Daphne Merkin. Voice box: women writing about writing about sex. *Nerve.com Webzine*. http://www.nerve.com/voicebox/WomenOnSex/

Schweickart, Patrocinio. 1997. Reading ourselves: toward a feminist theory of reading. In *Feminisms: An Anthology of Literary Theory and Criticism*, edited by Robyn R. Warhol and Diane Price Herndl, 609–34. New Brunswick, NJ: Rutgers University Press, 1997.

Shih, Shu-Mei. 1997. Nationalism and Korean American women's writing: Theresa Hak Kyung Cha's *Dictee*. In *Speaking the Other Self: American Women Writers*, edited by Jeanne Campbell Reesman, 144–64. Athens: University of Georgia Press.

Sidel, Ruth. 1997. The new American dreamers. In *Making Choices: Reading*

Issues in Context, eidted by Michael Cooley and Katherine Powell, 489–504. Boston: Houghton Mifflin.

Sills, Judith. 1996. *Loving Men More, Needing Men Less*. New York: Penguin.

Spivak, Gayatri. 1990. The making of Americans, the teaching of English, and the future of culture studies. *New Literary History* 21:781–98.

Sutton, Terri. 1995. Women, sex, and rock 'n' roll. In *Rock She Wrote: Women Write about Rap, Rock, and Pop*, edited by Evelyn McDonnell and Ann Powers, 376–81. New York: Delta.

Thoreau, Henry David. 1947. Walking. In *The Portable Thoreau*, edited by Carl Bode, 592–630. New York: Viking.

Young, Iris Marion. 1989. Throwing like a girl: A phenomenology of feminine body comportment, motility, and spatiality. In *The Thinking Muse: Feminism and Modern French Philosophy*, edited by Jeffner Allen and Iris Marion Young. Bloomington: Indiana University Press.

Lolita Talks Back:
Giving Voice to the Object

Timothy McCracken

What happens if the "object" started to speak?
                                                —Luce Irigaray

THERE IS THIS SMALL SCENE NEAR THE END OF TED DEMME'S 1996 movie, *Beautiful Girls*. Will (Timothy Hutton) has spent a snowy holiday at a ten-year high school reunion with mostly his male friends. In a moment of drunken honesty he tells his friend Mack (Michael Rapaport), about his infatuation with Marty (Natalie Portman),[1] his thirteen-year-old neighbor. Later as Will drives away, returning home, Mack comes up to Marty and says, "So, you're the little neighborhood Lolita?" To which Marty responds, "So, you're the alcoholic, high school buddy shit-for-brains."

With her sharp retort, Marty talks back to one male's placement of her as the objectified "Lolita." Marty's back talk is one small voice in a growing chorus of male[2] and female[3] voices descanting against the framing of Lolita as a downsized seductress. Because Lolita in Vladimir Nabokov's *Lolita* speaks very little, writers and interpreters have taken up her cause by speaking both *for* her and *through* her. But for Lolita to become a subject in her own right three things must be done: find the sources of the mis-readings of her character, review the critical interpretations of *Lolita* which confront traditional approaches praising *Lolita*'s aesthetic achievement while downplaying the subject matter, and hear Lolita's own story from her perspective.

Readers and writers are no longer willing to overlook *Lolita*'s pedophilic content in favor of the narrator's, Humbert's, elegant prose and Nabokov's claim of "aesthetic bliss" (Nabokov 1989, 314). When the focus shifts from Humbert to Lolita, she is transformed from passive and "safely solopsized" object into a subject with a voice (Nabokov 1989, 60). This speaking girl-subject, thus, resists the privileged status of the male's "aesthetic bliss"; her transformation from "nymphet" or "daemon" into subject awakens readers to her identity as a young girl in peril.

FRAMING LOLITA

The present misuse of the name "Lolita," perhaps, outstrips that of Mary Shelley's often misattributed "Frankenstein." In both cases, a similar error occurs: the monster creates a victim who—through the creator's treatment—is then framed as the ostensible monster. While Shelley's monster is mistakenly called "Frankenstein" (probably because his creator Victor Frankenstein never named him), Lolita *does* have a name: Dolores; yet in the cultural *lingua franca*, the name "Lolita" now carries serious connotative baggage. In a culture which calls a gun-toting teenage prostitute "the Long Island Lolita,"[4] which reviews *teenager fatal* movies as featuring "Lolita wannabes" and "Lethal Lolitas,"[5] and which has web-sites where a search of the name "Lolita" yields pornography, it is safe to say that the Lolita's name has, as Ellen Pifer noted, "very little connection with its original source" (71). While it might take a book-length study to chart how Lolita evolved from miss to myth, if Lolita is to "talk back" from a subject position, the sources of her misrepresentations need to be located.

Of course, some misrepresentations occur when those who use the term "Lolita" have not actually read Nabokov's novel. However, even for the literately informed, if close attention is not paid to Nabokov's "celebrated false leads" or Humbert's monstrous "incuriosity,"[6] Lolita may assume the role of a dangerous and magical being. Readers tend to trust the narrative voice and even a self-proclaimed monster may seduce more than little girls, and thus, for instance, Humbert's definition of the "nymphet" provides an example of not only Humbert's masked desire, but Nabokov's verbal sleight-of-hand: "Between the ages of nine and fourteen there occur maidens who, to certain bewitched travelers, twice or many times older than they, reveal their true nature which is not human, but nymphic (that is, demonic)" (14). Later, after he claims that he has been seduced by Lolita, Humbert describes his kidnapped stepdaughter as "the body of some immortal daemon disguised as a female child" (139).

It is through Humbert's descriptions that the reader may
begin to locate the "framing" of Lolita. She and her ilk are
"trouble," actively bewitching, bothering, and bewildering poor
Humbert. In addition, the subtlety of Humbert's rendering mis-
leads the reader into failing to notice the metamorphosis of Lolita into "daemon." Thus, while Humbert frames Lolita as a
preternaturally aware seductress and Nabokov challenges and
even flatters the attentive reader, Lolita achieves her erroneous
reputation. Consequently, while the readers' perceptions of Lolita teeter between the obvious and subtle shifts within the language of the framing itself, Lolita—as twelve-year-old suburban
American girl and object of a mature man's lust—disappears.[7]
    Soon after *Lolita*'s publication, however, the notion of Lolita
as merely a sexy young girl was challenged. Simone de Beauvoir contended that the "Lolita Syndrome" in '60s cinema was
not in fact about sexual young girls but rather about young girls
being *sexualized* by men. For de Beauvoir the "Lolita Syndrome" operates on the principle that as more adult women
begin to inhabit the adult male world, and "the child-woman
moves into a universe he cannot enter," the man fashions the
"nymph" into a portal for his personal redemption, a return
ticket into the lost arcadia of his youth. The man "abandons
himself to the charms of the 'nymph' in whom the formidable
figure of the wife and 'Mom' is not yet apparent" (23). Thus the
nymph's charms lie in her essential absences: "she is without
memory, without a past, and, thanks to ignorance, she retains
the perfect innocence that is attributed to a mythical childhood"
(de Beauvoir 12).
    In other words, "Lolitas" are not born—as Humbert would
have it—but fabricated by male desires. As the creation of the
male, she becomes *the* eternally young *tabula rasa* upon which
the older man may inscribe *his* new self. Little wonder, then,
that "Lolita's," especially in the movies,[8] are often portrayed by
pale blondes; she becomes, figuratively, the white cipher to be
filled in by the older man. Yet to become this blank slate, the
girl's own reality must be denied. And it is the reconstruction of
her reality that is the principle goal of both "Lo-centrism" and
"white ink" re-writings of Lolita.

LO-CENTRISM

Michael Wood recognizes,

the "actual" Lolita is the person we see Humbert can't see, or can
see only spasmodically. In this sense she is a product of reading, not

just "there" in the words, but because she is what a reading finds, and I would say needs to find, in order to see the range of what the book can do. She needs to be "there," that is, and she needs to be found. (117)

She is located in the spaces between the words, spectacularly present by her very absences. This is the heart of a Lo-centric criticism: to find the absent/present Lolita. It is the reader who must recreate her either through or between Nabokov's elegant but polyphonic prose. How she is found within the white spaces that surround Humbert's words form the debates among *Lolita*'s readers. With Nabokov's centenary upon us and with "nymph mania"[9] in the air, the number of books and articles devoted to Nabokov and his real or misappropriated Lolita are too numerous to even list.[10] Yet given the approach to give voice to Lolita, the salient criticism is that which attempts to locate Wood's "actual" Lolita. Lo-centric critics do not necessarily, however, embrace Wood's "adventure in reading" when he says that neither Humbert nor Nabokov should play a role in our reading: "We do need to see that the important differences between these figures [Nabokov or Humbert] are going to be textual (unless we happen to be friends of or victims of Humbert) matters of reading" (105). There are three critics who, although not victims of Humbert (and often no friend to Nabokov either), see themselves as spokespersons for Lolita's pedophilic plight. Trevor McNeely, Linda Kaufman, and Elizabeth Patnoe speak up for the largely silent Lolita by trusting not the teller but the tale that Humbert and Nabokov tell.

For Trevor McNeely the tale of the subject matter *does* count. Risking the philistine's position, McNeely dismisses the aesthetic approach so publicly embraced by Nabokov and others as "nihilistic" because "a great work of literature cannot be just verbal trickery; beautiful patterns in themselves mean nothing" (143). Rather, McNeely sees Nabokov deliberately choosing pedophilia because since it is "the most universally despised . . . vile . . . beyond all dispute and discussion evil," Nabokov "sets himself up for the ultimate triumph as a jokester." McNeely claims that *Lolita*'s "perfect novelist hoax" forces readers to side with both Humbert's claims of a deep and magical romanticism and with Nabokov's own indifference to morality[11] while ignoring "the sexual slavery and abuse of a twelve-year-old orphan" (137).

A primary example of Humbert's bogus literary alchemy is when, in comparing himself to Dante and Petrarch, the ever-erudite Humbert in his hymn to nymphet love attempts to turn grubby and criminal pedophilia into far more romantic nympholepsia. McNeely, however, points to two crucial distinctions between Humbert and the two real poets. While the first distinction is that chastity was paramount to both Petrarch and Dante, the second is even more revealing of and damning to Humbert's pretensions: both Dante and Petrarch, as McNeely points out, loved the girls not because the girls were children but the poets loved the girls when the poets themselves were children.

While McNeely articulates such tricks within *Lolita*, Linda Kaufman examines how "the inscription of the father's body in the text obliterates the daughter's" (152). Kaufman's aim is to combine clinical studies of incest with feminist and deconstructive strategies to discover that "the greatest love story of the twentieth century . . . indicts the ideology of love and exposes literature's complicity in perpetuating it" (166). For Kaufman, there is no woman in *Lolita*, but a girl's body which is "framed between the horror of incest and aesthetic *jouissance*, between material reality and antimimesis, between pathos and parody" (166). Lolita is thus a missing child, absent from the text, and thus absent of a life. To be blunt: " 'Lolita' is a word; Humbert is flesh" (156). Echoing French feminist theory, Kaufman locates the problem by noting how Lolita's body is inscribed:

> By thus inscribing the female body in the text, rather than consigning it to the hazy and dolorous realm of abstract male desire, or letting it circulate as the currency of exchange between male rivals, one discovers that Lolita is not a photographic image, or a still life, or freeze-frame preserved on film but a *damaged child*. (164, my emphasis)

Kaufman tries to find, as does Michael Wood, an authentic girl who for Kaufman is not only damaged, but who is also, to use a more political word, "disappeared" in the text. Lolita is not in *Lolita* because she has been silenced and objectified. It would seem that for McNeely and Kaufman the more we look for Lolita the more she is not there.

To find the mind inside this obliterated daughter's body is Elizabeth Patnoe's aim in "Lolita Misrepresented, Lolita Reclaimed: Disclosing Doubles." Patnoe uses Bahktin's notion of heteroglossia to extract Lolita's thoughts from what Humbert says. Concentrating on the "Enchanted Hunters Motel" chapter in which Humbert and Lolita have sexual intercourse, Patnoe notes there is a "double drama." This double drama is not only in the standard doubling between author and narrator, but also "an extreme kind of double-voicing" between Humbert and Lolita (96). This language incorporates not so much a "he said, she says," but rather a "he said, she might have thought."

To reclaim Lolita from the status of seductress, the Enchanted Hunters section needs to be deconstructed from Lolita's point of view. Patnoe reiterates what is now a leitmotif in Lo-centric criticism: readers can be easily misled by Humbert's verbal badinage, failing to recognize "the narration that is countlessly described as 'love-making' and seduction . . . can only be described as rape" (85).

Critical to this section is that Humbert wants the reader to believe two extraordinary things. One is—as he has so artfully foreshadowed—that Lolita is the seducer: "it was she who seduced me" (132). The other is Humbert's claim that "I am not concerned with so-called 'sex' at all. Anybody can imagine those elements of animality. A greater endeavor lures me on: to fix once for all the perilous magic of nymphets" (134).

First, as to Lolita's supposed seduction, Humbert's obsession is an artfully constructed black hole from which no light of Lolita (the light of *his* life) can escape. Thus, in speaking for Lolita, in locating the Lolita in *Lolita*, Patnoe asks how much are we to believe Humbert's contention that the sex was consensual between a delusional man in his forties and his silenced twelve-year-old stepdaughter.

But it is in her response to Humbert's proclaimed irrelevancy of the descriptions of the sex act that Patnoe makes her most potent points. The morning after the deed is done, Humbert tells us: "[A]s she was in the act of getting in the car, an expression of pain flitted across Lo's face. It flitted again. . . . No doubt, she produced it for my benefit. Foolishly, I asked her what was the matter. 'Nothing you brute', she replied" (140). Patnoe asks: "Are we to entirely believe the man who believes that Lolita's second expression of pain is 'reproduced' for his benefit? Does she really smile when she calls Humbert a brute?" (97). He cannot talk about the sex because it is not magic which drives him on but lust—a lust that is indifferent to the pain of the other. The pain caused by "the certain discrepancies" between Humbert's size and hers we are to believe is mutual and magical; yet, later as they sit in the car and Lolita cannot move, she tells Humbert that he "had torn something inside her" (141).

Perilous magic indeed. Here Lo-centric criticism reaches its critical mass: Humbert's wish to fix the perilous magic of the nymphet is magical for him, but perilous for Lolita. Searching for the Lolita closer to life than fantasy, McNeely foregrounds the relevancy of *Lolita*'s pedophilia, Kaufman searches though the spaces trying to locate the damaged Lolita, and finally Patnoe articulates the realities of Humbert's desires and actions. But while criticism can contest, negotiate, rethink, and reframe, it cannot rewrite *Lolita*.

WHITE INK LOLITAS

It is interesting to note that one of the very few moments of tenderness in *Lolita* is when Humbert finds Lolita again after three years, "hopelessly worn at seventeen," pregnant, and needing money to start a new life with her young husband (277). Humbert begs her to leave with him and as he begins to cry, Lolita says, "No, honey, no." Humbert says "[s]he had never called me honey before" (278). It is the pregnant Lolita, sensitive to his tears (as he never was to hers), who shows the first faint glow of empathy. This empathy ignites Humbert's brief epiphany concerning *her* life with him. Leaving with Humbert is, as Lolita says, "quite out of the question." "She groped for words. I supplied them mentally . . . '*You* merely broke my life' " (279). Finally and for one brief moment, he takes in her emotional life and temporally understands what it must have been like to be a little girl sexually abused by a fully grown man.

Writing from within the speaking body of—in this case—the young girl is the central feature of "white ink revisions." The phrase "white ink," taken from Helene Cixous' "The Laugh of the Medusa," describes a woman's acts of writing as the means to "put herself into the text—as into the world and into history—by her own movement" (334). This writing to and from women will "break out of the snare of silence," a silence that is key in perpetuating the "magic" of nympholepsia. For Cixous, "flesh speaks true" and thus from the woman's bodily experience of the world her writing will have "at least a little of that good mother's milk. She writes in white ink" (339). The white ink versions rewrite Lolita with an emphasis on the broken lives of the girls, not the broken hearts of the men.

Cixous is arguing for the creation of "a new history," a history written from within a women's body.[12] White ink versions parallel Lolita's experience and give voice to the heretofore silent object. White ink therefore not only empowers the individual woman writer, but also provides a cultural counter-memory—in this case—to Humbert's protestations of the "magic" and "romance" of pedophilia.

Only one of the following texts overtly acknowledges *Lolita* as its source and thus these white ink versions are not necessarily deliberate rewritings of *Lolita*; however, each of the following texts have parallel moments to *Lolita*. These texts attempt to give voice to the supposedly "blessedly" ignorant girl-child and thus give lie to the notion that these man-child encounters are either romantic or harmless.

Let us take, for example, that nearly archetypal "dirty, dirty old man" moment when the little girl sits on the big man's lap (141). Humbert is reading the Sunday paper and "hot little Haze" in a fit of rebellion informs "big cold Haze" that she will not go to church with her. Rather, she decides to hop on Humbert's lap disturbing more than his reading of the paper. Humbert uses this moment and Lolita's movements to reach orgasm. "Safely solopsized" Lolita is assigned various roles from being an Eve holding a "banal Eden-red apple" into "Lola the bobby-soxer" finally "my little Carmen." In his "self-made seraglio" Lolita says exactly eight words: "Give it [her apple] back" and "Oh it's nothing at all," referring to a bruise on her thigh (60). During the whole scene, we get exquisite detail of Humbert's exquisite torture, build up, and orgiastic release.

The reader, however, is supposed to see that Lolita's unconscious lap dance and Humbert's semiconscious orgasm is a kind of chaste rape: he got off but "Blessed be the Lord, she had noticed nothing" (61). However, as our Lo-centric critics have posed, how are we to know what Lolita knows? Her silences are deafening and her words, few and far between, are filtered through Humbert. Thus "the monster of incuriosity" has no idea what Lolita or any little girl would feel.[13]

As we read into the white ink versions, it becomes clear that the only way for Lolita to survive the abuse is for her to dissociate from the moment. Two recent examples present different takes on a lap scene from the girl's side. First, there is this lap scene from Dorothy Allison's *Bastard Out of Carolina*. While his wife, Anney, goes into labor, her husband, Glen, waits with his stepdaughter, Bone, outside the hospital in their Pontiac. Toward dawn, Glen pulls his sleepy twelve-year-old stepdaughter into the front seat and we get a much different version from the one that Humbert narrates:

He was holding himself in his fingers. I knew what was under his hand. I'd seen my cousins naked, laughing and shaking their things and laughing hard but this was a mystery, scary and hard. His sweat was running down his arms to my skin smelled strong and nasty. He grunted, squeezed my thighs between his arm and his legs. His chin pressed down on my head and his hips pushed up at the same time. He was hurting me, hurting me!

I sobbed once, and he dropped back down and let go of me. . . .

I pulled away, and it made him laugh. (47)

What is significant here is not only Glen's callus indifference—he will brutally rape her later in the novel, but of what actually happens to Bone's psyche. Bone begins to wonder if, in fact, it was a dream and but she asks "how I could have bruised myself in a dream?" (50).[14]

This dissociation from the moment is repeated in Paula Vogel's 1997 play, *How I Learned to Drive*. Near the end of the play, Uncle Peck offers his little eleven-year-old niece, Li'l Bit, a chance to drive. To "learn to drive" this little girl must sit on his lap. One of Vogel's intriguing techniques is that of having various Greek Choruses take over certain roles as the drama unfolds; in addition to reenacting its ancient role as society's conscience, the chorus here also adds a distancing quality to the girl's perception of the moment.

TEENAGE GREEK CHORUS: Not so fast, Uncle Peck!
(Peck puts his hands on Li'l Bit's breasts. She relaxes against him, silent, accepting his touch.)
TEENAGE GREEK CHORUS: Uncle Peck—what are you?
UNCLE PECK: Keep driving. (He slips his hands under her blouse.)
TEENAGE GREEK CHORUS: Uncle Peck—please don't do this—
UNCLE PECK: —Just a moment longer . . . (Peck tenses against Li'l Bit.)
TEENAGE GREEK CHORUS: (Trying not to cry.) This isn't happening.
(Peck tenses more, sharply. He buries his face in Li'l Bit's neck and moans softly. Teenage Greek Chorus exits, and Li'l Bit steps out of the car. Peck, too, disappears.) . . .
LI'L BIT: That was the last day I lived in my body. (90)

As told from the girl's point of view, it would be impossible for Humbert to gauge what Lolita knows or feels since her survival of the moment would dictate Lolita *not* acknowledging Humbert's actions. Since the source of the violation is the body, she must abandon her body to survive the assault.

The reason she must live out of the body is the shock of realizing that as the thirteen-year-old "Lolita," Lucky Lady Linderhof, writes: "Love wasn't written there. Lust, desire, obsession, yes, but never love" (Prager 177). Emily Prager's *Roger Fishbite* is the only novel currently in print that actually is an acknowledged parody of *Lolita* and of "the icon that the character Lolita has become" (end page). Lolita's story is paralleled in *Roger Fishbite* and Lolita talks back.

Like Humbert, Lucky writes her book from prison after she tracks down her stepfather, Roger Fishbite, in Disney World where he has gone with another thirteen year-old, the child model, Evie Naif. Knowing who the real enemy is, Lucky fires over Evie's head killing Roger with one bullet to the chest.

Prager's political agenda is quite clear beginning with her dedication: "To all the little girls I've met who have started out in desperate circumstances" and through her numerous references to child abuse and the sexual slavery of children. Her novel overtly aims to rewrite any notion of romance between girl and man. Indeed, in a direct reversal of Humbert's bogus claim of not being interested in "so-called 'sex'" but "to fix the perilous magic of nymphets," Lucky notes "I am not so much interested in the pornography of the affair as in chronicling the sort of man who initiates it" (93). This is the man for whom:

> a Catholic school uniform, even on a mannequin, does more than a whole album of grown-up nudes. A man whom Carter's white underpants titillate worlds beyond the classiest catalogue of frilly lingerie. A man whose knees, at the sight of a training bra on a flat chest, shake like Jell-O. (11–12)

Prager's target is the serious damage such a man can do. There are two lap scenes where we begin to see Fishbite in action: "He sat me on his lap, which was not all that comfortable for some reason, and let me type at the manual" (29). Like Humbert, Roger claims to be a writer but he never writes anything except his damning diary entries. This diary is not found by Lucky's mother, as it is with *Lolita*'s Charlotte Haze, but by Lucky herself where she reads Fishbite's confessions of his true nature.

The second lap scene implies that Lolita may have known something was up with Humbert, but could not acknowledge it:

"Sometimes when I am sitting on his lap at the manual, he moves all around and fidgets and it doesn't seem very grown-up. And he sighs and sweats all up. I don't like him very much then and I leave pretty quickly" (31). Lucky may be naïve, but she is neither indifferent nor unaware of Fishbite's strange behavior.

After Fishbite reenacts Nabokov's convenient killing off Lolita's mother with a car, Lucky is whisked away alone with Fishbite in a direct rewriting of Nabokov's "Enchanted Hunters" chapter. Alone with Fishbite and sharing Lolita's ignorance of her mother's death, Lucky tells her side of the "seduction." When at The Lake Innuendo Motel on a heart-shaped bed and Fishbite's fingers play across one of Lucky's nipples, she feels an "explosion in my brain, the psychic shift from being there to being once removed. You know the phrase 'beside myself'? I was from then on in" (85). There is no joy, no seduction. Rather as Lucky writes:

> with that tiny gesture I was changed forever. It was as if some doors shut in my brain and others opened, and cynicism, once an unknown quantity, sloshed along with hormones in my blood. *He wasn't what he seemed.* How easy to write and how hard to understand (85–86).

Lo-centric criticism meets white ink Lolitas to form a vibrant countermemory to Humbert's fancy prose and romantic assertions. Humbert is not what he says; he is the seducer, not the seduced. And of course, he is blessedly ignorant of the pain of the other: "it was astounding how self-centered he was. Another person's pain was like a picture on the wall to him, an object you could take off and put in the closet if it gets in your way" (92).

After he has brushed her breast, Lucky freezes and "Fishbite continued on, *blissfully unaware of possible trauma*, seemingly convinced . . . that despite our differences in age, height, weight, and batting average, we were in the same ballpark" (86, my emphasis). This is the end of the magic, here in the bulk of this big man is the peril to the young girl. He—not she—is "blissfully unaware." In his thoughtless touch, Fishbite changes the trusting child to stunned cynic, the naïve girl to wary woman. She is never "safely solopsized" as long as her pain is unheeded and her person unseen.

ICEBERGS IN PARADISE

Although Humbert always paints himself as a romantic, as Lucky says, men like Humbert and Fishbite "wouldn't know love if it came up and kissed 'em"(150). Nymphet "love" is revealed at its heart to have no heart. Amy Bloom's fourteen-year-old narrator, Elizabeth, describes the hands of her high school English teacher she sleeps with as "[r]omantic hands, but I hated how they felt on my skin, and when I saw them moving down my body, I closed my eyes" (66). In Joyce Carol Oates's *You Must Remember This*, the uncle graphically describes sexual intercourse with his fifteen-year-old niece without Humbert's romantic glossing:

> What he was crazy for was pushing himself inside her as far as he could without hurting her too much . . . stretching her tight little cunt, it was only a matter of an inch or two, or three, but Jesus how he loved it and Enid being so small so like a child her ass small enough to be gripped in his hands." (188)

In Toni Morrison's *The Bluest Eye*, eleven-year-old Pecola Breedlove is attacked by her father: "But the tenderness would not hold. The tightness of her vagina was more than he could bear. His soul seemed to slip down to his guts and fly into her, and the gigantic thrust he made into her then provoked the only sound she made—a hollow suck of air at the back of her throat" (163).[15]

No poetry or paradise for Lolita and her white ink sisters. When the object talks back, when writing comes from the body of the girl, she becomes a subject who creates a countermemory. The new, white ink history of Lolita is that it was never magic or love or paradise for her, just lust. Any other explanations are, as Lolita said to Humbert's affections, "romantic slosh" (133).

NOTES

1. Natalie Portman is the young actor who turned down the role of Lolita in Adrian Lynne's version of *Lolita* claiming that Nabokov's story was "too disturbing" (Tom Russo, "Natalie Wouldn't," *Entertainment Weekly*, 26 January 1996).

2. The screenplay of *Beautiful Girls* was written by Scott Rosenberg. In this climate of sensitivity to the sexualization the young girl, there are works

by men who are aware of the troublesome and potentially destructive construction of "Lolitas." There are several recent novels by men revealing an awareness of the dangers for the girl in having sex with older men. Some of these works are Brian Hall's *The Saskaid*, Russell Banks' *The Sweet Hereafter*, Frederick Busch's *Girls*, Max Frisch's *Homo Faber*, A. N. Wilson's *Dream Children*, and Jonathan Lethem's *Girl in a Landscape*.

3. The subject of incest and pedophilia in women's writing has a long history. Karen Jacobsen McLennan's *Nature's Ban: Women's Incest Literature* (Northeastern, 1997) is a collection of stories dating from medieval times to the present. More recently, there are novels by various writers which take on the issue; some not mentioned in this essay are Joyce Carol Oates' *First Love*, Amy Bloom's *Love Invents Us*, Kristy Gun's *Rain*, A. M. Home's *The End of Alice*, and Beryl Bainbridge's *Awfully Big Adventures*.

4. In late April 1999 when Amy Fisher publicly apologized to her victim, Mary Jo Buttafuoco, New York radio station WCBS called Amy Fisher "the Long Island Lolita." On 18 May 1999 cable TV station A&E ran a story on Amy Fisher in which again she was dubbed the Long Island Lolita and the parallels between Nabokov's novel and the Fisher-Buttafuoco affair, especially in that in both stories "the young girl seduces the older man" were noted. To reclaim Lolita, Elizabeth Patnoe begins by asking this central question: "Why isn't the definition of 'Lolita' 'a molested adolescent girl' instead of a 'seductive' one?"(83). Patnoe asserts, "with so many co-opted Lolita myths circulating in our culture, readers come to Lolita inundated with a hegemonic reading of evil Lolita and bad female sexuality, an overdetermined reading that then imposes itself upon is own text" (84).

5. The underage characters in the films *The Crush* (1992), *Poison Ivy* (1992), and *Freeway* (1997) have been referred to as "Lolitas." *The Rolling Stone*'s title of its review *Poison Ivy* was "A Nineties Lolita from Hell" (28 May 1992, 59). However, what we have here is a new breed of downsized, suburban, headhunting Salomes—not Lolitas—who represent the age's current fear of the ancient scorned nymph—-the teenager *fatale*. Of course, this is bound to happen when Lolita is seen as "a girl of the nineties" as John Marks called her in *U.S. News & World Report* (70–71).

6. An excellent academic website for the literary *Lolita* can be found at www.libraries.psu.edu./iasweb.nabokov.

7. Lionel Trilling, for example, states, "Perhaps Humbert's depravity is the easier to accept when we learn that he deals with a Lolita who is not innocent, and who seems to have very few emotions to be violated" (qtd. in Bloom, 11).

8. See Marianne Sinclair's *Hollywood Lolitas: The Nymphet Syndrome* (London: Plexus, 1988) for an interesting review of the parade of pale young blondes who triumphed, briefly, in Hollywood.

9. Richard Goldstein's trilogy of articles in *The Village Voice* (10 June 1997: 3–40; 17 June 1997: 47–51; and 24 June 1997: 46–48) is a fascinating and relevant tour through the cultural images of the sexualized "beautiful child."

10. An excellent and thorough bibliography can be found by accessing the Penn State site listed in note 6. More recent items not included are Annette Michelson, "Lolita's Progeny" *October* 76 (spring 1996): 3–14; Douglas Anderson, "Nabokov's Genocidal and Nuclear Holocausts in *Lolita*," *Mosaic*, 29, no. 2 (June 1996): 73–90; Elizabeth Freeman, "Honeymoon with a Stranger: Pedophilic Picaresques from Poe to Nabokov," *American Literature*, 70, no. 4 (December 1998): 863–97; and in the same issue, Fredrick Whiting, " 'The Strange

Particularity of the Lover's Preference': Pedophilia, Pornography, and the Anatomy of Monstrosity in *Lolita*," 832–62.

11. Nabokov was clear on his position in an interview with Herbert Gold. When Gold commented, "Your sense of immortality of the relationship between Humbert and Lolita is very strong," Nabokov replied: "No, it is not *my* sense of the immorality of the Humbert Humbert-Lolita that is strong; it is Humbert's sense. *He* cares, I do not. *I* don't give a damn for public morals in America or elsewhere" (*Strong Opinions*, 93).

12. See also Ann Rosalind Jones, "Writing the Body: Toward an Understanding of *l'ecriture feminine*" (1981).

13. Vladimir Alexandrov's discussion of the couch scene is indicative of the ironies within Humbert's narration of events. Alexandrov notes that immediately after Humbert has achieved his satisfaction, Lolita "stood and blinked, cheeks aflame, hair awry." If she doesn't know anything how do we explain Lolita's visible disturbance? (63).

14. This attempt to make the abuse a dream is not solely the provenance of women writers. After thinking of suicide after her father has again forced himself on her, the fourteen-year-old Nicole Burnell in Banks' *The Sweet Hereafter*, says: "But I didn't know how to get hold of any sleeping pills, so I gave it up and instead tried to make what happened in the car coming home from the Ansels' like I only dreamed it" (175).

15. All of these Lo voices bespeak a new history and signal what Humbert called "icebergs in paradise" (285). In the novel, these "icebergs" were when those brief moments "tenderness and azure" with Lolita were repeatedly shattered by Humbert's unquenchable lust.

WORKS CITED

Alexandrov, Vladimir. 1993. *Lolita*. In *Lolita*, edited by Harold Bloom, 169–94. New York: Chelsea House.

Allison, Dorothy. 1992. *Bastard Out of Carolina*. New York: Dutton.

Banks, Russell. 1991. *The Sweet Hereafter*. New York: HarperCollins.

Bloom, Amy. 1997. *Love Invents Us*. New York: Vintage.

Bloom, Harold. ed. 1993. *Lolita*. New York: Chelsea House.

Beauvoir de, Simone. 1972. *Brigitte Bardot and the Lolita Syndrome*. New York: Arno Press & *The New York Times*.

Kaufman, Linda. 1993. Framing Lolita: is there a woman in the text? In *Lolita*, edited by Harold Bloom, 149–68. New York: Chelsea House.

McNeely, Trevor. 1993. 'Lo' and behold: solving the *Lolita* riddle. In *Lolita*, edited by Harold Bloom, 134–48. New York: Chelsea House.

Morrison, Toni. 1994. *The Bluest Eye*. New York: Penguin.

Nabokov, Vladimir. 1989. *Lolita*. New York: Vintage International.

———. 1973. *Strong Opinions*. New York: Vintage International.

Oates, Joyce Carol. 1989. *You Must Remember This*. New York: Dutton.

Patnoe, Elizabeth. 1995. Lolita misrepresented, Lolita reclaimed: disclosing doubles. *College Literature* 22 no. 2: 81–104.

Prager, Emily. 1999. *Roger Fishbite*. New York: Random House.

Vogel, Paula. 1997. *How I Learned to Drive*. New York: Theatre Communications Group, Inc.

Warhol, Robyn R. and Diane Price Herndl, eds. 1991. *Feminisms: An Anthology of Literary Theory and Criticism*. New Brunswick: Rutgers University Press.

Wood, Michael. 1994. *The Magician's Doubt: Nabokov and the Risks of Fiction*. Princeton: Princeton University Press.

I Will Not Wear that Coat: Cross-Dressing in the Works of Dorothy Allison

Connie D. Griffin

"Until we can understand the assumptions in which we are drenched we cannot know ourselves."
—Adrienne Rich, *When We Dead Awaken: Writing as Re-vision*

Likening her survival of father-daughter incest to the biblical story of Joseph and his coat of many colors, Dorothy Allison writes in her memoir, *Two or Three Things I Know for Sure*, that soon after she left home, began to write, and published her autobiographical novel, *Bastard Out of Carolina*, she began to realize that other people could no longer see her. Rather, they saw only the metaphorical coat that she wore—its colors so vibrant that they hid the complexity of the individual behind the horror of her childhood experience of incest. Insisting that she is more than the coat that others see, Allison slips in and out of genres like outfits she is trying on in order to elude the reification of textual representation, in order to enact the human joy and suffering behind the textual reading. Allison's cross-dressing among genres engages in telling her story via memoir, autobiographical novel, short stories, essays, and poetry; by refusing stasis she reclaims the right to self-representation. Resisting the father's gaze, she cries:

> I did not want to wear that coat, to be told what it meant, to be told how it had changed the flesh beneath it, to let myself be made over into my rapist's creation. I will not wear that coat, not even if it is recut to a feminist pattern, a postmodern analysis.
> (1995, 71)

In disrobing herself of the limiting identity of incest victim forced upon her by her stepfather's desire, rage, and rape, Allison claims authority over her body. In refuting external inter-

143

pretations of her history, Allison refuses any paradigm, even a feminist one, that would "recut" her history and identity in a more simplified form, thus claiming authorship of her story. Rejecting the "make-over" of a postmodern analysis, she attempts to avoid the reductionism of any purist textual analysis. Instead, Allison reaches for a far more complex series of readings of her life, articulating the interactive nature of a politics of identity that is cross-cultural in its symbolics; and in claiming the flesh beneath that coat as her very own, Allison foregrounds the mediating role of language in self-construction, but refuses to surrender herself entirely to language.

LIFEWRITING: LIFE AND WRITING

Allison's oeuvre to date constructs hybrid literary formulations, blurring and blending traditional boundaries between genres. Setting fact and fiction within a dialectic of truth-telling she constructs an autobiographics of self-re/presentation that strives for the emotional and psychological truth of a specific situation rather than its absolute factual nature.[1] In entering into history and memory from this angle, Allison writes from a place of deep psychological struggle; as she tells us in the preface to her collection of short stories entitled *Trash,* her drive to write derives from an instinct for survival.

Titling her preface "Deciding to Live," Allison began to write, she informs her reader, "to shape [her] life outside [her] terrors and helplessness" (9). She began to write to move beyond the humorous stories she had always told about her family "in a drawl that made them all funnier than they were," and in so doing she moved into a subterranean level where her "hidden" stories resided, stories that came "rising up [her] throat. . . . like water under pressure . . . pushing [her] fear ahead of it" (9). Three years passed between Allison's writing of the hidden stories and her reading of them, even to herself, but when she did she writes that she realized just "how thin and self-serving [her] funny stories had become" (9).

For Dorothy Allison, as the first reader of her work, "those stories were not distraction or entertainment, they were the stuff of [her] life. . . . [and] holding onto them, reading them over again, became a part of the process of survival" (10, 11). Writing in so passionate a register redirects the reader's attention from a singular focus on the text—the beauty of the syntax, the rhythm of the prose, the effects of alliteration and metaphor—to the life behind the words, the flesh beneath the coat, the longing and the suffering that existed long before the storytelling began, and that will continue long after it ends.

Allison's fear of having that life mis-read is triple: she fears postmodern reductionism to textuality; she fears feminist censure for her sexual politics; and she fears the outside gaze that tries to return her to her childhood status of victim. Her anger at having her life's struggles and scars reduced by postmodernist critics to words on a page, rebutted by feminists as politically injurious to the movement, and read by her readers as victimization compels Allison to assert authority over her body, agency over her identity, and authorship of her story. Thus, her story/telling reclaims the right to self-definition and self-representation.

FRAMES, FRACTURES, AND FATHERHOOD

Reconstructing the cultural frame of reference that situates her in the background, Allison foregrounds her identity as southern, white, working-class, and lesbian. Writing against the cultural construction of patrilineal authority and its powers of defining legitimacy, Allison's project demonstrates that subjects always exist within the confines of legal and cultural definitions, even when they are defined as *outside* such categories.[2] Thus, the title of Allison's autobiographical novel, *Bastard Out of Carolina*, denotes not only the geographical state of her protagonist's birth—South Carolina—but the legal, social, and patriarchal state of her birth—illegitimacy—identifying a complex sense of subjective dis/location from birth onward. Dispossessed by the state, exiled from maternal protection, exploited by paternal desire, Allison is in search of a self-concept that will shift her identity from object to subject within a cultural con/text that locates her and her story as "trash"; for just as the laws of kinship locate Allison "outside" the boundaries of legitimacy, literary canonical law declares Allison's self-representational narratives as minor and therefore marginal.[3]

Taken as a whole, Allison's work may be read as a critique of the moral judgment to which her life and literature have been subjected. Allison's writings criticize a culture and a canon that create a center and margin, an inside and outside, major works to which minor are subjected, high art and low. Thus, just as her title "Bastard" signifies illegitimacy within a patrilineal cultural, social, and legal system, the title "Trash" echoes this reality, while signifying illegitimacy within a literary system that constructs a center and its margin.

Finding oneself positioned outside the culturally constructed center creates a keen awareness of centric thinking; such an *excentric* perspective empowers its subjects with a lens that provides a clarity of vision about the hegemonics of social constructionism and therefore the radical power of deconstruction. Meanwhile those subjects who traditionally have been privileged with culturally centric status experience today's multicultural sensibility as a fracturing of societal values, selfhood, and authority. Indeed the decentering of centric status has come to be described by postmodernists as a kind of lamentable death of self, subject, and authorial presence. This creates a nostalgic vacuum for *what has been,* canonically and culturally, and often calls forth an angry reactionism by many who have comfortably fit the norms of the dominant cultural, political, and symbolic systems and who are frustrated by the appearance of ex-centrics[4] who previously were content to live in the gaps and cracks created by the center-margin paradigm.

One example of attempts at restoration of those boundaries that have been eroded by the influx of the previously marginalized is Alastair Fowler's argument in *Kinds of Literature* that an "overextension of political iconoclasm" has begun to pervade literary studies, an iconoclasm "inappropriately directed against legitimate authorial privilege" (266). Setting forth a paradigm of literary genres in terms of what he defines as "family resemblances" Fowler writes that the producer of "generic resemblances is tradition: a sequence of influence and imitation and inherited codes connecting works in a genre. As kinship makes a family," he argues, "so literary relations of this sort form a genre" (42).

Fowler denies that his literary genealogy is hierarchical and exclusive even as he argues that the expansion of the canon and college curriculum in the name of something called "Women in Literature may be justified." However, he sets up a dangerously dichotomous terrain of legitimacy and illegitimacy, clearly defining literature as a "kinship" system in which "legitimate authorial privilege" derives from either inheritance or mimicry. Like the legitimate and the illegitimate child, one inherits rights replete with patrilineal privilege, the other does not.[5]

Story/Telling

Allison's drive to tell, written not only against powerful external exclusionary forces, but also internalized voices that collab-
orate against her telling—her father's threats, her mother's
fears,[6] her sisters' vulnerability—finally broke through, and although she believed that "no one would want to hear the truth
about poverty, the hopelessness and fear, the feeling that nothing [she] did would ever make any difference and the raging resentment that burned beneath [her] jokes" (1994, 22), the day
finally came when the price of silence was too great for Allison.
She writes in "Deciding to Live":

> I had been a child who believed in books, but I had never really
> found me or mine in print. My family was always made over into
> caricatures or flattened into saintlike stock creatures. I never found
> my lovers in their strength and passion. Outside my mother's stub-
> bornness and my own outraged arrogance, I had never found any
> reason to believe in myself. But I had the idea that I could make it
> exist on those pages. (9)

Striving to believe in herself, motivated by the possibility of a
more accurate representation of the complex matrix of her identity and history, Allison refuses to force her family to "fit the
myths of the noble poor generated by the middle class . . . , that
romanticized, edited version of the poor," nor will she succumb
to liberal intellectualism's notions of her history; she writes:

> The poverty portrayed by left-wing intellectuals was just as roman-
> tic, a platform for assailing the upper and middle classes, and from
> their perspective, the working class hero was invariably male, righ-
> teously indignant, and inhumanly noble. . . . There was a myth of
> the poor in this country, but it did not include us, no matter how
> hard I tried to squeeze us in. (Class 17–18)

Allison's point, that the poor are culturally represented in
American history and literature, but that their representation is
a mythic version that bears little relation to the reality of lives
lived in poverty, lifts her literary project well out of a personal
search for self-representation and places it within one of the
most significant debates of the day—literary and historical representation of the culturally marginalized. Allison's story/telling
challenges cultural assumptions of centric thinking as univer-

sally representational by exposing them as misrepresentational of her kind.

To tell her story, then, so as to come to a fuller understanding of "the question of family and loss and betrayal,"[7] to represent the people of her past and present, Allison is required not only to enter into an autobiographical journey that leads her back to the geographical place of her birth; but by entering into the larger historical framework of literary representation she is simultaneously required to shatter cultural misrepresentations that run the gamut of the political spectrum. Allison's project of representational revision requires that she foreground how the personal is woven by a complex web of political economics within which she was caught as a child growing up. In coming to terms with her history, Allison represents the construction of her subjectivity as multicultural; that is, it derives from many differing and contradictory aspects of personal and political arrangements. Coming to see the self that she has become as having taken shape within a kaleidoscope of forces, Allison posits a subjectivity that is fluid, a self that is always changing depending upon the particular circumstances in which she finds herself.

Thus, just as Allison refuses to be confined by a specific genre, juxtaposing and integrating autobiography and fiction, short stories and essays, deferring any final fixed notion of generic appropriateness, she also refuses to be culturally fixed within a specific category of identity. Drawing on sophisticated literary devices for her self-representational narratives, Allison's considerable body of work to date demonstrates that she represents her subjectivity, not as an escape from gender, race, social class, or sexual identity, but rather with the intention of creating a new kind of subject, one that defers any final fixed definition.[8]

Self-assertion, like self-knowledge, is central to Allison's literal and literary return to the place of her birth and childhood conditioning, and serves to deconstruct the constructions of illegitimacy; only after such a disassembling takes place can she reconstruct a self who has shed the coat that would hide the history behind the story/telling. Allison writes:

> I grew up trying to run away from the fate that destroyed so many of the people I loved, and having learned the habit of hiding, I found I had also learned to hide from myself. I did not know who I was. . . . Hide, hide to survive I thought, knowing that if I told the truth about my life, my family, my sexual desire, my history, I would move over

into that unknown territory, the land of they, would never have the chance to name my own life, to understand it or claim it. (Class 13–14)

Describing running away from home and its destructive fate as a process that eventually became one of habitual "hiding," Allison's realization of internalization becomes painfully apparent when she comes face to face with the reality that "you take your world with you" (1995, 4). It is only then that she makes the decision "to reverse that process," to claim her family, history, and "to tell the truth not only about who [she] was but about the temptation to lie" ("Class" 34). Thus, Allison's writings suggest that transformation is achieved through the enactment of return, a return to the past for the purpose of revision, revision for the sake of representation; that is, a reclaiming of representational status that serves the purpose of self-recreation. Through self-representation, then, Allison retrieves her identity from its former state of misrepresentation and represents a subjectivity of her own making.

PATRIARCHY, POWER, AND SOCIAL PRACTICE

In Michel Foucault's analysis of how social power operates, special subjects and relations of power intersect within multidimensional networks, with multiple forces interacting to construct social phenomena. Included in this web are individual relationships and practices, competing discourses, institutions, laws, customs, and social rituals. Within this paradigm, relationships of power are exercised by a kind of generalized "surveillance" that creates socially constructed norms. It is this network, which Allison describes as "an intricate lattice," with which she must negotiate.

My aunt Dot used to joke, 'There are two or three things I know for sure, but never the same things and I'm never as sure as I'd like.' What I know for sure is that class, gender, sexual preference, and prejudice—racial, ethnic, and religious—form an intricate lattice that restricts and shapes our lives, and that resistance to hatred is not a simple act. Claiming your identity in the cauldron of hatred and resistance to hatred is infinitely complicated, and worse, almost unexplainable. (1994 23)

Negotiation of the "intricate lattice" of social systems of con-
straint, disregard, and even hatred requires Allison to transform
historical and literary objectification of her identity into subjectivity. Allison takes the flattened characters of literature that
misrepresent the various classes and communities within which
she lives her life and breathes life into them, making them real.
Writing her way out of the paternalism of illegitimacy, Allison
enters into history and literature as a self-defined legitimate
subject.

In choosing to enter the literary landscape through an autobiographics of self and story, Allison's self-representation is expressed through a genre that only recently has begun to gain
status as legitimate literature—autobiographical fiction. Traditionally when a genre achieves legitimacy, it does so through an-
drocentric definition; autobiography and autobiographical
fictions are no exception. The traditional autobiographical
canon, as it has been constructed by literary critics, traces a patrilineal trajectory back through Eurocentric male experience,
with a few rare exceptions. However, while the autobiographical canon has been predominantly a masculinist one, it has been
posited as "humanist"; it is upon this definition that the notion
of universal representation is built. Such a genealogical framework has constructed a Western autobiographical tradition that
invokes, in the words of Sidonie Smith, "a specific notion of
'selfhood,'" creating a frame of reference that defines what
Smith has described as "self-representational spaces with centers, margins, and boundaries."[9]

It is important at this point to note that although postmodernist tenets in their masculinist form have begun to fracture traditional notions of centricity, such a fracturing is possible because
a purportedly representational subject has been constructed. In
other words, masculinity can have its deconstructive moment
only because of its particular constructivist historical stance—
the masculine subject as universal. This paradigm is problematic for subjects who have not had an opportunity to see what
shape selfhood might take should their self-representational images appear on the historical and literary landscape. Because
marginalized or illegitimate subjects have been relegated either
to nonrepresentational status, or they have been misrepresented, such subjects narrate processes of self-construction, not
deconstruction.

The problem is not differences between male and female, but
a dualistic symbolic system that has projected onto male and fe-

male a culturally defined "masculinity" and "femininity." Such a symbolics also becomes hierarchical when what is defined as "masculine" accrues authoritative "representation" and is given the privilege of defining and interpreting sociocultural, literary, and historical representation. It isn't men—in their numerous guises—who are the problem; it is the setting up of masculine subjectivities as representative so that cultural representations of the "masculine" are held forth as synonymous with that which is deemed "human." "Femininity" then necessarily becomes polarized as masculinity's "opposite," and therefore cannot resonate as humanistically "representative." Through this logic, women's autobiography is relegated to a position of "other" in literary history. The consequence of such a gendered hierarchy is that female experience and its symbolics are permitted to resonate locally, but rarely universally. In this way women's symbolics are read as minor, while men's are read as major; women's as local, men's as universal.

As Elizabeth Fox-Genovese has noted, narratives (like subjects) do not exist outside of symbolic systems, but take shape within the frequently hidden ideological assumptions of the cultural symbolics by which they are shaped. Thus, women who would enter into self-representation do so as writer of one text (autobiographical representation) and reader of another (a dominant sociocultural symbolic system that sets women within a limited subjectivity). However, as Thomas Kuhn's social scientific studies have demonstrated, paradigmatic shifts are not only possible, paradigms themselves are fluid processes that only appear to be in a state of stasis because subjects come to self-definition from within their defining structures. As such, no symbolic system is static, but rather is a multidimensional dynamic that exists in a constant state of renegotiation.

The historian Joan Scott alludes to this when she argues that the more productive postmodernist analyses might more accurately be described as "epistemological phenomena." Because such an approach insists that we consider identity as historical—"produced, reproduced, and transformed in different situations and over time"—it suggests that it is not only possible to intervene in history and effect cultural change, but that this is an inevitable, ongoing process. Perhaps it is no coincidence, then, that the feminist movement, which began to address issues of women's individual and collective identity and to revise masculinist representations of female subjectivity, intersected a predominantly male-defined postmodernist movement, which began to come to terms with the decentralization of male identity and to experience and express this as a disintegration of subjectivity. The distance between these two theoretical perspectives, although they intersect and interact within a particular historical and cultural moment, is to be found in their effects on subjectivity. Postmodernism's experience of the disintegration of subjectivity set up a paradigm into which subjects defined and regulated by cultural definitions of "femininity" enter at great risk, primarily because this is the very conceptual field from which women have sought liberation. In order to enter into postmodernist disintegration, one must already be writing from a subjective position that has achieved a representational status of integrity, of wholeness. In other words, one must have garnered centric status to experience the loss of de-centering.

The postmodern experience and expression of the death of that subject, as it traditionally has been represented, can certainly be constructive then for "subjects of that type," as Patricia Waugh has so aptly argued (2). Simultaneously and happily, such a deconstruction provides a newly created representational space for "other" subjects to tell their stories, to share "other" perspectives on a history and a literature that inaccurately have presumed to be representative of the cultural experience in its entirety. Thus the politicization of identity categories, what Adrienne Rich has described as a "politics of location," is a contemporary response to a long history of exclusionary politics, a vortex that has created a cultural, literary, and historical vacuum that warrants the current eruption of self-representational literature. The expression of such a "politics of location" in ex-centric contemporary autobiographics articulates a paradoxical position—one of location and dislocation simultaneously. Rather than mutually exclusive positions, however, marginalized subjects narrate a process of shuttling back and forth between them in order to construct a fully present self within a previous representational absence. Contemporary women's self-representational literature, faced with a no-win choice between misrepresentation and nonrepresentation refuse both. Instead, writers such as Dorothy Allison provide new paradigms for representation of subjectivity. For example, Allison represents a subject who is in a constant state of being and becoming, of deconstruction and reconstruction. Far from lamenting authorial annihilation, Allison's narratives weave cycles of disintegration with those of reintegration, thus creating a subjectivity that is achieved through a fierce life force that strives to survive, and does so through the act of story/telling.[10]

Linking subjectivity and story, Allison foregrounds the act of writing in reconstructing the self, creating a direct connection between coming to self-understanding and the act of writing. A final powerful scene in Allison's memoir represents a dream where she is standing by herself at the bottom of a pile of bricks, which represent the "rubble" of her life, each brick providing a story that she needs to know in order to create a self that can live with integrity. She must pull herself up through the rubble around her and to do so she must rely on the strength of her own body, her ribs have become a ladder for pulling herself up by, her strength is in pulling herself out, out of the chaos of history and memory. Allison stands at the bottom of a "rubble" of stories out of which she chooses to make herself over, not in someone else's image, but in an image of her very own making.

Allison began to tell stories so that she might survive amid a familial and cultural milieu of devaluation; and yet, through the process of telling, she comes to acknowledge that, as an adult, she now is responsible for her own survival. Although heart-wrenching, the closing image of her memoir is a hopeful one as she pulls herself out of the rubble of her life, rib by rib. The scene suggests that shattering is essential to healing, but one cannot remain in such a broken state for long, but must put the pieces back together again, must reassemble some semblance of self and most often in a new form. And this she does through the process of storytelling. So that by the time she has arrived near the conclusion of her memoir, she is able to write: "Two or three things I know for sure and one of them is that telling the story all the way through is an act of love" (1995, 90). Although Allison now has multitudes of readers, as well as many critics who analyze her work, she makes it clear in her memoir that it was not the idea of readers that set her storytelling in motion: "If I could convince myself, I can convince you. But you were not there when I began. You were not the one I was convincing. When I began there were just nightmares and need and stubborn determination (1995, 4).

Allison's storytelling is circular; it curves back in on itself, creating repetitive scenes, and then it circles out from the vicious cycle of repetition to tell the story even as the story changes through the telling.[11] Such textual self-reflexivity—"narrative that includes within itself commentary on its own narrative conventions"[12]—draws attention to literary codes and conventions, and yet simultaneously draws attention "to the conventionality of the codes that govern human behavior," revealing how "such codes have been constructed and how they can therefore be changed" (Greene 2).

Stories, like subjectivities, are not one-dimensional, nor are they all-encompassing. They speak the "truth," but never the whole truth. Allison's work suggests that storytelling literally saved her life, but that even so she is not about to reduce experience to the textuality of the story. The telling of the story is merely a means, albeit a significant means, to understanding, to surviving. The writing of the story is a process, each story a rib to grip in her long climb upwards out of the rubble of her past and into her present sense of selfhood. Yet, behind every story told, every story written and read, is the actual, lived experience that serves as the heartbeat for the story. Behind the word is the lived experience. Behind the telling is the necessary silence of the child in the midst of her abuse. When Allison moves into the narrative representation of the experiences that drive her fear of telling and her need to tell, she focuses on the suffering that took place behind the formation of a self that took "damage like a wall, a brick wall that never falls down," she foregrounds the experience behind the story that is nonnegotiable, the experience that will forever remain historical fact. And she locates it at a specific time and place in history: "I was five, and he was eight months married to my mother" (1995, 38, 39). In the midst of telling this part of her history, Allison's childhood pictures are inserted: a child with her sister at the beach, a child holding a doll, a child at an Easter picnic, a child in front of the family Christmas tree, a child mostly smiling, mostly looking for all the world like the happy picture that childhood is so often represented to be.

> Behind the story I tell is the one I don't. Behind the story you hear is the one I wish I could make you hear. Behind my carefully buttoned collar is my nakedness, the struggle to find clean clothes, food, meaning, and money. Behind sex is rage, behind anger is love, behind this moment is silence, years of silence. (1995, 38–39)

Her spatialization of history, her acknowledgment that other stories always exist behind the stories that get told, sets forth an argument that when any story is written others remain unwritten. Consequently, the apparent coherence and unity of the text is an illusion that is, in fact, created by a process of selection, exclusion, and arrangement. Such a contextual perspective, incorporating a kind of social network of stories, complicates the notion of any singular truth, instead placing the storyteller in the position of constantly negotiating stories and the various versions to be told, those to remain untold. In Allison's case this has meant not only a dynamics of self-re/presentation that serves to correct cultural misrepresentation, but also an internal dialectic between what is spoken and what is silenced, what is represented and what remains absent from the representational narrative. For Allison, as well as others previously marginalized, it has meant a serious literary project of reclamation, which is not only a reclamation of the right to recut the representational coat that she will wear, but also to name the flesh that lives beneath it as her own. It is nothing short of the reclamation of a life and the integrity with which it intends to be lived.

NOTES

1. It is my argument that in the process of "telling," one's autobiography becomes a poetics of autobiography, or *autobiographics*. As such, I foreground the constructed nature of self-representational narratives. I do this in order to acknowledge the mediating process of language in the representation of life. Thus, I situate *autobiographies* in relation to, but separate from, the autobiographical tradition as it has come to be defined by autobiography studies. Leigh Gilmore argues in *Autobiographics* that there is a "crisis in critical approaches to the discourses of women's self-representation," and suggests that such a crisis "can be characterized as a kind of contractual dispute around gender and genre, in which the 'terms' [of traditional autobiography studies] seek to define legitimacy within autobiography's discursive nexus of identity, representation, and politics" (1994, 2).

2. Gilmore points out that those who are "placed outside" are always somehow "found" on the margins, "the margins being constructed as a 'place' quite literally 'without history' " (1994, xiii). This "place," I would argue, is a place of fluidity; it is always changing depending upon the various interactions between subjects.

3. Cultural canonical constructions have created frames of reference that define what Sidonie Smith has described in *De/Colonizing the Subject* as "self-representational spaces with centers, margins, and boundaries." So, when women and other marginalized subjects set out to carve representational spaces for themselves, the very act itself of intervening in exclusionary traditions illuminates the arbitrarily constructed limits of a "tradition."

4. Ex-centricity, as used here, posits a position for self-representational subjects that is both spatial and temporal. The "ex" denotes historical time, or post-centric models of being, and it also denotes space, a place beyond centric

thinking. Such a paradigm represents marginal thinking as intentional, em-powered, and deconstructive of centric thinking.

5. In drawing on Derrida's essay, "The Law of Genre," Mary Jacobus (1984) has shown how Fowler's preoccupation with cultural "legitimacy" is both gendered and embedded in a conservative politics.

6. In her collection of essays entitled *Skin*, Allison writes of the internal-ized voices that silenced her childhood need to speak of her experiences and that continue to have their repressive effects on her adult decisions to write about her life. Like a ventriloquist, the early voices speak on, creating a chorus of internal voices across time and space. "Always in the back of my mind there was my mother's whisper: 'They'll send you to detention. You'll wind up in the county home and your life will be over. You don't want to do that,' " (53).

7. See "Shotgun Strategies," 1994.

8. This is not to suggest a purist postmodernist reading of Allison's subjec-tivity, a perspective that would likely place her everywhere and nowhere si-multaneously, that certainly would disconnect the life lived from the text written. It is, rather, to implicitly argue that it is because of the disorienting nature of such multiplicitous situatedness that the shaping of self through story, the performativity itself of the autobiographical act, is gathered into the story's subject just as surely as the author's life itself.

9. See *De/colonizing the Subject*.

10. It may be difficult to get at what is behind and beyond the culturally dominant except through the symbolics of a culturally dominant language; however, it is significant that contemporary writers from the cultural margins posit a world that is made up of far more than linguistic constructions. These writers profess a profound belief in the story, while stressing that it is not "all." Such a position gives their works a creative optimism, a joyfulness in the reflexive act of narrative self-construction that does not falter in futility, nor does it flounder in nostalgic regret.

11. Gayle Greene, in *Changing the Story: Feminist Fiction and the Tradition*, describes feminist fiction as invoking a "pattern of circular return" that enacts "repetition with re-vision, a return to the past that enables a new future." Greene's findings suggest that feminist narratives are engaged in "the trans-formation of closed, 'vicious' circles to liberatory cycles," as "fixed structures of the past shift and open out into processive forms that accommodate change" (16).

12. In *Changing the Story,* Gayle Greene looks at the self-conscious fiction of Doris Lessing, Margaret Drabble, Margaret Atwood, and Margaret Laurence, which she reads as exploring women's efforts at liberation in relation to prob-lems of narrative form; she describes such fiction as "destabiliz[ing] the con-ventions of realism in a project of psychic and social transformation" (1).

WORKS CITED

Allison, Dorothy. 1992. *Bastard Out of Carolina*. New York: Plume-Penguin.

———. 1988. "Deciding to Live." *Trash: Stories*. Ithaca: Firebrand.

———. 1994. "A Question of Class." *Skin: Talking About Sex, Class & Litera-ture*. Ithaca: Firebrand.

———. 1995. *Two or Three Things I Know for Sure.* New York: Dutton-Penguin.

Foucault, Michel. 1980. *Power/Knowledge: Selected Interviews and Other Writings, 1972–1977.* Translated by Cohn Gordon et al., edited by Cohn Gordon. New York: Pantheon.

Gilmore, Leigh. 1994. *Autobio-graphics: A Feminist Theory of Women's Self-Representation.* Reading Women Writing. Cornell University Press.

Greene, Gayle. 1991. *Changing the Story: Feminist Fiction and the Tradition.* Bloomington: Indiana University Press.

Kuhn, Thomas S. 1962. *The Structure of Sciental Revolutions.* Chicago: University of Chicago Press.

Rich, Adrienne. 1986. *Blood, Bread, and Poetry: Selected Prose 1979–1985.* New York: W.W. Norton and Company.

Scott, Joan W. 1988. *Gender and the Politics of History.* New York: Columbia University Press.

Smith, Sidonie and Julia Watson, eds. 1992. *De/Colonizing the Subject: The Politics of Gender in Women's Autobiography.* Minneapolis: University of Minnesota Press.

Part 3
Vintage Re-(Per)Versions

Instructions for Survival— or Plans for Disaster? Young Adult Novels with Mythological Themes

Elise Earthman

Myth has long been recognized as a powerful human resource; in 1947 Richard Chase commented that in myth we find "a compulsive technique for controlling experience," and that through myth we can summon "that supernatural force the savages call *mana* and [compel] it to do one's bidding" (Chase 47). His antique reference to "savages" aside, the comment still has relevance, especially in his use of the word *mana* which we may read not only as supernatural force, but also as "power," and "authority." John Vickery echoes this idea, much more recently arguing that one of the central functions of myth is "to provide contact with that transrational but empirical power called . . . the numinous [and] . . . to perpetuate and focus the significance of that awe, wonder, and above all vitality that is the human response to the experiential that lies both within and without the individual" (288). He goes on to connect myth to literature, arguing that literature's ability "to move us profoundly is due to its mythic quality," and that the true function of literature "is to continue myth's ancient and basic endeavor to create a meaningful place for human beings in a world oblivious to their presence" (297). But has myth created a meaningful place for *all* humans? Many women readers have felt that it is not only "the world" but mythology itself that has been oblivious to their particular presence.

In an essential article on revisionist mythmaking, Alicia Ostriker discusses the explosion of work since 1960 by women who have become "thieves in the house of myth" by rewriting the patriarchal texts of classical mythology; such transformations, Ostriker argues, "are corrections; they are representations of what women find divine and demonic in themselves; they are retrieved images of what women have collectively and historically suffered; in some cases"—and this is the heart—"they are instructions for survival" (69), written by women, for other women. Such texts are oppositional in that they self-consciously call attention to the patriarchal ideology encoded in the myths, yet when women write themselves into mythology they are also making a home for themselves in that "inhospitable terrain" and in so doing are, in Ostriker's words, using "one significant means of redefining ourselves and consequently our culture" (71). Such possibilities for redefinition through myth would be particularly attractive to women writing for an audience of young women who are still in the process of defining (rather than redefining) themselves, and indeed, within the body of adolescent literature we find a number of books that rewrite myth, three of which I will discuss here: Patricia Galloway's *Snake Dreamer*, Cynthia Voigt's *Orfe*, and Donna Jo Napoli's *Sirena*.

Why worry about what young girls are reading? Recent studies by Mary Belenky and her colleagues on women's psychology, Carol Gilligan and her associates on the psychology of adolescent girls, and the 1992 report from the American Association of University Women, called *How Schools Shortchange Girls*, have brought to our attention some very disturbing findings about the schooling of adolescent girls. To pull together many different threads from this body of work into a single, more manageable skein, I'll summarize by saying that at adolescence, the self-esteem and self-confidence of girls decline, the conflicting expectations for women in our society "provide greater stress and fewer coping resources for girls," and they suffer from the "hidden curriculum" of the schools, which continues to reinforce gender stereotypes (AAUW 10). Also at that time, young girls begin to silence themselves rather than risk conflict that might lead to isolation and to disconnect in multiple ways: psyche from body, voice from desire, thoughts from feelings, self from relationship (Brown and Gilligan 23). For many girls—not for all but for many, because the readership of adolescent literature is quite large—reading in general and young adult literature in particular can at least potentially offer girls support in this difficult period of their lives. I say "potentially," because studies have shown that not all reading has a salutary effect; Angela McRobbie, for example, has shown that teen magazines can represent a powerful force in reconciling British girls to their futures, rather than empowering them to take control of those futures. But other researchers have shown the positive effects of reading: Janice Radway, Linda Christian-Smith, and Amy Bowles-Reyer, for example, have shown that young women in particular read "to learn how to solve their problems" (Bowles-Reyer 257); they also put themselves in the role of the heroine, learn about themselves, feel better about themselves, and become more open-minded and better decision-makers. Darcy Miller has also documented positive changes in the adolescents' "self-concepts, future aspirations, and attitudes" when young adult literature is read and discussed by "at risk" high school girls (443). So literature clearly has the power to effect changes in young women's lives, and young adult novels that rewrite mythology would appear to offer young women a way to make a meaningful place for themselves in the world.

Three adolescent novels, written by women and published after the 1992 AAUW report, take up mythological themes. What kinds of models do they present to young women readers? Do they offer to girls the chance to participate in a new kind of myth that might allow them to connect their intimate, private selves with the power and authority that myth has the ability to confer? What kinds of "instructions for survival" do young girls find in these books? We will find that although what Galloway and Voight achieve is ultimately disappointing, in *Sirena* Donna Jo Napoli has created a character from whom young girls may draw the courage to be themselves.

The ideas of Mary Russo, who has written extensively on the idea of the female grotesque, will help to frame the consideration of these books. Russo has discussed the notion of a woman "making a spectacle of herself," which she labels as a "specifically feminine danger " (213). To describe such a spectacle, she uses a double meaning of the word "stunt": 1) the extraordinary act of a risk-taking woman (as in the stunt flying—stunting—of Amelia Earhart), and 2) the dwarfed and distorted (stunted) creatures of a sideshow, which represent "a well-known cultural presentation of the female body as monstrous and lacking" (22–23). Russo sees this monstrous female body as connected with the Bakhtinian notion of the grotesque in that it is identified with "the visceral. Blood, tears, vomit, excrement—all the detritus of the body that is separated out and placed with terror and revulsion . . . on the side of the feminine" (2). Interestingly, these notions become very relevant when we consider novels whose stories are connected to mythology.

In *Snake Dreamer*, Priscilla Galloway updates the Medusa story by introducing her main character, sixteen-year-old Dusa, through her horrific nightly dreams about snakes, "twenty or thirty snakes that twisted about, hissing horribly"; in being "consumed by their rage," she herself becomes a spectacle, as her back arches, her "arms and legs [jerk] violently," and "spittle drool[s] from her mouth" (prologue, unnumbered page). Traditional medical science, in the person of the kindly family doctor, throws up its hands, helpless to identify or cure Dusa's problem. It appears, early in the novel, that she is doomed to be a freak, a prisoner of her nightmares, stunted in her development as a young woman.

Help arrives, though, in the form of two women who embody Russo's other form of a female spectacle: Drs. Teno and Yali Gordon, Greek researchers who are a medical doctor and a psychologist, respectively. Teno and Yali practice high-risk therapy with the patients that traditional medicine cannot help, "snake dreamers" like Dusa who come from all over the world to be cured at their clinic on a Greek island. The Drs. Gordon fit squarely into the tradition Russo sees as being embodied by Amelia Earhart: they both fly small planes, which they maintain themselves; Teno can keep a large yacht on course, "blindfolded"; and these activities come to them as naturally as breathing. Dusa reflects on their abilities: "she couldn't help feeling that Teno flew as she'd always flown, as if the plane's wings had somehow grown out of her shoulders . . . she belonged in the air, totally relaxed, totally in control" (56–57). These women exert enormous power over Dusa, who gives herself to them completely; she ultimately allows them to call forth the snakes that torment her, and they assure her, "Don't be afraid . . . we can control them" (94). They are extremely powerful and, for a time, positive figures.

Dusa, for her part, is very much out of control; she exhibits the symptoms of dissociation that Gilligan and her associates see as typical of her developmental stage: she is literally separated from all that's familiar (her mother, her home); she has been separated from her friends and acquaintances by her condition; she dreams of being a head separated from her body; and she senses she is fighting the snakes for possession of her mind. She feels she cannot trust her eyes, ears, or intelligence. She looks to the Gordons to save her, to rescue her from her freakish condition. She trusts them so much that she puts aside the uncomfortable and disturbing feelings she comes to have about them, ignoring the inner, truthful voice that is telling her to beware.

Dusa convinces herself that the Gordons can make her whole, but in fact they have a much more sinister intent: to make their sister, the Medusa, whole. For Teno and Yali aren't embodiments of Russo's "aerial sublime" (25) after all, but are rather themselves disguised freaks, as Lucy, another patient whom Dusa discovers locked in a tower, can clearly see; Lucy "sees auras . . . shapes within shapes, shapes beyond shapes" (184). Lucy perceives the monsters within Teno and Yali: "Almost always, I could see both shapes at the same time. Think of two naked breasts, sagging old woman's breasts, jutting out from Teno's navy jacket!" (184). Interestingly, what is grotesque about these two women are not the characteristics traditionally associated with the Gorgons of legend, the snakes, wings, or tusks, but the breasts of an old woman—probably grotesque enough in the eyes of a teenage girl concerned with appearances above all. For her insight, Lucy is "rewarded" by Teno and Yali by being imprisoned, comatose and anorexic, a grotesque skeleton of a young woman who must be kept from speaking the truth at any cost.

Dusa, longing to still feel connected to the Gordons, remains disconnected from herself by refusing to listen to what her inner voice is telling her. She argues with herself that they've nurtured her and taught her—how to run the boat, how to make soup. In her mind, anyone so competent could not be bad. She's seduced throughout by comfortable images and objects: the pink marble bath, the delicious food (which she fears may be drugged but eats anyway), and in one unintentionally comical moment, she tells herself that Yali can't possibly be a Gorgon, because "all her tops had logos" (132) and she wears Pierre Cardin jeans!

In the end, it is the Medusa herself who saves Dusa from the evil Teno and Yali. After they have used a hypnotized Dusa to find the head that Perseus in antiquity had separated from Medusa's body, they reassemble her in their laboratory ("Frankenstein territory," thinks Dusa [142], a place where a freakish woman will be made) and bring Dusa and Lucy into her presence. Lucy is turned to stone, but Dusa survives to have a heart-to-heart talk with the Medusa.

In antiquity, the Medusa, it turns out, "never [wished] to kill anyone . . . in me, victim and killer come together" (204).

Though in modern times it was her snakes reaching out to connect that created the snake dreamers, it was Teno and Yali, in
amplifying the snake dreams, who did harm. The Medusa shows
Dusa her hideous face, as well as her more beautiful human
face, and Dusa realizes that "They are both you, aren't they?"
(221). Dusa and the Medusa part, having deeply bonded with
one another, and the Medusa tells Dusa that the girl can summon her whenever she likes, through the snakes that will remain with her always. Dusa is reunited with her mother, and
the story ends with her going back to her life, determining to
study archaeology and psychology, ready to be a happy and productive young woman in the world.

Although Galloway is, through her transformation of the Medusa myth, presenting a reasonable metaphor for the psychological difficulties that face a girl at Dusa's age—the loss of
voice, the dissociation, the desire for connection even at the expense of the self—in the end, I believe she has not provided her
young readers with "instructions for survival" of those difficulties. Dusa herself seems terribly shallow, easily seduced by an
elegant bathroom and other creature comforts ("Monsters or
not," she muses at one point, "Teno and Yali kept a well-stocked
kitchen" [156]). She develops a crush on Perse, a young man
who stands in for the Perseus of antiquity, that seems particularly silly, given the difficult situation in which she finds herself
on the island at the Gordons' mercy. She also seems more than
a little dense; despite the fact that her name is clearly connected
to "Medusa" and that she has studied the myth rather extensively in school, she takes an incredibly long time to register the
fact that "Teno" and "Yali" are names awfully close to the
"Stheno" and "Euryale" of legend, and that the sister that the
Gordons/Gorgons refer to could be the Medusa. We could argue
that in these ways she reflects the typical situation of the adolescent girl; but then we could have hoped that through the myth,
Galloway would challenge this condition and tell a story that
could be more empowering to girls like Dusa who are reading.
Dusa is unable to help Lucy, who remains in the Gordons'
power and is turned to stone; the Gordons/Gorgons are defeated
by Perse, not her; and Dusa returns to being a "good girl,"
whose snakes from time to time "[rouse] comfortably, then [set-
tle] once more in her mind" (231).

Most disappointing of all is the characterization of the Medusa, who as victim loses much of her potential power; she
claims she was an instrument of those (her sisters, Perseus,

Athena) who used her for evil ends—"their weapon, nothing more" (204). Although Dusa does understand that the Medusa has both lovely and hideous faces, the Medusa's hideous face is never "owned" by either the mythological character or the young adult woman as a normal and even necessary part of a woman's personality.

Since this is a story of a young woman among women, not a romance (except for the romantic Perse subplot, the Perseus part of the story plays very little role in this modern retelling), I think we may look farther than Freud's vision of the Medusa as devouring and castrating woman in interpreting the use of the mythological figure here. If we may think of the Medusa as representing a girl or woman's "dark side," the anger, the powerful feelings, the ambitions, and the desires that are driven underground as a relatively unfettered girl moves into being a culturally acceptable woman, then this vision of the Medusa as basically a several-thousand-year-old "nice girl" is very unsatisfying indeed.

Galloway, instead of presenting a Medusa who accepts and controls her power, who says, in effect, "Yes, my anger sometimes has turned people to stone, but hey—they deserved it," gives us a Medusa who is only a weapon in the hands of others, who "never wished to kill anyone" (204), who has an "ocean of pain" in her "deep, dark eyes" (208). And Galloway's portraits of Teno and Yali are, in their way, even more insidious; she presents to us two wonderfully competent and powerful women who, of course, turn out to be monsters in reality, an extremely conservative vision of the modern career woman as ruthless bitch.

In *Orfe*, Cynthia Voigt, an extremely popular young adult writer, makes the interesting choice to switch the genders of her characters: The Orpheus of myth becomes a young woman, Orfe, a singer and songwriter; the Eurydice figure becomes Yuri, a young man whom Orfe loves and whom, for a while at least, she rescues from drug addiction.

The music that Orfe composes, which she ultimately performs in a band called "Orfe and the Three Graces," has extraordinary power. As her friend Enny, the novel's narrator (parallel to Persephone in the myth), says, "I didn't want the music to end, not once, not ever. I felt embraced, empowered. Secure in my own strength . . . released from the prison of myself" (32). Her power, for a time, tames the beast of Yuri's drug addiction; he listens to her and he, too, is empowered, to go into a detox and rehab program. However, through no fault of his own (he is "dosed" on his and Orfe's wedding day by his old companions), he sinks back into his drug-infused underworld, and it's up to Orfe to try to save him. True to the myth, of course, she is unable to do so, and he remains where he is in "the house of death" (117), miserably addicted.

At Orfe's last performance with her band, she meets her own end: After performing "The Icarus Song" atop a set of bleachers in a gymnasium, Orfe seems to be "calling [the audience] forward" (114). The crowd, overwhelmed with her music and pressing to be near her, rushes up the bleachers, causing them to collapse, killing Orfe.

Throughout the ages, the Orpheus myth has been one that has focused intensely on the male as artist, as powerful creator; therefore, a transformation of the protagonist into a woman might present interesting possibilities for questioning that focus and for seeing a young woman character as a powerful artist. Although representations of Orpheus over the millennia have emphasized various parts of the legend, in almost every case, Orpheus is triumphant in the end, over death, over chaos, through the power of his song.

Although Voigt's Orfe is a young woman, she is an androgynous character, unencumbered (as was Amelia Earhart) by an excessively female body. When Enny re-meets Orfe as an adult (they had been in school together as children), she is struck with the ambiguity of Orfe's appearance: she "could have been taken for a scrawny young man or a slender young woman; it didn't matter which" (21). Not at all pretty—in fact, according to Enny, "just barely not unattractive" (23)—Orfe nevertheless has an "arresting" appearance, one that "[makes] you want to look and keep on looking" (23). Clearly her appeal comes from her art, her voice, rather than from a stereotypic female attractiveness.

Yuri, on the other hand, is physically attractive, even beautiful, in a way that counters male stereotypes, with "curls [that] hung like the tendrils of grapevines," and a body that "relaxed into curves" (78) when he sat. He is non-stereotypical in other ways as well: he enjoys dancing, cooking, and cleaning up afterward; he is always agreeable, whatever others want to do; and he is content to watch Orfe rehearse and perform. One of Enny's boyfriends remarks that it's "not the usual attraction [Yuri] has," but then hastens to add that he's "not putting him down as unmasculine" (96). And yet Yuri is not traditionally masculine, in a number of ways that are perhaps less appealing: he lacks self-esteem, he has little faith in himself (one reason he will not leave his drug habit is because he is sure he will disappoint Orfe again), and he cannot face the pain he knows will come with being sober, the pain of life outside the underworld of addiction.

What does Voigt gain by her mythological cross-dressing? Will young girls be encouraged by Orfe's story, to imagine new possibilities for themselves as young women, to see themselves as artists, harnessing chaos to create art? Unfortunately, in the end Orfe does not present any more positive instructions for survival than does *Snake Dreamer*.

Orfe, as a character, combines Russo's two forms of the female grotesque. She is, in the one hand, a talented and ambitious musician whose music is so powerful it "makes people go out and do things" (42), such as feeding the homeless; on the other hand, when we first meet her, she is making her mark in the club scene as a singer with a punk band, whose signature song is something called "Current Events." In this song, the lead singer assaults Orfe with horrifying headlines from the daily news, to which she repeatedly responds, "It makes me sick," until at last, overcome, she vomits on the stage—and we return to Russo's notion of the grotesque as being connected to the visceral, to bodily fluids identified with the feminine. Orfe, to her credit, leaves this band and stops her spectacular vomiting on stage, but her public sees this as a loss; her fans have come specifically to see this spectacle, because it provides a release for them. Orfe says, "Sometimes I think I just act out what they feel, what they're feeling, sometimes" (35).

Although Voigt, who is a much more accomplished writer than Galloway, has done some interesting things with the Orpheus myth, Orfe as a character, though much less a victim than is Dusa (or the Medusa), presents conflicting messages for young women readers.

Orfe is extraordinarily talented and is able to use that talent in powerful ways, but the effects of that power ultimately destroy her because she cannot control the response that people have to her. Perhaps Orfe's strongest talent is for creating chaos, a talent she seems to have had since childhood; whatever game Orfe joined into "broke . . . down into chaos" (11), and when she sang, even on the playground, "rules seemed impotent" (12). She can purify people: Yuri sees Orfe as "someone like a flame . . . a flame like fire to burn you clean" (66). In one way, Orfe seems to have it all—she is able to express her deepest feelings and inner vision while at the same time retaining her connection to others. Indeed, her empathy and ability to express what others, male and female, cannot draw people powerfully to her. But her powers are inadequate to save Yuri from addiction, and it is the uncontrolled connection to others, the very connection that adolescent girls seek in this moment of their development, that kills her. And unlike the Orpheus of the traditional myth, who in continuing to sing beyond death (after he is ripped to pieces by the Maenads, his head and lyre float down the river Hebrus to the island of Lesbos, where Apollo himself protects the head) illustrates "the animating and vitalizing power of the beauty and pleasure of song" (Segal, 13), Orfe seems not to live beyond herself. The book ends abruptly with Orfe's death, and except for a brief mention that Orfe's portion of the royalties from the album, *Yuri's Dreams* (note that the dreams are Yuri's, not Orfe's), are sent to Yuri and continue to support him in his addiction, Voight says nothing about any effect that Orfe's music might continue to have after her death.

In *Sirena*, Donna Jo Napoli takes on an interesting myth, that of the Sirens who lured sailors to their deaths with their singing. Since little was written of the Sirens in classical mythology, Napoli has a fresher imaginative canvas on which to work; she is not as restrained, as Galloway and Voigt are, by the ancient story, and though Napoli writes Sirena into an existing story (that of Philoctetes and his role in the Trojan War), she does so in a way that allows her much freedom in the creation of her character.

Napoli writes of the Sirens, or mermaids, shortly after the time of their birth; when we meet them, they are seventeen and have yet to work their magic on men. Half fish and half goddess (their parents were the parrotfish "Little Iris" and Eros), they are, as Napoli imagines them, doomed to mortality unless they can make a human man love them, a curse placed upon them by the nymph Rhodope, who was jealous that their mother had caught Eros' eye.

Sirena, part of a group of ten mermaids on the island of Anthemoëssa, shares her sisters' excitement at the prospect of making men love them and attaining immortality. They have tried going to where men live, but were driven away by men who tried to harpoon them and catch them in nets—and who looked at them as monstrosities, clearly not objects of love. So they have returned to their island to wait for a ship to capture, so that the men, shipwrecked on their island, will have "time to look beyond our crossbred selves and fall in love" (5).

From the first, we see that Sirena is different from her sisters in a number of ways—she is a risk-taker, an adventurer, and something of a loner compared to her extremely social "school" of sisters. Her sister, Alma, warns her that "someday you will pay for your independence" (8). Indeed, when the cost of immortality becomes clear to her—many men drown during the shipwreck because they do not swim, and the remaining men die on the rocky island, which has no fresh water, cursing the Sirens as "wretched misshapen monsters of the deep. Seductresses of evil" (14)—Sirena refuses to participate further and even tries to save the next shipload of human men by arguing with her sisters, who respond, "You aren't always sensible." Her sisters don't care if the men die, because "they will love us first" (35), thereby assuring the Sirens' immortality; Sirena, in despair, says, "We have become the monsters they said we were" (36) and leaves Anthemoëssa to live alone on Lemnos, an island where, because of its history, she is sure that men will never go. And she vows never to sing again.

At this point, we might feel that Sirena shares one important characteristic with adolescent girls—she silences herself. But Sirena vows silence not as a way of hiding her real feelings, of concealing her figurative "monstrosity" as adolescent girls do in order to be accepted by the group, but as a way of being true to herself: alone on Lemnos, rejecting the fate that Rhodope's curse has put on the Sirens, she asserts that "I am a monster in body . . . but I am decent in soul" (43). She finds the solitude and freedom there to be herself, and though lonely, she is happy and unafraid, believing that "If I yield to fear, my life will become small and dry, until no pleasures touch me at all. I must allow myself adventure" (45).

When the man Philoctetes is abandoned on Lemnos by his shipmates and left to die, Sirena's convictions are tested. Suffering from a serpent bite on his leg, a consequence of his having offended the goddess Hera, the man lies feverish and unconscious on the beach, and Sirena is moved to tend to his wound and bring him food. As he recovers, she continues to help him, and though she tries to keep herself concealed, she finally responds to his requests that she show herself.

Of course, Sirena grows to love Philoctetes; however, she does not lose herself in the process. They share food and stories, reveal their strengths and weaknesses, become friends. Sirena is

very aware that she could seduce him by singing and win immortality, and since Philoctetes is perfectly capable of continuing to live on Lemnos after being bewitched by her (unlike the
men who couldn't survive on Anthemoëssa), she struggles with
her urges: "No one would be harmed. A cost-free prize of eternity." But since gaining immortality would involve both deceiv-
ing Philoctetes and giving in to the curse of Rhodope, Sirena
continues to maintain her silence and integrity. Though the
world constructs her identity as monstrous, she holds on to
what she knows she is inside.

When an encounter with a bear inland forces Sirena to sing
(charming the bear is the only way to keep from being eaten),
Philoctetes hears her, is also charmed, and falls in love with Sirena. Though crushed that she has won his love under false pretenses, Sirena accepts both Philoctetes' love and immortality,
since she has no way to undo what was done.

The ten-year "marriage" of Sirena and Philoctetes is a relationship of equals. Determined to be neither Rhodope nor
Hera's victims, they live a life filled with the pleasures of each
other and of life on the island. Yet they also argue and debate,
differing significantly, for example, on the role that honor plays
in life: for Sirena, honor comes from living "a decent, honest
life" (135), while for Philoctetes, "true honor [is] to be the main
character in a tale of courage" (194). And of course Philoctetes
worries that Sirena will grow tired of him as he grows old and
she remains young and beautiful; she assures him that she will
not.

When fate offers Philoctetes the chance to resume his place
in such a tale—Odysseus and his men arrive to tell Philoctetes
that the war with Troy cannot be won unless he arrives to kill
Paris—his departure seems fated, and Sirena's visit to Mother
Dora, mother of the nymphs and surrogate mother to the sirens,
seems to confirm this. Still, Philoctetes says that he is willing to
stay on Lemnos. Sirena's belief that he only offers this possibility because he is enchanted leads her to ask the question she
has never before asked: "When did you first think you loved
me? . . . Was it when you heard me sing to the bear?" When he
replies that he loved her *before* that, and that her singing only
made him love her more, Sirena realizes that he is not bound to
her by the gods' manipulations, that she does have a choice. She
lets him go, to take his place in the tale of courage that is the
Trojan War.

We might be tempted to see Sirena as the embodiment of a

stereotype—the self-sacrificing woman who puts aside her desires for the sake of the man she loves—and in one sense, that is true, for she decides in the end that it's more important for Philoctetes to be able to live out his version of honor than it is for her to fulfill her own needs by having him with her. But Sirena has never stopped being her own person throughout their long relationship, and it is because she has become an integrated, rather than dissociated, woman/mermaid that she can make the choice she does.

In many ways, Sirena's development from a young, innocent mermaid to a mature being follows the typical pattern of the adolescent girl. Happy and free while young, she takes risks, swimming with squid who could eat her, enjoying her solitude away from her sisters, acting very much as an individual who doesn't care whether she has the approval of those around her—and she receives the disapproval of both her sisters and Mother Dora. But following their initial encounters with men, Sirena accepts that her form renders her monstrous, and for a time participates with her sisters in trying to disguise what they are, "picking lilies and tying them with bunches of seaweed to their tails in an effort to cover all but their lovely brown breasts" (5). That they are monstrous is shockingly confirmed when the men shipwrecked on Anthemoëssa kill her sister Cecelia, shouting "Vicious whore from hell!" But rather than either accepting the men's construction of her identity or submerging her own identity so that she is acceptable to her sisters, Sirena chooses a third path: to live in solitude, separating herself from both her sisters and humans, so that she can more fully be herself and live a life of dignity and honesty. She refuses, in Russo's sense, to "make a spectacle of herself," either as a monstrous hybrid fish-woman or as a creature of wonder who can make any human man lose himself in love for her. Her "stunts," soaring leaps with schools of squid or long, sensual swims with porpoises, occur where no one, not even Philoctetes, can see them and are solely for her own enjoyment. Though troubled from time to time with worries that she's freakish (she becomes upset when Philoctetes tells her the tale of the half-human Minotaur), as she matures, Sirena accepts herself and is at peace with herself.

At one point, Napoli suggests that the love of Sirena and Philoctetes is "doomed" (153), but by the end of the novel, we see that this is not so. Because she has steadfastly clung to her own identity and made room for the fulfillment of her own needs, Sirena is able to see that Philoctetes should have this opportunity too, that his honor requires that he avenge the death of Achilles and help the Greeks win the war. Thus, she participates in her own "tale of courage" by encouraging him to go.

In *Sirena*, Donna Jo Napoli uses the bare outline of the sirens' story to create a transformation of the myth that indeed does contain "instructions for survival" for young girls: accept yourself as you are; do what you know is right, no matter what the crowd suggests; don't forget your own needs as you please another person. The consequences may not always be pleasant— Sirena, at least at the end of this part of her story, is alone—but she has refused to be dishonest and deceptive, and she has not traded her soul, her identity, for acceptance or gratification at any time.

Myth offers strong possibilities for young women readers of adolescent novels, possibilities that at least in two of these novels remain largely unrealized. In some ways, *Snake Dreamer* and *Orfe* mirror some of the problems that young women face as they move toward adulthood, but neither serves as a positive model that could aid in that development. *Sirena,* on the other hand, in the guise of what might appear a traditional story of "doomed love," offers a portrait of an adolescent who successfully accomplishes several important developmental tasks: identity formation and the development of independence and integrity. Young women readers of *Snake Dreamer* and *Orfe*, rather than finding "instructions for survival," will learn little that will help them negotiate the Scylla and Charybdis of their adolescence, and will have to look elsewhere, to *Sirena* or perhaps to the work of poets such as Adrienne Rich, Rita Dove, or June Jordan, in order to be able to claim the numinosity of myth for themselves.

WORKS CITED

AAUW Educational Foundation and Wellesley College Center for Research on Women. 1992. *How Schools Shortchange Girls: The AAUW Report.* New York: Marlowe & Co.

Bowles-Reyer, Amy. 1998. "Our Secret Garden: Young Adult Literature in the 1970s and the Transmission of Sexual and Gender Ideology to Adolescent Girls." Diss. George Washington University.

Brown, Lyn Mikel , and Carol Gilligan. 1992. *Meeting at the Crossroads: Women's Psychology and Girls' Development.* New York: Ballantine Books.

Chase, Richard. 1996. "Myth as Literature." In *Literary Criticism and Myth,* edited by Robert A. Segal, vol. 4, *Theories of Myth*, 47–66. New York: Garland.

Christian-Smith, Linda K. 1990. *Becoming a Woman through Romance*. New York: Routledge.

Galloway, Patricia. 1998. *Snake Dreamer*. New York: Delacorte.

Miller, Darcy E. 1993 "The Literature Project: Using Literature to Improve the Self-Concept of At-Risk Adolescent Females." *Journal of Reading* 36: 442–48.

Napoli, Donna Jo. 1998. *Sirena*. New York: Scholastic.

Ostriker, Alicia. 1982 "The Thieves of Language: Women Poets and Revisionist Mythmaking." *Signs: Journal of Women in Culture and Society* 18:68–90.

Radway, Janice A. 1991. *Reading the Romance: Women, Patriarchy, and Popular Literature*. Chapel Hill: University of North Carolina Press.

Segal, Charles. 1989. *Orpheus: The Myth of the Poet*. Baltimore: The Johns Hopkins University Press.

Vickery, John B. 1996. "Literature and Myth." In *Literary Criticism and Myth*, edited by Robert A. Segal, vol. 4, *Theories of Myth*, 283–305. New York: Garland.

Voigt, Cynthia. 1992. *Orfe*. New York: Scholastic.

Galatea: Rewritten and Rewriting

ELLEN PEEL

FOR CENTURIES WESTERN CULTURE HAS FELT THE POWERFUL appeal of the myth that Ovid tells about Galatea and Pygmalion: after the sculptor creates the statue of a perfect woman, he falls in love with it, and Venus brings the statue to life (281–82).[1] From Ovid's time onward through contemporary times, the story has sustained its hold on us: it has been evoked in myriad ways—ranging from male influence upon a living woman (William Shakespeare's *The Taming of the Shrew*) to male creation of a female robot (Lester del Ray's "Helen O'Loy"). The myth and its variants flourish not only in literary texts but also in films such as *Educating Rita*, *Pretty Woman*, *Weird Science*, and the little-known but unforgettable *Frankenhooker*.[2] Some retellings explicitly recall the myth—as in George Bernard Shaw's *Pygmalion*, whereas in others the myth simply serves as a latent pattern, though in some cases that pattern may result from actual influence. Although beyond the scope of this paper, it would also be rewarding to pursue the pattern in non-Western cultures where actual influence would be extremely unlikely, if not impossible. Consider Murasaki Shikibu's classic from eleventh-century Japan, *The Tale of Genji*, in which the hero trains a girl from her youth to be his ideal love object. The existence of such widespread examples suggests that, while patriarchy takes varied forms in specific cultures, the Galatea and Pygmalion myth may nonetheless serve as a helpful paradigm for many of those forms.

The most intriguing aspect of this myth's reception is that, despite the fact that it represents patriarchal values, almost every version of its countless retellings offers at least some critique of those values. Subversion bubbles up as if from the unconscious of the text. Some feminists believe, along with Audre Lorde, that "the master's tools will never dismantle the master's house" (112), but I find that the master's texts, when rewritten, can at least shake the foundations of that house.

176

A vital technique for shaking up patriarchy by means of rewriting has been called "mimicry" by the French psychoanalyst and philosopher Luce Irigaray. Her writings emblematize how one can detect and exploit the weaknesses in systems deeply influenced by patriarchy—in her case linguistic and philosophical systems. Institutionalized and intersubjective, language may seem particularly impervious to resistance. The pervasiveness of patriarchy makes it hard to find any tools other than the master's, and so Irigaray practices the kind of rewriting she calls mimicry (*mimétisme*): by quoting or imitating patriarchal language in certain ways, she causes it to criticize itself. Irigaray states: "There is, in an initial phase, perhaps only one 'path,' the one historically assigned to the feminine: that of mimicry. One must assume the feminine role deliberately. Which means already to convert a form of subordination into an affirmation, and thus to begin to thwart it" ("Power," 76). So, if patriarchy makes women into looking-glasses for men, if even feminist writers must act as mirrors, they can at least transform what they reflect.

Irigaray herself employs mimicry in *Speculum of the Other Woman*, quoting extensively from Freud, Plato, and other master thinkers of the West, but in order to use their words against them. Her book's very title may be read not only in patriarchal ways, such as "instrument for invasively probing the other, i.e., Woman," but also in feminist ways, such as "mirror controlled by the woman who is other than expected." The object might turn out to be a subject. So even a few words, seemingly rewritings that merely parrot patriarchy, can be rewritings in another sense—new, challenging writings. Irigaray's mimicry provides one instance, suggestive of numberless other possibilities, of how feminists confronting the ostensibly invincible system of "the master's house" can in fact make it teeter. Such possibilities are what is evoked by the Galatea and Pygmalion myth when we recognize the vein of subversion that runs through it.

I propose to discuss different versions of the same story, but—as narrative theorists and folklorists can tell you—it is hard to determine how much the versions of a story can change before they cease to be "the same story" (Propp, ch. 1). We would probably agree to consider a story to be a retelling of the Galatea and Pygmalion myth even if the created being were not made of ivory, for few of us would think of the statue's material as a necessary component of the myth. It might, however, prove harder to reach agreement on other components. At the risk of some arbitrariness, I have decided that, to belong to the Galatea and Pygmalion tradition, a story must at least include one person who literally or figuratively creates another, and this story should usually include the creator's falling in love with the creation. As we shall discover, the creative process feeds the love, and the love feeds the creative process. Usually the creator is male and the creation is female, though we shall observe some fascinating variations on that pattern.

Sometimes the process of creation is physical, one person literally making another —a biological impossibility made possible in such stories by magic, science fiction technology, or delusion on the part of an observer. At other times no physical creation occurs, but one person exercises a tremendous influence on another. Of course, while characters influence each other in almost all literature, this does not mean that most literature evokes the Galatea and Pygmalion myth. Jane Austen does not, for instance, present Darcy as a Pygmalion who utterly transforms Elizabeth Bennet. To count in my definition of the Galatea and Pygmalion tradition, a story with no physical changes has to tell of influence that forms or profoundly transforms a person's identity, as in some recountings of Abélard's influence on Héloïse.[3] Thus there are more ways to create than sculpting in stone; in fact, in some stories the object of desire is a powerful projection, formed solely in the creator's imagination.

The compelling magnetism of the Galatea and Pygmalion myth is based in large part on the appeal of a wish that comes true. What could be more romantic than having a lover who magically fulfills all your desires? What could be more romantic than magically fulfilling all your lover's desires? Underneath the magic of this success story, however, lies something disturbing, unsettling. In the traditional versions of the story, Pygmalion's success consists of controlling his creation, and her success depends on pleasing him by being controlled. Such a story appeals to both sexes in societies where men wish to control women and where women wish to please men—or where women *need* to please men.

I am not the first to find something unsettling in the original myth. In fact, one can argue that Ovid himself affords a peek beneath the romantic surface, insofar as he presents the myth as one bawdy tale among others in *The Metamorphoses*, as a sort of dirty joke about someone who builds a sex doll. And, as Bonnie MacDougall Ray says, the myth has undergone "many metamorphoses" ever since "the third century B. C. . . . The figure of Pygmalion [has] represented an idolator, papist, melancholy outcast, madman, artist, neo-platonic lover, onanistic loner, and a courtier" (Abstract). In some of these interpretations Pygmalion certainly falls short of being a romantic ideal. Thus when I read the myth as a metaphor for something disturbing, I am joining a long line of earlier readers.

Yet I differ from most of those readers in one significant way: they focus their gaze on Pygmalion (even if that gaze is critical), whereas I am focusing on his creation, Galatea.[4] Or, rather, I am focusing on the figure who would be Galatea, if she had a name. Significantly, Ovid and other ancient writers never referred to her by name—apparently she acquired one only in the 1740s.[5] (For clarity, however, I consistently refer to her as Galatea.) My emphasis on the creation rather than the creator grounds a threefold thesis: the myth is an exquisite allegory for the unequal relations of women and men in a male-dominated, or patriarchal, society; a surprising number of rewritings of the myth question aspects of that inequality, albeit in a limited way; and, finally, some rewritings subvert the inequality more radically.[6]

I focus on Galatea because my inquiry emphasizes gender and sex, especially female gender and sex, and sexuality, especially heterosexuality, and in these ways my critical reading differs from most past readings.[7] I am asking why the sculptor is male while the sculpture is female. It is no coincidence. After peeling off the story's romantic surface, we need to notice the underlying misogyny. We are not told that Pygmalion likes women in general and loves his statue-woman best: instead, Galatea is the only woman he loves, for it was disgust with women in general that prompted him to sculpt her figure in the first place. As Thomas Bulfinch retells the tale, "Pygmalion saw so much to blame in women that he came at last to abhor the sex, and resolved to live unmarried" (65).

And, more importantly, regardless of his attitude toward other women, problems are raised by his creation of this ideal, nameless woman. His love for the statue can, by definition, be based only on her physical traits, rather than emotional, spiritual, or intellectual ones. He is subject—she is object. In addition to her originally inanimate nature, she is further objectified in that she is his creation: she is the passive object upon which he acts. Even when she comes to life, passivity persists. As Susan Gubar says, "Not only has he created life, he has created female life as he would like it to be—pliable, responsive, purely physical" (292).

Created as his ideal, she embodies his desires. Although Galatea does not look like Pygmalion, she is, as the embodiment of his desires, metaphorically a self-portrait of her creator, a representation of self rather than other.[8] Pygmalion has rightly been compared to Narcissus, a man in love with his own reflection (Ray 86). Irigaray centers her book *Speculum of the Other Woman* on the idea that Western patriarchy constructs women as mirror images of men—not literally to look like men but to be controlled by, and thus reflect, men's wishes. Patriarchal society considers men as the norm, in contrast to women, who are deviations from that norm: two-dimensional, inferior reflections. Even when Galatea comes to life and would seem to become a subject in her own right, her subjectivity can be no more than a reflection of Pygmalion's, because he has constructed her as a sort of double, projected out of his own desires. She is his wish come to life.

Her resemblance to him stems not only from having him as a father but also from having no one as a mother. Ordinary creation of a human being requires two parents, whereas Galatea has only one. Since Pygmalion is, in the most basic sense, a single parent, he produces a child who is more like him than if half her traits came from a mother.[9] In fact, as his (desire's) looking-glass reflection, she resembles a clone more than a child.

If she is like a child, their eventual union has undercurrents of parent-child incest; if she is like a clone, it is hard to say whether their union is between parent and child, between two siblings, or between Pygmalion and himself. In any case, incestuous undercurrents come to the surface when Ovid goes on to recount the tragedy of Galatea and Pygmalion's great-granddaughter, Myrrha, who commits incest with her father (282–89).[10] Thus, threads of narcissism and incest, of claustrophobic mirroring, run through Pygmalion's story at various points, suggesting the solipsism that lies at the extreme of male domination.

I want to make clear that I am not condemning Pygmalion as if he were a real person who needed a dose of consciousness-raising. Even if he had really existed, his attitudes would have been understandable, given the attitudes of ancient times. Nor am I objecting to the myth as a whole. Instead, I am expressing admiration for it because of the clarity with which it allegorically represents the relations of many women and men in male-dominated society. Male domination means that men "create" women in two senses: they create notions of what women are and should be, and they create real women insofar as they have the power to cause women, by force or persuasion, to do what men want.[11]

It is striking that almost every rewriting of the Galatea and Pygmalion myth is an instance of mimicry, questioning patriarchy to some degree. I call a rewriting a "limited" or a "strong" critique, depending on how much the text engages in subversion, the rattling of the master's house. Interestingly, although all the critiques are challenging the role of gender, sex, and sexuality in patriarchy, the strength of the challenge does not correlate in any simple way with literal gender, sex, and sexuality associated with a given text. We might think that the degree of subversion would depend on whether the author were female, male, or—in a film—collective, or on whether the creator/creation relationship were heterosexual, queer, or not erotic; in fact, it turns out that, say, female authors or nonheterosexual relationships do not necessarily make for the strongest critiques. Issues such as the author's sex and gender and the characters' sexuality do come into play, but in a much more complex way, often differently in different texts.

The less critical versions, the limited critiques, question some patriarchal values while retaining other crucial ones. Some versions, for instance, rely on ambiguity to avoid a wholesale rejection of patriarchy. There is much debate about whether Kate, Shakespeare's bold shrew, has been tamed by the end of his play. We wonder whether the playwright has achieved his happy ending by letting Kate retain a last portion of independence or by depriving her of it.

Other limited critiques of the myth tell of a man who tries to perfect a living woman and, in doing so, destroys her. In Nathaniel Hawthorne's "The Birthmark," for instance, a scientist is revolted by a birthmark on the cheek of his beautiful wife and projects onto it all his dissatisfaction with earthly frailties. After he convinces her to loathe it herself and to submit to his attempt at removing it, he eradicates the birthmark, but his wife dies in the process. The story condemns him for sacrificing nature to an abstract ideal. Similarly, in the story "Adieu," Honoré de Balzac condemns a man who kills his former mistress in the process of curing her insanity. The men in both works are blamed for trying to sculpt a living woman into the form they desire. These stories do not fully eschew patriarchal values, however, for both glorify the women's suffering as martyrdom, and both to some extent exalt the men as tragic, heroic over-reachers who deserve pity and a sort of admiration.

Another type of limited critique offers variations on the model of male creator and female creation. Such variations, by indicating that the creator need not be male or that the creation need not be female, challenge the patriarchal construction of men as subjects in relation to women as objects. A relation that might seem natural or inevitable is thus revealed as only *one* possibility. It may be no coincidence that some of the authors who risk such variations are themselves women—female creators; indeed every female-authored text implicitly challenges the notion that creators are always male.

Yet the author of one of the most resonant rewritings, herself a female creator, did not, in departing from the paradigm, choose to make the creator character female. Instead, Mary Shelley made the created character male: both Frankenstein and his nameless monster are men. Her book's subtitle is "The Modern Prometheus"; I would like to suggest that another Greek myth is more lightly inscribed—Frankenstein is also "The Modern Pygmalion." The monster's maleness throws into relief what is only hinted at in the original myth—the reflection of the creator in the creation, his second self: although Frankenstein does not set out to create a second self and shudders at any similarity between himself and the monster, in fact the two are doubles in a number of ways. One can read the novel as an exposé of the tragic consequences that stem from Frankenstein's narcissism, his botched attempt to give life alone, without a woman. The novel, unlike the standard Frankenstein films, further subverts the original story by endowing the monster with poignant subjectivity and the eloquence to express it, both of which the myth never permits Galatea to demonstrate. By giving him such subjectivity, the novel suggests that even an object—a creation—can become a subject.

On the other hand, the monster's maleness may also betray a limitation in the critique: perhaps Shelley, writing in 1818, could endow a Galatea figure with subjectivity only by turning her into a male. Frankenstein does start to make a female companion for his monster, then dismembers his handiwork. Because Victor fears his creatures will reproduce and probably for a host of other reasons such as fear of female sexuality and hatred of the male monster, the scientist destroys the female creation—but what is Shelley's motive for having him do so? The aborted process of creating the female monster might represent the

nineteenth-century author's own inability to give as much selfhood to a female creature as to a male one. It is as if Shelley
expressly introduced the possibility of a female monster and
then quashed its creation, lest one assume a female object could
take on subjectivity as easily as the male does. We are tantalized,
and then the notion is abruptly censored. Thus Shelley's decision to make both Frankenstein and his monster male—while
challenging the patriarchal link between man and creator,
woman and creation—nonetheless also returns to patriarchy in
a subtle way.

"Pygmalion," a limited critique by H. D. (Hilda Doolittle), also
presents both creator and creation as male, for her sculptor
makes statues of gods, not of a mortal woman. He says, "I made
the gods less than men/for I was a man and they my work;" yet
he now doubts his powers (71). The statues come to life, speak,
move, but only to torment him:

> each of the gods, perfect,
> cries out from a perfect throat:
> you are useless,
> no marble can bind me,
> no stone suggest.
> . . .
> each from his marble base
> has stepped into the light
> and my work is for naught. (72)

Sources of anguish rather than love, they cause him to ask
whether he is subject or object: "am I the god? / or does this fire
carve me / for its use?" (73). As in *Frankenstein*, the original
myth is challenged, for some power shifts from subject to object;
however, again as in *Frankenstein*, perhaps it is only the maleness of the object, here accomplished by the elision of Galatea,
that makes the shift possible.[12] Actually Galatea has been elided
in several ways: one female mortal has been replaced by multiple male immortals, whose divinity indeed makes it easier to
represent them not only as subjects but as creators. So Pygmalion's loss is not Galatea's gain. Furthermore, the sculptor, while
profoundly questioning himself, is still the speaker throughout
the poem, for we hear even the gods' voices only as quoted by
him. Like many a Romantic hero, he may be suffering agonizing
self-doubt, but not enough to fall silent.

Fay Weldon has produced another rewriting that deviates

from the pattern of male creator/female creation. In *The Life and Loves of a "She-Devil,"* both figures are female. In fact, they are a single character: a formerly docile housewife who, enraged by her husband's infidelity, turns herself into a "she-devil." She completely transmogrifies her body and her personality. This is no feminist triumph: revenge being what drives her, she remains obsessed with her husband—hardly liberation. Her re-creation of herself includes excruciating plastic surgery (to make herself shorter, for instance), and the body she so badly wants, and gets, is just like that of her husband's mistress. Although the protagonist analyzes her former exploitation and revolts against it by seeking power, she is no more a paragon of feminism than Hans Christian Andersen's Little Mermaid, who willingly undergoes mutilation for love and of whom the she-devil could be a grotesque parody. This Galatea may create herself, but she fails to love herself.

One of the the best-known limited critiques to vary the sex of characters is by Shakespeare: Paulina, in *The Winter's Tale,* punishes King Leontes for his jealousy by telling him Queen Hermione is dead. After years of suffering have reformed the king, Paulina says she will show him a statue of his late wife. The so-called statue descends from its pedestal and turns out to be Hermione, whom Paulina has kept hidden all that time. The play certainly illustrates how the power of one woman can help another get revenge on male tyranny; yet Paulina's solution causes almost as much pain to the innocent queen as to the king. Although Paulina deserves credit for metaphorically bringing Hermione back to life, Paulina also deserves some of the blame for having metaphorically killed her, for having objectified her. Jealous Leontes wanted a wife he could control completely, a wife he could, in effect, paralyze; ironically, to save Hermione, Paulina has herself had to paralyze the queen.[13] This play resists patriarchy largely through patriarchal methods.

As shown in the examples just given, rewritings of the myth have tended to stay within the basically heterosexual framework of the original. Even in *Frankenstein*, H.D.'s "Pygmalion," *The Life and Loves of a 'She-Devil,'* and *The Winter's Tale*—texts where creator and created are the same sex—their relationship is not homosexual, for the creator does not fall in love with the creation (though an interesting play might be written about Paulina and Hermione during the supposedly lost years). Some queer texts, however, can be read as analogues to the Galatea and Pygmalion story; for instance, Namascar Shaktini has found traces of the myth in Monique Wittig's *The Lesbian Body*. Wittig defies tradition by making both lover and beloved female and by going beyond the conventional Petrarchan praise for teeth like pearls and lips like cherries, instead celebrating the beloved's veins, viscera, and lymphatic system. Despite the charm of such originality, the emphasis on separate body parts, no matter how celebratory, is all too reminiscent of patriarchal violence against women, the ultimate objectification; even if intended to criticize the violence by laying it bare, Wittig's tactics are problematic, diluting her critique.

In contrast to these limited critiques of the myth, there exist what I call strong critiques, rewritings that subvert the myth much more drastically. Some such versions drain the original plot of romance by pitilessly revealing its male narcissism, without the hedging that goes on in texts like Hawthorne's "The Birthmark." In "The Statue," Artur Lundkvist writes of a man whose inadequate love turns his wife into stone (22); in "He Says He Doesn't Want to Change Her," Rebecca McClanahan Devet presents a man who metaphorically chisels away at his wife while assuring her, "I love you / just the way you are." With a lighter tone, *Stage Door* unmasks the sleazy intentions of a producer vaunting himself as a Pygmalion who will "mold" a young actress, his Galatea. Both "The Sand-Man," by E. T. A. Hoffmann, and "The Mannequin," by Germaine de Staël, make fun of men who mistake mechanical dolls for real women. The men immediately fall in love with the dolls, which possess, along with beauty, the alluring feature that they agree with everything the men say. Although the men do not literally create the dolls, they, like Pygmalion, project or inscribe their desires onto blank female pages.

Balzac recounts a similar strong critique, with an extra twist. In "Sarrasine," the story that Roland Barthes analyzes in *S/Z*, Balzac wryly tells of a sculptor who falls in love with a beautiful opera singer, La Zambinella, but is horrified when he eventually learns the singer is a castrato—a man and therefore an image of the sculptor's body rather than of his desires. It is hard to say, though, whether he is bothered more by La Zambinella's resemblance to him (maleness)—which he rejects as unthinkable—or by the fact that an unexpected difference (castration) also exists. Like the men in the Hoffmann and Staël versions, the sculptor has been projecting his own wishes onto the beloved, ignoring all hints of his mistake. In none of the three versions does the

Pygmalion figure physically create the Galatea figure (though
Balzac's sculptor does reproduce her in a statue), but all three
texts testify to the creative power of projection.

The sculptor's tunnel vision also foreshadows that of a more
recent male character, Gallimard in *M. Butterfly*, by David
Henry Hwang: a man named Song, pretending to be a beautiful
actress, gets Gallimard to fall in love with him. Explaining why
he and other men play women's roles in the Peking Opera, and
in effect boasting about his own success as a seductress offstage,
Song says, "only a man knows how a woman is supposed to act"
(63). This comment, which could apply as well to Balzac's
singer, implies that if what men in patriarchy really want is a
mirror, that role may best be filled by another man. It is as if
the sculptor and Gallimard direct a paradoxically homophobic
homoeroticism toward the objects of their desires.

Although La Zambinella and Song have a good deal in common as performers onstage and off, Hwang's character is the
more active subject. Song intentionally seduces Gallimard,
prides himself on his success, and refers to himself as an "artist"
(62, 63). Not merely a blank screen for another's projections, not
merely an actor reciting another's lines, he is also an improvi-
sor, even a sort of playwright—in short, a creator. It is as if this
Galatea is created by both Pygmalion and herself. So, while *M.
Butterfly* resembles the other texts just discussed—all mock the
projections of male narcissism—Hwang's play also differs from
the rest because the feminine object of the projections is not
blank. For this reason *M. Butterfly* has affinities with another
group of retellings as well.

These versions offer an equally strong critique of the myth by
granting Galatea subjectivity and independence. Claribel Alegría's "Galatea before the Mirror" is a particularly bitter example:

> I've become accustomed these past days
> to lament my good fortune
> in front of the mirror
> everything
> I have everything
> you modelled me perfectly Pygmalion
> you covered me with gold
> with silks
> with perfumes
> you taught me how to act
> at every moment

how to modulate my voice
I feel you're satisfied with your creation
and perhaps you even desire me.
I don't love you Pygmalion
you didn't arouse in me
the spark of love
my perfection isn't mine
you invented it
I am only the mirror
in which you preen yourself
and for that very reason
I despise you.

This poem gives subjectivity to Galatea, the object, for she is able to see herself and to reflect upon that reflection. As a subject, she has a voice, and the poem is wholly in that voice. She has not created herself, but she has created these words, words that in turn reinterpret, if not recreate, the sculptor's creation. What is more, Galatea is criticizing Pygmalion, and in an especially devastating way, since she is not disputing that he made her "perfect" but is instead disputing the very foundation of that act, the very notion of making someone perfect. Her speculations and her expression of them occur, significantly, "before the mirror," for she is aware that in Pygmalion's eyes she mostly exists visually, as a physical being. Indeed she recognizes that for him she herself serves as a mirror. It makes ironic sense, then, for her to address him while looking at her own mirror image, since in a complex way her reflection is his.

Some rewritings not only tell of Galatea's autonomy but also record Pygmalion's discomfiture at what he has wrought.[14] The classic example is Shaw's *Pygmalion*, along with *My Fair Lady*, the Lerner and Loewe musical that interprets Shaw's play. By making Eliza Doolittle into a lady, Henry Higgins is unwittingly giving her power, power that breaks out of his control and that draws him to her. (Her rise in class does, however, deprive her of the power to earn her living as she used to, by selling flowers on the street; now she must marry or find enough money to open her own flower shop.)

Another strong critique is offered by Christa Wolf, in "Self-Experiment: Appendix to a Report," which presents a woman who is turned into a man and then rebels, to the displeasure of the male experimenters. The pattern is complicated, for the woman on whom the experiment is done is herself one of the experimenters, so that the very process of objectification turns both the object and one of the subjects from a female into a male. Moreover, one wonders whether the rebellion is fueled by the fact that the object once was female, or that he now is male, or that he is subject as well as object.

Finally, the rarest and most fascinating examples of thoroughgoing subversion are those in which the female figure shows independence but the man is not discomfited—he is delighted. The lighthearted film *Mannequin* introduces a department store mannequin who comes to life when a window dresser falls in love with her. Yet she is no Sleeping Beauty, no woman who exists only when recognized by a man. This Galatea figure is actually more creative than her lover: her advice enables him to design captivating window displays. Furthermore, before becoming a mannequin, this heroine was both alive and resistant to male demands: she was born in ancient Egypt and was turned into a twentieth-century window model because she prayed to the gods to save her from having to marry a man she did not love. While not having created her modern self, she did have the strength to refuse the earlier self that ancient society presented to her.

In surveying the Galatea and Pygmalion myth and its rewritings, I have stressed their subversive force, the many instances of what Irigaray calls mimicry. I have talked about various limited critiques: one rendering gives voice to attacks on patriarchy but ends ambiguously, and other versions condemn men for exercising fatal control over women but applaud the men's overreaching and the women's martyrdom. Still other limited critiques present creator and creation as members of the same sex, a move that breaks the linkage between men and subjectivity, women and objectification. But some of such stories seem unable to imagine women as subjects, and others present female subjects who exert baleful power over female objects. I have also discussed strong critiques of the myth: some variations mock the narcissism of a man who projects his own desires onto his beloved—figuratively, or even literally, onto an automaton; in other versions it is a feisty Galatea herself who mocks her creator. And in one retelling it is Galatea's very independence that Pygmalion loves. Even the limited critiques have condemned some patriarchal assumptions; meanwhile the strong critiques have attacked patriarchy for its absurdity as well as its injustice, frequently telling of how male domination demeans men as it oppresses women. Together, the two sorts of critiques comprise an impressive gamut of ways in which rewritings of the original myth have shaken it—weaknesses in the edifice of patriarchy that range from almost imperceptible cracks to yawning abysses. On close inspection, even the original story displays a crack, for it is Venus, an exemplar of female power, who actually brings the statue to life.

Furthermore, both types of critique go beyond suggesting why patriarchy should change to suggesting that it can change, that it has weak spots. If the original myth is largely an allegory for the power of patriarchy, then the critical retellings can serve as allegories for the vulnerability of patriarchy. Male domination has existed for centuries; given specific historical circumstances, however, it has not always taken the same form and, most significantly, it has not always consisted of a seamless, self-perpetuating system. Sometimes, as in Shaw's *Pygmalion*, female power slips through its grasp. Often the system damages itself, as when Frankenstein sows disaster in his attempt to avoid female creators and female creations. The very pervasiveness of critique throughout the myth's different versions raises the possibility that patriarchy's vulnerabilities are inherent, as if it were unconsciously undercutting itself. Just as the original myth contains the seeds of all its retellings, so patriarchy contains the seeds of its own subversion.

NOTES

1. I am grateful to Dolora Cunningham, Deborah Russell, Elise Earthman, Jo Keroes, and Elizabeth Sommers for their comments on this essay.

2. Jo Keroes discusses *Educating Rita* and *Children of a Lesser God* as examples of "Pygmalion Refused," since "Rita refuses the erotic consequences of her transformation . . . [and] Sarah Norman refuses transformation altogether" (106).

In some films (as in some literature) the characters differ in sex from those in the myth: for example, in *The Witches of Eastwick*—based on a John Updike novel—it is female creators who conjure up a male sex object, and the Adonis-like creation in *The Rocky Horror Picture Show* is constructed by a drag queen. In *Rocky Horror* this mad scientist and his minions also transform people into statues and back again, by throwing a switch to "Medusa" or "de-Medusa" them.

3. E.g., Jean-Jacques Rousseau's *Julie ou La Nouvelle Héloïse*.

4. For example, the central metaphor in J. Hillis Miller's *Versions of Pygmalion* links the sculptor, not the sculpture, to a narrative's "author, reader, or critic" (vii). Susan Gubar, in her discussion of "The Blank Page," by Isak Dinesen, is one of the few to share my focus, but our essays, while beginning at the same point, take different directions. I go beyond her emphasis on two particular types of creation: the textual (the man who conflates women and

texts) and the physical (the woman who views her body as her only creative realm). Also, unlike Gubar, I stress how not only blank pages but rewritings of the myth itself can critique patriarchy.

5. Meyer Reinhold says "names began to be invented for the statue" during the myth's vogue in the early eighteenth century; around 1741 Thémiseul de Saint-Hyacinthe de Cordonnier wrote a work that "would appear to have contained for the first time the name Galatea for Pygmalion's statue" (317). Reinhold adds that "Rousseau's *Pygmalion* [written in 1762] popularized the name Galatea for the statue" (318).

6. I define "patriarchy" as the oppression of women. The innumerable specific instances of patriarchy are usually characterized by two salient traits: men generally have superior power, and norms associated with men are generally viewed as superior.

7. I use "sex" to refer to inborn traits that differentiate women and men, and I use "gender" to refer to acquired traits that tend to differentiate women and men.

8. Of course, all art to some degree represents the artist. But Galatea does so to a degree that is almost embarrassingly literal—even comic. On women and literalization, see *Bearing the Word: Language and Female Experience in Nineteenth-Century Women's Writing*, by Margaret Homans. Simone de Beauvoir discusses how patriarchy positions woman as other.

9. Since Pygmalion knows that no woman or other man helped create Galatea, she embodies not only his desire for sex and love, but also his desire to create offspring alone. As Gubar says, "he has evaded the humiliation, shared by many men, of acknowledging that it is he who is really created out of and from the female body. Our culture is steeped in such myths of male primacy in theological, artistic, and scientific creativity" (292–93). I am grateful to Dolora Cunningham for mentioning, in this connection, that some men have an "obsession . . . with legitimacy."

10. Their son is Adonis, with whom Venus falls in love (Ovid 289). According to Philostephanus, Pygmalion's statue represents Venus (Hammond and Scullard 902, citing C. Müller, *Fragmenta Historicorum Graecorum*, 1841–70). In that case, she is Adonis's great-great-grandmother as well as his lover—another instance of incest.

11. One could argue that the sexes in the myth could just as well be reversed; after all, women also create notions of what men are and should be. But women do not have as much power as men over members of the other sex.

12. Despite its title, the poem says nothing of Galatea or even of a statue in the image of the goddess Venus. Even if one interprets "god," "man," and masculine pronouns as generic terms meant to include females, it is striking that, of the two gods specifically mentioned, one is male (Hephaestos) and the other is Pallas, born of Zeus, not of a mother.

13. Mary Ellen Lamb discusses both Paulina and Autolycus as Ovidian artist figures. Lamb presents Autolycus as the disreputable one and evaluates Paulina in a more straight-forwardly positive way than I do. Bonnie MacDougall Ray does not link Paulina to Pygmalion; instead Ray interprets Paulina as a "Hermione," a Venus figure, and sees Pygmalion in Leontes, as lover, and in Romano, as artist (ch. 5).

14. These creators are upset to learn their efforts have had unintended consequences. In *M. Butterfly*, Gallimard is upset too, but for a different reason—learning that he has been a creator at all.

WORKS CITED

Alegría, Claribel. 1993. "Galatea before the Mirror." In *Fugues*, translated by D. J. Flakoll, 85. Willimantic, CT: Curbstone Press.

Andersen, Hans Christian. 1980. "The Little Mermaid." 1837. In *Tales and Stories*, translated by Patricia L. Conroy and Sven H. Rossel, 34–58. Seattle: University of Washington Press.

Austen, Jane. 1813. *Pride and Prejudice. The Complete Novels of Jane Austen.* New York: Modern Library, n. d., 229–465.

Balzac, Honoré de. 1896. "Adieu." In *The Works of Honoré de Balzac*, translated by Katharine Prescott Wormeley, vol. 17. Boston: Little, Brown, 1888–96, 85–142.

Barthes, Roland. 1970. *S/Z: An Essay.* Translated by Richard Miller. 1974. Reprint, New York: Hill and Wang-Farrar, Straus and Giroux.

Beauvoir, Simone de. 1949. *The Second Sex.* Translated by H. M. Parshley. 1974. Reprint, New York: Vintage.

Bulfinch, Thomas. 1968. *Bulfinch's Mythology: The Age of Fable.* 1855. Reprint, Garden City, NY: Doubleday.

del Ray, Lester. 1938. "Helen O'Loy." In *Science Fiction Hall of Fame*, edited by Robert Silverberg, 42–51. Garden City, NY: Doubleday, 1970.

Devet, Rebecca McClanahan. 1987. "He Says He Doesn't Want to Change Her." In *Mother Tongue*, 54. Orlando: University of Central Florida Press.

Dinesen, Isak. 1957. "The Blank Page." In *The Norton Anthology of Literature by Women: The Traditions in Engish*, edited by Sandra M. Gilbert and Susan Gubar, 2nd ed., 1391–94. Reprint, New York: Norton.

Educating Rita. 1983. Directed by Lewis Gilbert. RCA.

Frankenhooker. 1990. Directed by Frank Henenlotter. Southgate Entertainment/Shapiro Glickenhaus Entertainment.

Gubar, Susan. 1985. " 'The Blank Page' and the Issues of Female Creativity." In *The New Feminist Criticism: Essays on Women, Literature, and Theory*, edited by Elaine Showalter, 292–313. New York: Pantheon.

H.D. (Hilda Doolittle.) 1925. "Pygmalion." In *Collected Poems of HD*, 70–73. New York: Horace Liveright.

Hammond, N. G. L., and H. H. Scullard, eds. 1970. *The Oxford Classical Dictionary.* 2nd ed. Oxford, Eng.: Clarendon-Oxford.

Hawthorne, Nathaniel. 1843. "The Birthmark." In *Hawthorne: Selected Tales and Sketches,* 3rd ed., 264–81. Reprint, 1964, 1970. New York: Holt, Rinehart and Winston.

Hoffmann, E. T. A. 1987. "The Sand-Man." 1816–17, translated by J. T. Bealby. In *The Best Tales of Hoffmann*, edited by E. F. Bleiler, 183–214. New York: Dover.

Homans, Margaret. 1986. *Bearing the Word: Language and Female Experience in Nineteenth-Century Women's Writing.* Chicago: University of Chicago Press.

Hwang, David Henry. 1989. *M. Butterfly.* 1988. Reprint, New York: New American Library.

Irigaray, Luce. 1985. "The Power of Discourse and the Subordination of the

Feminine." In *This Sex Which Is Not One,* translated by Catherine Porter with Carolyn Burke, 68–85. 1977 Reprint, Ithaca, NY: Cornell University Press.

———. 1985. *Speculum of the Other Woman.* Translated by Gillian C. Gill. 1974. Reprint, Ithaca, NY: Cornell University Press.

Keroes, Jo. 1999. *Tales Out of School: Gender, Longing, and the Teacher in Fiction and Film.* Carbondale: Southern Illinois University Press.

Lamb, Mary Ellen. 1989. "Ovid and The Winter's Tale: Conflicting Views toward Art." In *Shakespeare and Dramatic Tradition: Essays in Honor of S. F. Johnson,* edited by W. R. Elton and William B. Long, 69–87. Newark: University of Delaware Press.

Lerner, Alan Jay. 1956. *My Fair Lady; A Musical Play in Two Acts, Based on Pygmalion by Bernard Shaw.* Music by Frederick Loewe. New York: Coward-McCann.

Lorde, Audre. 1984. "The Master's Tools Will Never Dismantle the Master's House." In *Sister Outsider: Essays and Speeches by Audre Lorde.* 110–13. Trumansburg, NY: The Crossing Press.

Lundkvist, Artur. 1980 "Four Prose Poems." Translated by Diana Wormuth. *Scandinavian Review.* 4: 22–25.

Mannequin. 1987. Directed by Michael Gottlieb. Media Home Entertainment/ Heron Communications.

Miller, J. Hillis. 1990. *Versions of Pygmalion.* Cambridge, MA: Harvard University Press.

Ovid. 1960. *The Metamorphoses.* Translated by Horace Gregory. 1958. Reprint, New York: Mentor-New American Library.

Pretty Woman. 1990. Directed by Garry Marshall. Touchstone.

Propp, V. 1975. *Morphology of the Folktale.* Translated by Laurence Scott. 2nd ed. 1928. Reprint, Austin: University of Texas Press.

Ray, Bonnie MacDougall. 1983. *The Metamorphoses of Pygmalion: A Study of Treatments of the Myth from the Third Century B. C. to the Early Seventeenth Century.* Diss. Columbia University, 1984. Ann Arbor: University of Michigan, 8406537.

Reinhold, Meyer. 1971 "The Naming of Pygmalion's Animated Statue." *Classical Journal* 66:316–319.

The Rocky Horror Picture Show. 1975. Directed by Jim Sharman. Twentieth Century Fox.

Rousseau, Jean-Jacques. 1967. *Julie ou La Nouvelle Héloïse.* 1761. Reprint, Paris: Garnier-Flammarion.

Shakespeare, William. 1969. William Shakespeare: *The Complete Works.* Edited by Alfred Harbage. Baltimore, MD: Penguin.

Shaktini, Namascar. 1982. "Displacing the Phallic Subject: Wittig's Lesbian Writing." *Signs* 8:29–44.

Shaw, George Bernard. 1953. *Pygmalion: A Romance in Five Acts.* In *Four Plays by Bernard Shaw,* 211–320. 1913. Reprint, New York: Modern Library-Random House.

Shelley, Mary. 1992. *Frankenstein or The Modern Prometheus.* Edited by Johanna M. Smith. 1818, 1831. Reprint, Boston: Bedford-St. Martin's.

Shikibu, Murasaki. 1977. *The Tale of Genji.* Translated by Edward G. Seidensticker. 1976. Reprint, New York: Knopf.

Staël, Germaine de. 1987. "The Mannequin." In *An Extraordinary Woman: Selected Writings of Germaine de Staël,* Translated and edited by Vivian Folkenflik, 325–47, 396–97. New York: Columbia University Press.

Stage Door. 1937. Directed by Gregroy LaCava. Republic Pictures.

Weird Science. 1985. Directed by John Hughes. Universal.

Weldon, Fay. 1984. *The Life and Loves of a "She-Devil."* 1983. Reprint, New York: Pantheon.

The Witches of Eastwick. 1987. Directed by George Miller. Warner Bros.

Wittig, Monique. 1975. *The Lesbian Body.* Translated by David Le Vay. 1973. Reprint, New York: Morrow.

Wolf, Christa. 1978. "Self-Experiment: Appendix to a Report." Translated by Jeanette Clausen. *New German Critique* 13:109–31.

(Dis)Obedient Daughters: (Dis)Inheriting the Kingdom of Lear

SARAH APPLETON AGUIAR

A POPULAR TALE FOR FEMINIST REVISION, *KING LEAR* FORMS THE basis for several late twentieth-century novels written by women: Margaret Atwood's *Cat's Eye*, Anne Tyler's *Ladder of Years*, Laura Esquivel's *Like Water for Chocolate*, and, especially, Jane Smiley's *A Thousand Acres*. While the primary character focus for the novels differs in several of the revisions, "their stories suggest that a woman's identity may be better found by moving against, rather than following or embodying, prevailing myths about women" (Rozga 20). And whereas three of the novels discussed concentrate upon the damage done to Cordelia through her father's insistent ego, Smiley's novel finally allows Goneril her long-overdue rebuttal.[1] All of the mentioned works actively (dis)inherit the traditional legacy of *King Lear*'s portrayals, suggesting that the daughters must be viewed as more than mere archetypal figures.

"[Literary] Re-vision can be represented in two ways" according to Peter Erickson: "a conciliatory mode that urges moderation and balance or an oppositional mode that insists on a more uncompromising critical perspective" (167).[2] Yet, often the feminist revisionist writer combines both active oppositional and conciliatory modes in her writing, paradoxically both honoring the text she usurps, as well as simultaneously subverting the original text's authority. And while she may often write to recover a missing feminine authenticity that may have been lacking in the original work—writing a validation of women's roles from a re-conceptualized point of view—the feminist revisionist does not automatically attempt to supplant the original narrative. As Nancy A. Walker states, the aim of such a revision is that it becomes "*a* narrative rather than *the* narrative, a construct to be set alongside other constructs," removing absolutist authority from the original (6). For the feminist author, then, revision serves the triple purpose of renewing an established narrative, granting female characters subjectivity and complexity that had been lacking in the original narrative, and, to quote Walker, "expose or upset the paradigms of authority inherent in the texts they appropriate" (7).

Perhaps the most crucial step in rescuing misrepresented texts and female characters—after acknowledging the dilemma of course—is to reconstruct the textuality of the original narrative, creating an alternative version. Kim Chernin acknowledges, "The transformation of woman is a work of archetypal dimension and significance. To change fundamentally the nature of woman, it would be necessary to transform the archetype itself" (148). And thus, feminist revisions of male-authored female characters do attempt to broaden the outlines of the feminine archetypes, in some cases rescuing vilified characters, and in others, adding dimensions to flatly represented women.[3]

The purpose of re-envisioning a maligned female antagonist is not to "clear" her name so much as it is to re-evaluate the original conception of the type, finding a clearer, more woman-centered reading of the character, as well as to relocate the motivations for her behaviors and to interrogate the "traditional" framework that created her. A well-known example, Hélène Cixous' landmark essay, "The Laugh of the Medusa," significantly revises the male-written myth of Medusa, contending that Medusa was not ugly but beautiful, yet no less angry, powerful, or dangerous than she had been depicted (246). Cixous challenges the traditional "gaze" leveled at Medusa—the one that finds her terrifying—and questions the criteria that have supported the judgment against her. De-establishing the basis for the pronouncement condemning Medusa, Cixous proposes alternate parameters of estimation, re-valuing a woman who was once denounced. Yet, it is also critical to acknowledge that Cixous refuses to disempower Medusa, to render her benignly innocent or to remove the locus of her power: her rage and vengeance.

Shakespeare's plays, as narratives constituting part of the very core of western patriarchal literature, are crucial targets for feminist revisionists. These writers engage in broadening the often two-dimensional heroines of the plays, such as Naylor's revisioning of Miranda in *Mama Day*, or participate in the "rescue/reclamation" of villainesses, such as Smiley's reconception of Goneril and Regan. Yet many of the revisions written by feminists refrain from condemning Shakespearian literature with its adherence to patriarchal law and its often reductive representations of women. Feminine reworkings of the plays, for the most part, pay tribute to Shakespeare even as they reconstruct an alternative text.[4]

Jane Smiley's novel, *A Thousand Acres,* takes two of Shakespeare's most wicked women as its source: *King Lear*'s Goneril and Regan. Smiley, according to Walker, "reformulates Shakespeare's *King Lear* to give narrative authority to the female characters and thus to expose and question the patriarchal patterns that Shakespeare and his contemporaries took for granted" (7–8). Set in the American Midwest of 1979, *A Thousand Acres* recounts the story of the demise of the Cook family and the destruction of the family farm. The patriarch, Laurence (Larry) Cook, a contentious and disagreeable man, ceremonially divides his property among his three daughters; only this time, instead of the parceling off of a kingdom, Lear's division occurs as shares in a family-run farming corporation. As in *King Lear,* the narrative focuses upon the elder daughters' agreement to the division and the youngest daughter's refusal. However, Smiley's version of *King Lear*'s script deviates from the familiar tale as she adds details of the women's relationship with their father and, in particular, bestows motivations for the elder daughters' actions.

The narrator of Smiley's novel is Ginny, not the Cordelia character as is the case in many other feminist revisions of *King Lear.* Goneril finally gets to tell her side of the story of one of the most evil women in literature, the recipient of Albany's famous line: "Proper deformity shows not in the fiend / So horrid as in woman" (4.2.60–61). Mary Paniccia Carden allows, "Displacing the moral center of Shakespeare's plot, Smiley disrupts and de-centers discourses that position the father's perspective as the perspective of history" (182). In fact, Smiley's revision suggests that the primary transgression of Goneril/Ginny is not her ostensible cruelty to her father, but rather it is her insistence on retelling the story from the feminine/daughter perspective, depreciating Lear's perspective.

Like many of the traditional evil female characters in literature, Shakespeare's Goneril and her equally evil sister Regan seem to have no legitimate basis for their more depraved actions. Claudette Hoover recognizes, "influential critics of this century have agreed that since their motivations defy understanding, they must be regarded as representations, personifications, or symbols rather than individualized characters or even dramatic types" (49).[5] Marianne Novy notes, "Few of [Goneril's and Regan's] lines carry hints of motivations other than cruelty, lust, or ambition, characteristics of the archetypal fantasy image of the woman as enemy" (1984, 106). However, Stephen Reid notes that, given Lear's professed greater fondness for Cordelia, Goneril and Regan's initial stance is one of necessary "subservience" to their "tyrannical father" (228). He further posits that, as evidenced by Lear's towering rage at Cordelia's "momentary inability to express her love," Lear's behavior toward his daughters is "pathological": "The slightest sign of petulant behavior in Goneril was [probably] met by something close to absolute rage" (239). Thus, Goneril's behavior toward to her father, once she has gained power, might be recognized as not only having motivation—her rebellion against his tyranny—but also her own paternal training: she responds toward him as he would respond toward her.

Hoover also notes that in Shakespeare's revision of the earlier and anonymous *The True Chronicle Historie Of King Leir*, he masculinized Goneril and Regan (50). In Jungian archetypal theory, a woman who maintains an overly masculine psyche relies upon an unconscious identification with her animus.[6] Regan and Goneril, in becoming rulers—ironically not of their own volition—are then severely castigated for adopting the characteristics of a strong (read: masculine) monarch.[7] Perhaps, the reader may wonder, Lear did not really mean for his daughters to rule after all? Perhaps Lear's motivation was always an intention to demonstrate his own superiority? That is, he may have purposely desired his daughters' failures to adequately rule, sabotaging them when it became apparent that he was not, in fact, a necessity.

CORDELIA'S (DIS)INHERITANCE

As Goneril and Regan are always held in contrast to Cordelia, several feminist revisionists have examined the conditions of Cordelia's selfhood, rendering revised portraits of her refusal to profess an all-consuming love for her father. Moreover, these authors also posit the conditions of Cordelia's existence, and by extension, the conditions of her sisters' daughterhood as well. Atwood's *Cat's Eye* relates the consequences of Cordelia's rejection by her father and his patriarchal legacy.[8] Cordelia, youngest of three sisters, is trapped within a vicious legacy of self-hatred as she is subjected to the soul-withering nature of her father's scorn, a malicious behavioral pattern that she replicates with her friends. Having failed, somehow, like her namesake, to convince her father that she is worthy of his love, she is metaphorically banished from the kingdom.

Cordelia makes her appearance in the novel after protagonist Elaine returns from her summer with her family to find a new girl who is "lanky, sinewy" and dressed in "corduroys and a pullover," unlike the other girls who are wearing "summer skirts" (74). Thus, upon her first description, Cordelia is likened to a more masculine figure,[9] especially when compared to her older "gifted" sisters: Perdita and Miranda.[10] Cordelia quickly seems to assume a stance of strength and power as she brutalizes Elaine, yet the novel suggests that Cordelia is replicating her own treatment by her father: Cordelia and her sisters do not "joke or drawl when mentioning him. He is large, craggy, charming, but [Elaine has] heard him shouting" (77). Cordelia's "victim," Elaine, is torn between her fear of Cordelia's vicious behavior and her equally potent fear of Cordelia's rejection in an innocent yet deadly version of female/male, daughter/father patterns; and as Stephen Ahern asserts, "Cordelia uses Elaine in this classic patriarchal pattern of projecting what one is trying to escape/reject within oneself onto an 'Other' " (13).

Cordelia's tactics in tormenting Elaine are obviously repetitions and revisions of what have been said/done to her. For example, in one scene, Elaine is ostracized from the other girls by Cordelia until she thinks over everything she's said that day "and [tries] to pick out the wrong thing"—a clearly parental admonition (122). Cordelia also repeats classic paternal reprimands: "What do you have to say for yourself?"; "You should have your mouth washed out with soap"; "Look at yourself! Just look!" (123, 143, 168).[11] Elaine recognizes that Cordelia has been ruled by fear; she relates, "Cordelia's father . . . makes wry jokes, his smile is like a billboard, but why is she afraid of him? Because she is" (175). Elaine, whose own father is benign, does, however, understand that "Darkness brings home the fathers, with their real, unspeakable power" (175).

During dinner with Cordelia's family, the "wolfish" father complains to Elaine, " 'I'm hag-ridden' " (263).[12] Cordelia's father, as a revised King Lear, is a tyrannical and unpacifiable ruler/father. Although Cordelia obviously strives for her father's love and acceptance with her "dithering, fumble-footed efforts to appease him," it is equally obvious that she is never granted her desire "because she is somehow the wrong person" (264). Elaine also reports that Cordelia's father "can make you feel that what he thinks of you matters, because it will be accurate, but what you think of him is of no importance" (263). Atwood suggests that Lear's rejection of Cordelia is far more perverse than merely an egotistical father having a temper tantrum because his daughter won't lie to him. Atwood's Cordelia clearly models herself upon her father, acting in a masculine manner and adopting his own traits; she believes that she may find some sort of perfection in her father's eyes by mirroring him. Yet, in order to emulate her father, she must also engage is his hatred/disdain of women; thus, she must also hate her self.[13] Cordelia will never please her father, except, possibly, by total erasure of her self in metaphorical or literal death. And indeed, Atwood's Cordelia *does* disappear.

Anne Tyler's *Ladder of Years* recounts the story of motherless daughter, Delia Grinstead, the youngest of three, who like her namesake, ultimately becomes the daughter who best demonstrates her love for her father. Delia, however, finds that in her attempt to please him, she sacrifices herself completely, even marrying his assistant and never leaving her father's house. In her care of her father, she fails to gain her own identity; and following her father's death, Delia at age forty finds herself adrift, a grown-up who has never emotionally grown beyond daughterhood.[14] The novel relates Delia's journey as she walks away from her family for over a year, creating the necessary autonomy she never possessed, even though Delia does choose to return to her family at the end of the novel, as is the case in many female *Bildungsroman* novels.

Ladder of Years revises *King Lear*, becoming a powerful feminist *Bildungsroman*, enacting subjectification for a woman rather than relating a tale of destruction. Delia's experiences mirror those related by Rita Felski in her definition of the female *Bildungsroman*: they are "difficult and painful," such as when her son finds her and asks her to come home, but her journey is presented as one of her "necessary steps toward maturation" (135). Felski writes,

Individual development requires some kind of recognition of the contingency and uncertainty of experience; this form of knowledge is counterposed to the deceptive myth of romance, the ideological fiction of idyllic married bliss which provided an already written script without space for the articulation of dissent. (136)

Delia's unquestioning devotion to her father in *Ladder of Years* suggests a naivete that stifles her ability to be a mother and wife within her own family. Thus, what appears to be selfish abandonment as Delia walks off of a beach with very few possessions and no explanation is actually the only means by which Delia will be able to fulfill her familial "responsibilities." She will return because she chooses to, and not because she is required to.[15] Tyler, in invoking *King Lear*, suggests that his daughters are destined to failure because they have never been allowed to develop self-love and self-gratification. In subjugating their selves, voices, desires, and ambition to the patriarch's influence, the Gonerils, Regans, and Cordelias must quell their own requirements to develop and mature.

Tyler also suggests at the perhaps inadvertent cruelty of the father who selfishly allows his daughter to profess an all-consuming love. While Delia had never left her father's house, marrying his junior partner and continuing her childhood habits—wearing girlish clothing, reading trashy romance novels, Delia's new personality—Miss Grinstead—reads mature classics, wears adult clothing, procures employment, maintains her own rented room. Delia's new life is a time-warped and fast-forwarded version of the life she never had, and thus she finally is able to grow up. And it is only this maturing process that had been truncated that will allow her to cope autonomously with life without her father.

Adrienne Rich, in *Of Woman Born* argues that "The loss of the daughter to the mother, the mother to the daughter, is the essential female tragedy. We acknowledge Lear (father-daughter split), Hamlet (son and mother) . . . as great embodiments of the human tragedy; but there is no presently enduring recognition of mother-daughter" (103). Laura Esquivel's novel, *Like Water for Chocolate*, as a partially inverted retelling of *King Lear*, does focus upon such a mother-daughter split. Daughters Rosaura and Gertrudis portray Regan and Goneril, and Josefita known as Tita, the protagonist/heroine, is a version of Cordelia, a Cordelia who has been successfully forced to profess an ultimate love and remain with her parent: Mama Elena. Like Lear, Mama Elena insists on unconditional devotion from her daughter Tita; Tita is obligated by family custom to remain single and care for her widowed mother as long as Mama Elena shall live. And also like Lear, Mama Elena is not interested in a truthful protestation of love for her from Tita, only abject acquiescence to her will.

Mama Elena, "represented through the filter of awe and fear," refuses to allow Tita to marry her "true love," Pedro, and instead, marries Rosauro to Pedro, who agrees so that he might remain close to his beloved Tita (de Valdés 79).[16] Tita, obedient daughter, agrees in enforced silent anguish. Yet Mama Elena is not triumphant in her daughter's resignation to her will, implying that perhaps Lear too would remain unsatisfied had Cordelia mouthed a tritely dutiful response, or even sacrificed herself completely to her father. Because she has tyrannically compelled loyalty from Tita, Mama Elena can never accept Tita's compliant devotions. She cannot trust Tita, knowing that Tita has not chosen to care for her mother of her own free will, a lesson Lear never learns.[17]

Ultimately, Tita is driven mad by sacrificing herself to Mama Elena's will, "screaming wildly, 'Here's what I do with your orders! I'm sick of them! I'm sick of obeying you!' " (98). At this, Tita's first real rebellion, Mama Elena sends for a doctor to take Tita to an insane asylum for her insubordinance, banishing her daughter from the "Queen-dom." Bereft of compassion (even though she too has experienced a thwarted romance), Mama Elena remains implacable; it takes the redundancy of paralysis below the waist (Mama Elena had negated her own sexuality long before she was attacked by bandits), for her to allow Tita to return. However, she still refuses to accept Tita's love: "It was as if Mama Elena's spit had landed dead-center on a fire that was about to catch and had put it out. Inside [Tita] felt the effects of snuffing the flame; smoke was rising in her throat, tightening into a thick knot and clouding her eyes and making her cry" (127). Esquivel suggests that Lear's narcissistic self-love, like Mama Elena's, would also have smothered Cordelia if she had not remained true to herself. In addition, Esquivel demonstrates that Lear, perhaps, would not have been placated if Cordelia had, in fact, lied; he may have continued his demands, disinheriting her (as he does with her sisters) as soon as she gave evidence—valid or not—that she had indeed lied.

GONERIL'S "(DIS)TRUST"

Jane Smiley stated in an interview that she "never bought the conventional interpretation that the sisters were completely evil" (Duffy). And therefore, the most significant revision of Goneril (and Regan) in *A Thousand Acres* is that Ginny is not an insensitive, defeminized, inhuman monster. Both Ginny and Rose embody the traditional feminine nurturing impulses; in particular, they have divided the care of their more than capable father between the two in addition to their own household duties.[18] On alternating mornings Ginny rises early and travels to her irascible father's house to make him his breakfast, "I set out sausage, fried eggs, hash brown potatoes, cornflakes, English muffins and toast, coffee and orange juice," a very hearty meal (29). She and Rose make dinner for him at the time he appoints, clean his house, and arrange their lives to suit his demands. Their lives are spent in service to their father, even though both are grown married women.

As in *King Lear*, Ginny and Rose have not been allowed to speak their own words. Goneril and Regan, in proclaiming their love for their father, speak a ritualized script, the one Lear had written for his daughters; and in *A Thousand Acres*, Ginny and Rose know only too well how to read their scripts.[19] Ginny says, "Of course, it was silly to talk about my 'point of view.' When my father asserted his point of view, mine vanished. Not even I could remember it" (176). In addition, Larry does not speak the truth; Ginny realizes, "There's always some mystery. He doesn't say what he means" (104). When Larry does speak, due to his massive ego, he expects his daughters to read his mind, to understand his implied subtexts. He has created an elaborate vision of reality: his *implied* word—which is subject to his immediate and arbitrary revision—is the law of the land.

Larry's refusal to allow his daughters autonomy, or to even acknowledge their humanity mirrors his awesome ego. His daughters belong to him; he allows them no space for their own husbands, or—in the case of Rose—children. The daughters' mother is dead, and as Ginny notes, "My mother died before she could present him to us as only a man, with habits and quirks and preferences, before she could diminish him in our eyes enough for us to understand him" (20). Only the youngest, Caroline, has managed to escape, to move away and become a lawyer, due in large part to Ginny and Rose's mothering of her and sheltering of her from their father's all-consuming influence.

Ostensibly for tax purposes, Larry impulsively decides to incorporate the farm, the thousand acres, and divide the shares among his daughters. None are prepared for this as Larry has maintained an unrelenting authority over his farm for all of his adult life. As in *King Lear*, the two eldest accept—automatically shielding their bewilderment and misgivings, while the youngest hesitates. Larry ruthlessly cuts Caroline out of the family, never even allowing her to speak, in a portentous demonstration of how he deals with obstruction.

Immediately the plan goes awry. Larry fumes about his own imposed retirement, spending hours glaring out the window as his sons-in-law work the fields. As Carden notes, Larry "feels he has lost the 'respect' that goes with ownership" (189). He soon starts drinking heavily and becomes more abusive than ever toward Rose and Ginny. In a revision of Goneril's and Regan's refusal to allow King Lear his one hundred knights and horses, Ginny and Rose, in this version, take away Larry's keys to his "horsepower" because of his repeated instances of drunken driving, including an accident.[20] Larry then "steals" a farm truck, and when confronted by his daughters, he rages and curses Ginny.

Larry Cook's curse re-invokes Lear's curse upon Goneril who has the "power to shake [his] manhood" (1.4.288). Larry's overreaction takes the form of misogynistic and inappropriate (especially for a father) venom:

> A wave of exhaustion waved over me. I [Ginny] said,
> "Fine. Do what you want. You will anyway."
> "Spoken like the bitch you are!"
> Rose said, "Daddy!"
> He leaned his face toward mine. "You don't have to drive me around anymore, or cook the goddamned breakfast or clean the goddamned house." His voice modulated into a scream. "Or tell me what I can do and what I can't do. You barren whore! I know all about you, you slut! You've been creeping here and there all of your life, making up to this one and that one. But you're not really a woman, are you? I don't know what you are, just a bitch, is all, just a dried up whore bitch." (195)[21]

As Hoover argues in regard to *King Lear*, the "anti-sexual" curse of Lear is inexplicably directed toward Goneril's femininity (60–61). Likewise, Oates questions *King Lear*'s yoking together of feminine evil and sexuality: "It is not dramatically clear why the sisters' cruelty to their father should be related to sexual desire" ("Promised"). However, numerous references are made to Goneril and Regan's "perverted" sexuality; Lear himself alludes to Goneril and Regan as being embodiments of "everywoman," complaining:

> Down from the waist they are Centaurs,
> Though women all above.
> But to the girdle do the gods inherit,
> Beneath is all the fiends'.
> There's Hell, there's darkness, there's the sulphurous pit,
> Burning, scalding, stench, consumption, fie, fie, fie!
>
> (4.6.123–29)

In *A Thousand Acres*, the malice of Larry Cook's curse carries a doubly horrific significance as Rose is in remission from a cancer that has taken one of her breasts and Ginny has suffered numerous miscarriages.[22] Furthermore, Larry's charge of "whore" is abhorrently ironic. Both Lear's curse and Larry's curse point toward an underlying hatred of all that is feminine within their articulated desires for their daughters to be barren. And while *King Lear* never explains the patriarch's loathing of the feminine, *A Thousand Acres* illuminates the genesis of Larry Cook's antipathy.

After Larry curses his daughters and rages off into a storm, the action, as Keppel notes, stays with Rose and Ginny rather than Larry (109). It is on this night that Rose broaches the subject of Larry Cook's sexual abuse of his older daughters: "He went into your room at night" (190). When Ginny fails to remember, she considers that perhaps it was only Rose who had to endure the incest because Rose was "prettier." Rose responds, "Prettier doesn't make any difference. You were as much his as I was. There was no reason to assert his possession of me more than his possession of you. We were just his, to do with as he pleased, like the pond or the houses or the hogs or the crops" (190).

Ginny eventually gains partial recollection of her childhood; she remembers beatings by her father, a continual sense of being "naughty"—"disobedient, careless, destructive, disorderly, hurtful to others, defiant", and a childhood disgust with her body (300). In a toneless recitation, Ginny recalls:

And so my father came to me and had intercourse with me in the middle of the night. I could remember pretending to be asleep, but knowing he was in the doorway and moving closer. I could remember him saying, "Quiet, now, girl. You don't need to fight me." I didn't remember fighting him, ever, but in all circumstances he was ready to detect resistance, anyway. . . . I never remembered penetration or pain, or even his hands on my body, and I never sorted out how many times there were. I remember my strategy, which had been desperate limp inertia. (302–3)

In denying his daughters' femininity, even while he avails himself of their bodies, and by suddenly making them rulers of the Kingdom, Larry has initiated new possibilities of freedom and power for his Ginny and Rose. Each adopts the grasping nature of her father; each becomes consumed by the idea of possession; each subdues her hated false façade that Larry had insisted she maintain. Yet both Ginny and Rose mistakenly believe that Larry desires that his daughters develop a new strength inherited from him, when in fact, he wants them to fail; he wants *his* power to be validated through their failures.

Cashing in on public sympathy after his "expulsion" into the storm becomes known, Larry acts like a man who has become senile due to ill-treatment; yet Ginny notices, following Harold Clark's (Gloucester's) obviously plotted and rehearsed denunciation of Rose and Ginny, "A look of sly righteousness," spread over her father's supposedly addled face (237). In a self-destructive and infantile rage, Larry reunites with Caroline and through his pathetic masquerade persuades her to sue for repossession of the farm. This act has disastrous consequences as a court order mandates that all construction on the farm must cease. For Ginny, Rose, and their husbands, the order spells financial peril and, ultimately, forces the farm into bankruptcy. Larry's behavior, then, and not Ginny or Rose's, destroys the "kingdom."

In addition to providing Goneril/Ginny (and Regan/Rose) with a voice, Smiley also endows the reader with the missing end to *King Lear*; Smiley presents a vision of the "kingdom" after chaos ensues. In *A Thousand Acres*, the farm is bankrupt, sold off, Rose dies of cancer, and Ginny leaves. The full measure of Larry's actions unfolds. The kingdom he has striven to build, cheated for and sacrificed his wife and daughters for disappears into the anonymous acreage of corporate farming. In fact, as Ginny sorts through the possessions left before Larry's house is sold, she realizes that she wants nothing; none of the remaining possessions hold any meaning, just as the farm itself no longer holds any significance. Furthermore, Caroline abandons the farm as well. In this *King Lear*, Cordelia lives; yet she is unwilling to take responsibility for the kingdom/farm she supposedly has rightfully inherited through her virtuous allegiance to its king.

Keppel recognizes, "Whereas *King Lear* concludes with only

men remaining, as if to signal a return to the rightful patriarchal order, *A Thousand Acres* ends with only women, among them the sole representatives of the next generation [Pammy and Linda, Rose's daughters]" (113–24). And as Carden acknowledges, "While [Ginny] lacks traditionally defined rewards of femininity—she has no money, no house, no man, no children of her own—she has gained the alternate rewards of memory, knowledge, and voice" (197). Significantly, Ginny chooses as her exile the life Rose had imagined their mother would have lived had she the courage to leave her husband; working as a waitress and being an adoptive mother to her nieces, Ginny chooses to carry on her matrilineal identity and forego her patriarchal inheritance. Ultimately then, as Margaret Rozga notes, *A Thousand Acres* "is not a *King Lear* story"; Ginny, "the child of an exploited land now in exile, no longer the dutiful daughter, no longer innocent, fashions a revision and readies herself to present a new mythology" (28).

As Mieke Bal pointedly asks, how can women "rewrite themselves back into the history of ideology?" (132). In this regard, feminist writers have engaged in numerous revisions to uncover a depth that the ensuing ages may have stultified into caricature or stereotype. Yet, as Alicia Ostriker notes, feminist revisions of classic and mythic female characters, "contain no trace of nostalgia, no faith that the past is a repository of truth, goodness, or desirable social organization" (330). Quite the contrary. Feminist revisions seek to revalue the existence of the character—and her narrative—without re-presenting her as merely an "innocent victim," misunderstood within the paradigm she had previously inhabited. Cordelia and Goneril, telling history from their points of view, enlarge the scope of Shakespeare's vision and add dimensions to the breadth of the story. The reendowed legacy of Cordelia and Goneril is no longer tied exclusively to Lear's estate; these female narratives create their own wealth.

Notes

1. Alfred Harbage, as an example, in his introduction to *King Lear*, allows Goneril and Regan no excuses for their actions, contending, "to see a causal relationship between what [Lear] does to Goneril and Regan and what they do to him, or to interpret their aggression as normal revolt against parental domination, is simply to be perverse" (1061).

2. Erickson elaborates:

The first mode [conciliatory] tends to mitigate conflict and to maintain the continuity of Shakespeare's cultural role. Challenges are acknowledged and valued, but temporized: new departures are seen as modifications that confirm rather than disrupt the primary image of Shakespeare's positive influence. The second, the oppositional, mode does not deny but qualifies Shakespeare's greatness. Yet the qualification is so substantial as to reconstitute the tradition and to alter Shakespeare's status as the dominant artistic force. (167)

3. *King Lear*, Joyce Carol Oates recognizes, validates "a world in which the masculine archetype can do things wrongly, and yet never embody wrong"; however, conversely, the feminine archetypes can never embody virtue: "the ultimate tragedy is the experiencing as 'enemy' the entire female sex" ("Promised").

4. Marianne Novy, in her introduction to *Women's Re-Visions of Shakespeare: On the Responses of Dickinson, Woolf, Rich, H.D., George Elliot, and Others*, asserts that women authors "show a long historical record of women's identifications with a range of Shakespearean characters and, more surprisingly, with Shakespeare himself" (2). Novy determines that women writers share an "affinity" with Shakespeare: "Three images of Shakespeare have particular resonance for women's history: the outsider, the artist of wide-ranging identification, and the actor" (2). Many of these writers "associate Shakespeare, explicitly or implicitly, with qualities that they see as feminine" (5). The poet H. D., in invoking Shakespeare in her poetry, affirmed that she was "remembering Shakespeare always, but remembering him differently" (31).

5. Hoover refers to several critics including Paul A. Jorgensen (*Lear's Self-Discovery*), Robert B. Heilman (*This Great Stage*), John F. Danby (*Shakespeare's Doctrine of Nature: A Study of* King Lear), Maynard Mack (King Lear *in Our Time*), Marilyn French (*Shakespeare's Division of Experience*), H. S. Wilson (*On the Design of Shakespearean Tragedy*), and Bridget Gellert Lyons ("The Subplot as Simplification in *King Lear*").

6. According to Jung, for the female, the experience of encountering the animus is much different from a male's more positive experience in encountering his anima; her encounter manifests itself as an obstacle to her full development. While a woman "naturally" possesses *Eros*, the feminine emotional and intuitive elements, she also contains unconscious elements of *Logos*, the masculine intellect and rationalizing elements. Jung regards a woman's *Logos* as a "compensatory factor" needed to offset imbalance within the psyche (1959, 121). Yet, as he further clarifies, "Eros is an expression of [a woman's] true nature, while their Logos is often only a regrettable accident. It gives rise to misunderstandings and annoying interpretations" (1982, 171). Clearly, while Jung is concerned with the necessary integration of *Eros* into male consciousness as a move toward individuation, he does not regard *Logos* as a favorable characteristic for women.

7. Oates asserts that Lear

rail[s] against Goneril and Regan as if their attitude toward him, in subsequent scenes, sprang from something inherently feminine in their nature, even something erotic; but in fact both daughters are behaving toward the old King, at this point in the play, like rebellious sons who are testing their father's authority. There is nothing feminine about them at all. ("Promised")

8. Carol Osborne relates that "Cordelia feels alienated in her home environment because she is not as gifted as her two [older] sisters are" (102).

9. Cordelia's sexuality is confusing. For instance, "Breasts fascinate Cordelia, and fill her with scorn" (97). Moreover, Cordelia seems to lack traditionally feminine talents such as knitting (107). Atwood is perhaps insinuating that Cordelia, as the third and last daughter, is a disappointment to her father; he may have been hoping for a son. Cordelia may, unconsciously, be attempting to please him by acting like a male.

10. It is interesting to note that Perdita, Miranda, and Cordelia are all names of motherless Shakespearean daughters.

11. Elaine, when she rejects Cordelia, sees that Cordelia's behavior is "an impersonation, of someone much older" (205). Furthermore, Cordelia's mother is characterized in the novel as oblivious to her daughters, a mostly absent presence.

12. Cordelia's father in *Cat's Eye* is, of course, echoing Lear's curse upon the "unnatural hags," his daughters Goneril and Regan (2.4.273)

13. "The disgust expressed in [*King Lear*] toward women is more strident and articulate, and far less reasonable, than the disgust expressed in *Othello* and *Hamlet*" states Oates. Atwood, in evoking Shakespeare, accentuates the devastating consequences of that disgust upon an innocently bewildered daughter ("Promised").

14. Brooke Allen states, "Delia has played the child all her life" (31).

15. As Susan S. Kissel recognizes, "Forming new relationships with strangers has created a sense of [Delia's] own self-worth and enabled her to renew past family relationships in more positive, effective ways" (84).

16. In a humorously biting, yet innocently related anecdote, Tita tells that her mother could "crack sack after sack of nuts" and "take great pleasure in it": "Applying pressure, smashing to bits, skinning, those were among her favorite activities" (224). Tita's equating Mama Elena with a castrating image has a paradoxical validity: Mama Elena has tried to destroy Tita's sexuality.

17. Lear's final wish for himself and Cordelia is the selfish desire that he might be locked in a cell for the rest of his life with his daughter while each continually professes love to the other (5.2.8–18). Even after all of his trials and even after Cordelia's demonstrated proficiency at leading an army, Lear has still not recognized his daughter's autonomy; nor does he ever truly understand Cordelia's initial reluctance to flatter him.

18. Oates argues that "In purely psychological terms, Lear is the incomplete personality, the immature adult"; likewise, Larry Cook's demanding reliance upon his daughters shows not only a regal disdain for their preferences and familial responsibilities, but also a childish incapability for caring for himself ("Promised").

19. Carden notes, "As object rather than subject in the economy of Daddy's authority, [Ginny] is not to answer, interpret, or construct meaning, but rather to passively receive his speech" (188). I would add that the way Ginny is "supposed" to "listen" to her father is exactly how she was supposed to accept his sexual abuse: silently, fearfully, and with unquestioning compliance.

20. Ironically, it is Caroline who first suggests that Larry not be allowed to drive.

21. Lear's curse begs "Nature" to

> Suspend thy purpose if thou didst intend
> To make this creature fruitful.
> Into her womb convey sterility,
> Dry up her organs of increase,

And from her derogate body never spring
A babe to honor her.

(1.4.267–72)

22. Both women's maladies are more than likely the result of toxicity of the farm's well water, the consequence of their father's use of dangerous chemicals. These same chemicals may also have been the cause of the death of Rose and Ginny's mother, a fact that further serves to underscore Larry's misplaced priorities.

WORKS CITED

Ahern, Stephen. " 'Meat Like You Like It': The Production of Identity in Atwood's *Cat's Eye*." *Canadian Literature* 137 (summer 1993): 8–17.

Allen, Brooke. "Anne Tyler in Mid-Course." *The New Criterion* 13, no. 9 (May 1995): 27–34.

Atwood, Margaret. 1988. *Cat's Eye*. New York: Doubleday.

Bal, Mieke. 1987. *Lethal Love: Feminist Literary Readings of Biblical Love Stories*. Bloomington: Indiana University Press.

Carden, Mary Paniccia. 1997. "Remembering/Engendering the Heartland: Sexed Language, Embodied Space, and America's Foundational Fictions in Jane Smiley's *A Thousand Acres*." *Frontiers* 18:181–202.

Chernin, Kim. 1987. *Reinventing Eve: Modern Woman in Search of Herself*. New York: Times Books.

Cixous, Hélène. 1980 . "The Laugh of the Medusa." In *New French Feminisms*, edited by Elaine Marks and Isabel de Courtivren, 237–54. 1975. Amherst: University of Massachusetts Press. 237–254.

de Valdés, Maria Elena. 1995 . "Verbal and Visual Representation of Women: *Como agua para chocolate/Like Water for Chocolate*." *World Literature Today* 69, no. 1 (winter): 78–82.

Doolittle, Hilda (H.D.). 1949. *By Avon River*. New York: MacMillan.

Duffy, Martha. 1991. "*A Thousand Acres*." Review of *A Thousand Acres* by Jane Smiley. *Time*. 11 November: KT8.

Erickson, Peter. 1991. *Rewriting Shakespeare, Rewriting Ourselves*. Berkeley: University of California Press.

Esquivel, Laura. 1992. *Like Water for Chocolate*. New York: Anchor Books.

Felski, Rita. 1989. *Beyond Feminist Aesthetics: Feminist Literature and Social Change*. Cambridge: Harvard University Press.

Hoover, Claudette. 1984. "Goneril and Regan: 'So Horrid as in Woman.' " *San Jose Studies* 10, no. 3 (fall): 49–65.

Jung, Carl Gustav. 1959. *The Archetypes and the Collective Unconscious*. Translated by R. F. C. Hull. Princeton: Princeton University Press.

———. *Aspects of the Feminine*. 1982. Translated by R. F. C. Hull. Princeton: Princeton University Press.

Keppel, Tim. 1995. "Goneril's Version: *A Thousand Acres* and *King Lear*." *South Dakota Review* 33, no. 2: 105–17.

Kissel, Susan K. 1996. *Moving On: The Heroines of Shirley Ann Grau, Anne*

Tyler, and Gail Godwin. Bowling Green: Bowling Green State University Popular Press.

Novy, Marianne L. 1990. "Introduction: Women's Re-Visions of Shakespeare 1664–1988." In *Women's Re-Visions of Shakespeare: On the Responses of Dickinson, Woolf, Rich, H.D., George Elliot, and Others,* edited by Marianne Novy, 1–15. Chicago: University of Illinois Press.

———. "Patriarchy, Mutuality, and Forgiveness in *King Lear.*" In *Love's Argument: Gender Representations in Shakespeare,* edited by Marianne L. Novy, 150–63. 1984. Reprint, Chapel Hill: The University of North Carolina Press.

Oates, Joyce Carol. 1974. "Is This the Promised End?": The Tragedy of *King Lear.*" *Journal of Aesthetics and Art Criticism* (fall). <http://www.usfca.edu/facstaff/southerr/lear.html>.

Osborne, Carol. 1994. "Constructing the Self Through Memory: *Cat's Eye* as a Novel of Female Development." *Frontiers* 14, no. 3: 95–112.

Ostriker, Alicia. 1985. "Thieves of Language: Women Poets and Revisionist Mythmaking." In *The New Feminist Criticism: Essays on Women, Literature, and Theory,* edited by Elaine Showalter, 314–38. New York: Pantheon Books.

Reid, Stephen. 1970. "In Defense of Goneril and Regan." *American Imago: A Psychoanalytic Journal for Culture* 27:226–44.

Rozga, Margaret. 1994. "Sisters in a Quest—*Sister Carrie* and *A Thousand Acres*: The Search For Identity in Gendered Territory." *Midwestern Miscellany* 22:18–29.

Shakespeare, William. 1969. *King Lear.* Edited by Alfred Harbage. In *William Shakespeare: The Complete Works,* 1969. General editor, Alfred Harbage. New York: The Viking Press.

Smiley, Jane. 1991. *A Thousand Acres.* New York: Ivy Books.

Tyler, Anne. 1997. *Ladder of Years.* New York: Berkley Books.

Walker, Nancy A. 1995. *The Disobedient Writer: Women and Narrative Tradition.* Austin: University of Texas Press.

Mingling and Unmingling Opposites: Bending Genre and Gender in Ann-Marie MacDonald's *Goodnight Desdemona (Good Morning Juliet)*

BEVERLEY CURRAN

> That fiction, that lie that you can't change the ending! it's already pre-ordained, prescribed—just what the doctor ordered—in the incontrovertible logic of cause and effect.
> —Ana Historic, 147

IN A RECENT INTERVIEW, BANUTA RUBESS, THE DIRECTOR OF THE first production of *Goodnight Desdemona (Good Morning Juliet)*,[1] said the comedy was one of the first Canadian feminist plays to elicit interest among "the big boy theatres" because it was largely based on Shakespeare (65). According to the playwright, Anne-Marie MacDonald, the play is really a Jungian fairy tale: "The Shakespeare is the backdrop, the running joke, the means by which the piece is recognizable. It was the source. I was being mischievous by using Shakespeare as the source in the same way he used everyone else as a source" (142). Borrowing, bending, and blending her fascination with alchemy and Jung's collective unconsciousness with the "revered" texts of Shakespeare, the playwright turns the tragedies of *Othello* and *Romeo and Juliet* into a comedy through dramatic translation that celebrates uncertainty. Her re-reading/rewriting resists the constraints of the "unforgivingly previous"[2] Shakespearean texts which were recreations of bent and borrowed texts themselves. The Bard is "imminent and beyond thanks," acknowledges MacDonald, but his is not the last word. Rather, the play is "dedicated to you, gentle reader," and its process is an intimate collaboration with the woman viewer/reader.

The woman "reader" is located within the play in the form of

Constance Ledbelly, an underrated Renaissance scholar struggling to finish her dissertation. "*Romeo and Juliet* and *Othello*: The Seeds of Corruption and Comedy" argues that the fated death of the tragic hero in each play is unconvincing; the inevitability of the hero's destiny is based on a comedy of flimsy errors (a missing handkerchief and a delayed wedding announcement) which points to the "footprints of a missing Fool"[3] (21). Yet in spite of her own acknowledged consciousness of the mutability of genre, Constance faithfully accepts the script of her own destiny—and its accompanying invisibility. She willingly ghost writes essays and scathing reviews for Professor Claude Night, the man she thinks she loves, in return for a perfunctory acknowledgment for her "irksome proofing of the text" (24). The critical ethic which makes her seek the source of Shakespeare's tragedies and question the representation of the characters of Desdemona and Juliet does not extend to an evaluation of her own complicity in academic or emotional dishonesty. If Othello's selfhood is dependent on Desdemona's constancy, Constance's own identity is undermined by her fidelity to an inherited female role; she is resigned to her sense of her marginal worth.

In order to support her thesis by finding the hidden source of Shakespeare's tragedies, Constance hopes to translate the encrypted Gustav Manuscript. Claude Night scoffs at her efforts to "crack these obscure alchemical hieroglyphs," adducing the general academic view that the manuscript is unimportant: "I hate to see you turning into a laughing stock Connie . . . No one takes it seriously anymore" (23, 22). The translation—and Constance's own academic credibility—are dismissed with the sort of impatience one might expect from a scientist when asked about the merits of alchemy (or Jung, whose theories resist empirical verification.) But then, as Sherry Simon points out, "Both women and translators are the 'weak' terms in their perspective hierarchies, sexual, and literary" (52). And the nature of translation is at the least as problematic as the eccentric science where "mingling and unmingling opposites transforms base metal into precious gold" (13). Indeed, like the alchemical *nigredo*, translation is an intimate and conflated process, in which reading and writing, and the relationship between reader and writer, and the text and life, is always questioned.[4]

As a translator, Constance is engaged not only in linguistic code-switching, but also in negotiating meaning in an imaginative space which is nevertheless constrained by a text which precedes her reading. On stage, the doubled image of a woman reading and writing is evident from the earliest scenes of *Desdemona,* with Constance reading aloud, her green plumed pen behind her ear, ready for retrieval. When she reaches into the wastepaper basket to pull out a paper, she is instead pulled *into* the story, and implicated. The stage direction "warp" effects—sounds of "screeching wind and music"—are consciously theatrical at this point (28). MacDonald explains:

> I'm not looking for the illusion of reality. If I call for a fabulous effect, I want to see the strings . . . I don't want anything seamless and I don't want anything fixed. I love the idea that theatre is never the same two nights running, that it has a million different incarnations. (140)

Reaching for a different kind of story, Constance suddenly finds herself located within the Shakespearean text through her reading, falling into act 3, scene 3, of Othello, just in time to expose Iago's deceit and prevent Desdemona's death:

OTHELLO:	*Get me some poison, Iago, this night.*
IAGO:	*Do it not with poison.*
	[Iago hands a pillow to Othello]
	Strangle her in bed.
CONSTANCE:	No!
	. . .
	Excuse me please
	[She plucks the handkerchief from Iago's hose
	and gives it to Othello]
OTHELLO:	Desdemona's handkerchief! [*to Iago*]
	Which thou didst say she gave to Cassio!
IAGO:	Did I say that? What I meant to say—

(29–30)

While her intervention saves Desdemona, Constance is horrified at what she has done: "I've wrecked a masterpiece. I've ruined the play, I've turned Shakespeare's 'Othello' into farce" (30). Although she cannot yet enjoy the interference her body in the text has created, this is just the first display of the powerful possibilities of her "monstrous" reading.

Given the opportunity to engage in a dialogue with the characters of the play, Constance discusses Desdemona with Othello (the role played by the same actor that plays Claude Night); she tells him "how [Desdemona] fell in love with you, because she

loved to hear you talk of war . . . I've always thought she had a
violent streak, and that she lived vicariously through you" (32).
But before she can observe the same pattern of vicarious fulfillment in her own life, Constance is suddenly disconcerted by
Othello's appearance: "He's not a Moor" (32). In fact, he is
"Amour," the heart of the play being the desire of two women
causing slippage in the male text.[5]

If *Othello* is a play in which the interpretation of "external
signs, whether linguistic or presentational" is the central problem which faces the characters, *Desdemona* displays a preoccupation with the internal and the collective unconscious, as well
as the notion of accidental discovery in lieu of rigid cause and
effect (Dawson 73). "In the Jungian sense it's a matter of incorporating the shadow to work for you rather than against you"
(MacDonald 136). When Constance engages in narrative cross-
dressing, taking her lines from Othello, or putting Juliet in
tights and Romeo in "rose-hued silk," her reading is extending
the parameters of romantic love. Instead of interracial love, *Desdemona* turns on the desire of one woman for another.[6]

The possibility has always existed through Constance's reading: she has imagined Desdemona in detail and dreamed of
meeting Juliet a thousand times. Her reading has allowed her to
tutoyer the characters she loves, to write herself in, to find a
lover as intimate as a reader: "she who is you" (Marlatt 129).
But, as a critic, Constance resists the erotic attraction of words,
afraid of tampering with the text by imagining it otherwise. She
prefers a definitive border between the real and the imaginary:

> Oh Constance, don't be scared, it's just a play
> And Desdemona will look after you.
> Desdemona! I am verging on
> The greatest academic breakthrough of
> The twentieth century!
> I merely must determine authorship,
> But have I permanently changed the text?
> —You're floundering in the waters of a flood;
> the Mona Lisa and a babe float by.
> Which one of these two treasures do you save?
> I've saved the baby, and let the Mona drown—
> Or did the Author know that I'd be coming here,
> And leave a part for me to play? How am I cast?
> As cast-away to start, but what's my role?

(37)

The abundance of questions in *Othello*—"questions not infre-
quently answered by their own reiterated echoes"—persists in
Desdemona, and is emphatically intertextual, the trajectories of
reading (Mosian 49).

Constance is unaware of Iago's plan to exact revenge upon
her just as she does not recognize how she has been exploited
by Claude Night. Under questioning by Desdemona, though,
she does admit her resentment that her efforts went unre-
warded by Night; yet she only blames herself for her fate, na-
ively claiming, "never did he mean to hurt me" (40). But
Desdemona sees Constance's "ten years of ghostly writing for a
thief" as ten years in which Constance was "an inky slave in
paper chains" (40). And as enthralled by these stories as she was
by Othello's tales of war, Desdemona urges Constance to:

DESDEMONA:	. . . tell me tales of life in Academe. If there be cannibals that each other eat, And men whose heads do grow beneath their shoulders? These things to hear, I seriously incline.
CONSTANCE:	It's quite dog eat dog. And scary too. I've slaved for years to get my doctorate, But in a field like mine that's so well trod, You run the risk of contradicting men Who've risen to the rank of sacred cow . . . . . . I was labeled as a crackpot, by the sacred herd of Academe; and after years spent as a laughingstock, I finally came to think that it was true. But, Desdemona, now that I've met you, I want to stand out in that field and cry, "Bullshit!"
DESDEMONA:	Wherefore? And what, pray tell, may bullshit be?
CONSTANCE:	A kind of lie. For instance, Academe Believes that you're a doomed and helpless victim.

(41)

Desdemona is but one of a legion of "doomed and helpless"
women in literature. MacDonald recalls the proliferation of that
role when she remembers how, as a young actor at the national
Theatre School in Ottawa, she "figured that the ability to cry on
cue or to come across as a genuine hysteric was some sort of
a touchstone of authenticity." She now sees that belief as "an

indication of the kinds of roles women are so often faced with:
emotional barometers and representatives of vulnerability and
instability in general" (129). She continues:

> I feel like I've been crucified on the cross of the ingenue one too
> many times. Throughout theatre school I was forced to play a Che-
> khov character like a fucking gossamer thing, or a Shakespearean
> lady like a wimp. If you get a part with teeth in it it's usually nega-
> tive: the character is a bitch or suicidal. I always heard that if a girl
> could cry she had to be a good actress. The guys never had to cry.
> They had a lot of words to say and had fun things to do. They didn't
> have to be emotional to prove they were good actors . . . (140)

The critical resistance Constance exercised against the inelucta-
bility of Shakespeare's tragic story—and Desdemona's fate—is
in the process of being translated into a resistance against the
scripts already written for Desdemona's enactment.

Collaborating with the language Shakespeare used, in addition to her own versions, Constance begins to read through and
against that language, gaining access to her own story. In conversation with Desdemona, Constance's role as "bookish
mouse" is rewritten (39). She becomes "Constance, Queen of
Academe"; her unmarried status is translated into "virgin ora-
cle" (33). But if the two women collaboratively imagine themselves in a more positive light, Iago persists in perpetuating the
negative connotations of Constance's lack of a husband. While
Desdemona contends that it is a "vestal study that anoints her
chaste"; Iago counters that a "hag may seem a maid, when she
in truth is Satan's bride" (44). Even Desdemona can be swayed
by the fearful image of the "witch," the social equivalent of
"beetles and spiders who live in the cracks of the walls and
wainscoting" where chaos reigns (Douglas 103).

In fact, Constance does occupy an interstice between the text
and life, and within two texts at once: "where two plus one adds
up to one not three" (52). Guided by her reading, she next finds
herself in *Romeo and Juliet* as Mercutio and Tybalt prepare to
fight. "One Mona Lisa down, and one to go," thinks Constance
as she once again intervenes (52). She announces that Romeo
has wed Juliet and thereby averts the tragic consequences of
Shakespeare's play. The skirtless Constance re-invents herself
as "Constantine"; however, Romeo finds Constance as appealing as he once found Juliet: *"Did my heart love till now? For-
swear it, For I ne'er saw true beauty till this day!"* (54). Invited to

the baths ("Greekling, come splash with us!"), Constance de-
murs although she wonders for how long she might avoid their
"locker room" (55).

Yet, while Constance has indeed theatrically changed her
gender, she is as yet unable to break the bonds of gender construction and view herself as a creator rather than creation. She
rails, "Where's the Fool? Where's the damn Fool?! / How come
I end up doing his work?" (55). Constance persists in believing
that the "Fool" who is also the "Author" can only be a male even
when a ghost attempts to enlighten her. She eagerly inquires:

	Do you know something of the Manuscript?
	Do you know who the Author is?
GHOST:	A lass.
CONSTANCE:	I know, 'alas, alas poor Yorick,' so?!
	Who wrote this thing?
GHOST:	A beardless bard.
CONSTANCE:	A boy?
GHOST:	A lass!
CONSTANCE:	Oh here we go again, 'alas'!
	Who is the Author?
GHOST:	A Fool, a Fool.

Constance may not want to see herself as a Fool—just as she is
reluctant to admit her identity as the Author—because, as Mac-
Donald explains, "boys are the clowns and it's OK for a boy to
get laughs, but when a girl gets laughs it means she's not attractive. She's weird. . . . Poking fun at institutions is iconoclastic
and girls are not supposed to be rebels" (MacDonald 137).

With perhaps even greater reluctance, Constance is unwilling
to admit to her lesbian desires. When asked by Juliet if she be
of "Lesbos," Constance replies ambiguously: "I've never been
there in my life" (77). Nor does she admit any familiarity with
Sappho. When Juliet then insists "we'll compose an epic of our
own," Constance still protests "I'm not—you know—I'm not a
lesbian. At all. That's just a rumor. I've never been involved with
a woman. Unless you count that time in grade eight" (77). She
is almost seduced by Juliet, but finds herself in bed with Desdemona as well; each character urges Constance toward violence:

DESDEMONA:	Return with me to Cyprus; take this sword,
	And dip it deep to drink Iago's gorge.
	[Desdemona puts the sword into Constance's
	hand]

JULIET:	Remain! To one blade, we'll two hearts afix,
	Then sail together 'cross the River Styx.
	[Juliet puts the dagger into Constance's other
	hand]
DESDEMONA:	Nay, come and kill.
JULIET:	Nay, come and die.

(84)

But a new Constance has found the strength to say, "Nay nay!!
. . . both of you. I've had it with all the tragic tunnel vision
around here" (85). Rereading Desdemona and Juliet allows
Constance to break the dismal destiny script she had been acting and thus, compose her own script. Recognizing in Desdemona a gullibility and violence equal to Othello's, and in Juliet
a love of death greater than any other love, Constance realizes
that she cannot save the characters through her reading, but
she can save herself. The transformative reading does not
wholly destroy the "Mona Lisa" texts; it salvages the texts for
women's use, bending them toward the light. MacDonald clarifies that this experience is like

> Opening up a trunk that used to be filled with instruments of torture
> and now everything has been turned into toys. When you reclaim
> and transform ideas and methods that have been used against you
> as a woman, you become empowered. Subversion of this kind is
> healthy. (142)

This redemptive rereading enacts an immersive criticism
which welcomes uncertainty: "To live by questions, not by their
solutions" (85). Such criticism is at odds with the restrain and
" 'disinterestedness' with regard to a potential emotional or libidinal engagement by a text [which has been] integral to the
whole history of criticism and connoisseurship" (Pearce 194).
Constance's intimate positioning of herself within the text at the
same depth as the characters makes her (and us, gentle readers)
more aware of the options beyond linear academic reasoning.
Hers is a critical reading which is more responsive to, and more
compatible with texts encouraging immersion, not detachment.
As Lola Lemire Tostevin describes it in *Subject to Criticism*, this
is a critical reading/writing that occurs when

> a woman writer is no longer willing to perpetuate the image of some
> stereotypical "other," and she is no longer satisfied with simply un-
> masking traditional ideological constructs. . . . Where "woman"

had, traditionally, been a sign written by someone else, she must now construct herself as a sign constituted as subject and enunciator of her own discourse. (2)

The language of criticism and the lessons of reading are not hermetically sealed off from life. The story is not a solid construction built to contain us or exclude us; a woman reading is a woman writing her own story.

NOTES

1. The first production of *Goodnight Desdemona (Good Morning Juliet)* took place at the Annex Theatre in Toronto on 31 March 1988.

2. From Margaret Atwood's poem, "First Neighbours."

3. Or, as Michael Bristol notes, although "the play is grouped with tragedies in the first folio and has always been viewed as properly belonging to this genre, commentators have recognized for a long time the precarious balance of the play at the very boundaries of farce" (81).

4. And the two processes converge in Jung, according to Christine Gallant, who points out, Jung

> showed a willingness to entertain the possible import of psychological experience that is not necessarily empirically measurable, namely paranormal phenomena. . . . When he decided that the field of alchemy might contain answers to questions about the nature of the collective unconscious he was then pondering, he taught himself medieval Latin so that he could read the untranslated alchemical manuscripts. (78)

5. At the same time, the playwright is neither avoiding nor disinterested in the issue of race and its intersection with that of gender. There is a coy conflation of the two implicit in Constance Ledbelly's name and her role as an "inky slave" to the patriarchy, and casting could make this even more explicit.

6. In her first novel, *Fall on Your Knees*, MacDonald writes about both interracial and lesbian love.

WORKS CITED

Atwood, Margaret. 1970. *The Journals of Susanna Moodie*. Toronto: Oxford University Press.

Bristol, Michael D. 1996. *Big-Time Shakespeare*. New York: Routledge.

Dawson, Anthony. 1978. *Indirections: Shakespeare and the Art of Illusion*. Toronto: University of Toronto Press.

Douglas, Mary. 1966. *Purity and Danger*. London: Routledge.

Gallant, Christine. 1996. *Tabooed Jung*. New York: New York University Press.

Homel, David and Sherry Simon, eds. 1985. *Mapping Literature: The Art and Politics of Translation*. Montreal: Véhicule Press.

MacDonald, Ann-Marie. 1990. *Goodnight Desdemona (Good Morning Juliet)*. Toronto: Coach House Press.

————. Interview. By Judith Rudakoff. In *Fair Play*, 127–43.

Marlatt, Daphne. 1988. *Ana Historic*. Toronto: Coach House Press.

Moisan, Thomas. 1991. "Repetition and Interrogation in Othello: 'What needs this Iterance?' or, 'Can anything be made of this?' " In *Othello: New Perspectives*, edited by Virginia Mason Vaughan and Kent Cartwright, 48–73. Madison: Farleigh Dickenson University Press.

Pearce, Lynne. 1997. *Feminism and the Politics of Reading*. London: Arnold.

Rubess, Banuta. Interview. By Rita Much. In *Fair Play*, 49–73.

Rudakoff, Judith and Rita Much. 1990. *Fair Play Twelve Women Speak: Conversations with Canadian Playwrights*. Toronto: Simon & Pierre.

Tostevin, Lola Lemire. 1999. *Subject to Criticism*. Toronto: Mercury.

"On Which [we] *Looked* Up at Her": Henry James's and Jane Campion's *Portrait(s) of a Lady*

Jamie Barlowe

Like *THE PIANO*, JANE CAMPION'S PALME D'OR AND OSCAR-WINNING film of 1993, her 1996 cinematic adaptation of Henry James's *Portrait of a Lady* (1881) begins with a voice-over. To be more accurate, *Portrait* opens with voice(s)-over of women discussing what Campion has called the "mythology of love" (*Premier*).

> FIRST VOICE: "The best part of a kiss, I think, is when you see that head coming toward you, and you know that you are going to get kissed. That moment just before is so exquisite."
> SECOND VOICE: "I never ever felt the touch of another person my age and the sensation just flew through me."
> THIRD VOICE: "I love it. I love kissing."
> FOURTH VOICE: "We're addicted to that being entwined with each other, whether it was really positive, which it was at the beginning, or negative."
> FIFTH VOICE: "I get this really intense look in my eyes that says I am so mysterious and there is so much more to me than meets the eye . . . "
> SECOND VOICE: "I believe in fate so I believe that person will just find me or we will find each other some day."
> LAST VOICE: "It means finding a mirror and the clearest mirror and the most loyal mirror and that so when I love that person I know they are going to shine that back to me."

The voice-over is followed by a series of black-and-white "portraits" which depict "a multicultural group of modern-day young women relaxing outdoors, candid, open, natural" (Sklar). As Nancy Bentley has noted, the "screen is black [except for the credits] while we listen to the voices, and once the film adds the crucial dimension of the visual the women are silent" (175). The portrait-sequence of young women has been labeled as "ambig-

uous" by Robert Sklar; he argues that this scene "immediately
destabiliz[es] one's expectation of effortless transport into the
world of 19th century fiction. . . . for any viewer familiar with *The
Portrait of a Lady*, this seemingly bland sequence can be only
disquieting" (B7). The last "portrait" is of a young woman who
stares directly into the camera, and then fades into Isabel Archer's (Nicole Kidman) intense, but downcast gaze. As Sklar
asks, "What is the relation of these women to James's heroine,
Isabel Archer?" (B7).

Attempts to answer this question invoke feminist film theory's discussions of mainstream film[1] and its differences from the
cinematic strategies of feminist alternative filmmakers like
Campion.[2] As Sandy Flitterman-Lewis puts it,

> [I]n denying traditional modes of looking at the female body in favor
> of a camera that is both analytic and direct, [feminist alternative
> filmmakers] redefine pleasurable looking. . . . There is no fiction of
> the visual, no hidden position of seeing, but an acknowledgment of
> the spectator's desiring look manifested in an uncompromising and
> frontal way . . . [as] self-conscious strategies of resistance. (40)

Resisting mainstream filmmaking strategies, using women in
key production roles,[3] assuming an intelligent aware viewer,
and re-articulating the camera's gaze are all part of feminist alternative cinematic strategies and practices—what Lucy Fisher
describes as an "intertextual dialogue with their male counterparts" (qtd. in Mayne 24). Likewise, Pam Cook contends that
feminist filmmakers insist "that their assault on traditional cinema be seen and heard" (x). Judith Mayne argues further that

> Some of the most interesting examples of women's alternative
> cinema . . . take as a central figure the screen—not 'rather' than the
> gaze, but in relationship to it. The complex function of the screen
> must be taken into account, then, to better theorize . . . examples of
> women's cinema, but also, and perhaps most important, to better
> theorize just what it is women filmmakers have sought alternatives
> to. (42)

Feminist alternative cinema not only disrupts the frame,
breaks the mimetic illusion, shifts the gaze, and rearticulates
desire, but it also changes the way we think about the relationship of the actual female viewer (what feminist film theorists
have called historical spectators) to the hypothetical spectator
constructed by the film's narrative content and strategies and

its cinematic apparatus.[4] In Campion's films the hypothetical female spectator is closely aligned with a feminist spectator, with what E. Ann Kaplan has called the "contemporary female spectator (whose reading of films may be inflected by a feminist consciousness that suggests alternate interpretations [or] meanings 'against the grain')" (Flitterman-Lewis 9). In this essay I will argue that Campion's opening voice(s)-over and portrait-sequence function as her artistic and political acknowledgment of the complex relationships between the contemporary women in the opening sequence and Isabel Archer, between the actual historically and culturally situated female viewer in the film's audiences and the hypothetical female spectator that her film constructs, between herself as an end-of-the-twentieth-century feminist filmmaker and the nineteenth-century male author Henry James, and between the opening and closing scenes of her film and those of James's novel. Put more simply, Campion's opening sequence teaches female spectators how to view her feminist alternative film.

INTRODUCTORY SEQUENCE AND ITS RELATIONSHIP TO THE FILM NARRATIVE

The young women in the opening voice(s)-over and portrait sequence are not posited as the ideal hypothetical female spectator or ideal portrait of contemporary young "ladies"; Campion complicates the (often assumed) fixed position of the female viewer by giving us multiple voices and perspectives, as well as multiple portraits of women who might occupy complex, gendered subject-positions informed by race, class, nationality, and sexual preference.

Most critics and James scholars have overlooked the differences in the comments made during the opening voice(s)-over, lumping them together.[5] Instead, these voices function more as individualized descriptions spoken sequentially than as an interactive discussion or dialogue. Taken as a whole, the comments can be said to articulate, as Alan Nadel puts it, "the erotics of being kissed," as well as offering more encompassing, highly romanticized statements about fated love-partners and self-mirroring, hardly differing from nineteenth-century romanticized visions of love (181). As Campion has said, "I think that the romantic impulse is in all of us and sometimes we live it for a short time, but it's not a sensible way of living. It's a heroic

path and it generally ends dangerously. I treasure it in the sense
that I believe it's a path of great courage. It can also be the path
of the foolhardy and the compulsive" (*Premiere*).

Campion's contemporary women both resemble and depart
from current notions of nineteenth-century women's subjectivities and relationships to sexuality—those socially constructed
and those which perhaps defied the constructions, in other
words, "the foolhardy," "the compulsive," and the courageous.
The women in Campion's voice-over are certainly more verbally
open about pleasure and desire than their nineteenth-century
counterparts; as Virginia Wright Wexman has also noticed:
"The modern women we see and hear during the film's brief introductory sequence wear . . . comfortable attire, and, unlike the
Victorian Isabel, they are more aware of their bodies' sensual
needs, giving voice to the pleasure they derive from kissing and
the gratification of romantic love" (185). Wexman, however,
does not mention that some of the comments of the voice-over
women remain mired in the kind of romanticism that fundamentally and perhaps unconsciously motivates Isabel Archer,
as well as the female heroes of countless nineteenth-century
novels—particularly male-authored ones, even male authors
like James and Hardy who seemed aware of the often negative
consequences of romanticized, idealized visions of love and sexuality for women and for men.

By foregrounding the contemporary penchant for open conversations about sex and sexuality, as well as by having some of
the voice-over women mouth nineteenth-century romantic plat-
itudes, Campion represents the ways in which progress is
trapped by constraints built into the very constructions many
women are seeking to resist, rename, and revise. Thus, she
shows the immensity of the paradox contemporary female spectators face, often, like the women in the voice-over, without conscious awareness of the paradox. What Stella Bruzzi has said of
Campion's film *The Piano*, one could say of *Portrait* in that it
"enters into a . . . complex dialogue with women's sexual histories, since the present-day consciousness remains embedded exclusively within the nineteenth-century narrative" (235).[6]

Believing themselves free from traps like those Isabel Archer
discovers, or assuming that modern society avoids setting such
traps, constitutes false and dangerous positions for postmodern
women, Campion may be saying, as are Isabel's assumptions
about what elicits her desire. For example, early in the film Isabel is depicted as sexually charged by the power she feels when

she refuses men's offers of love, commitment, and marriage and by voyeuristic gazes at her. In one of the most controversial scenes in the film, as if to confirm her opening warnings, Campion represents Isabel's sexual fantasy of lying passively while being kissed and groped by Caspar Goodwood (Viggo Mortensen) and Lord Warburton (Richard Grant) all along being watched by Ralph Touchett (Martin Donovan). This fantasy comes on the heels of her curt rebuff of Goodwood and her earlier refusal of Warburton's proposal. As Bentley says, "Campion's imaginary love scene suggests not only that Isabel sexually desires both of the men, but that there is something erotic for her in refusing them in marriage (this is the moment that James describes as charged with a 'throbbing' excitement from the 'enjoyment she found in the exercise of her power')" (176). Bentley also notes that "Campion's scene incorporates another dimension of the plot, one that is especially crucial to the visual terms of the film. . . . Merged as part of Isabel's fantasy, Ralph's watching is presented as part of the makeup of her own desire" (176).

Unlike Bentley and Priscilla Walton, I do not think that the cause of the eventual disruption of Isabel's sexual fantasy is her awareness of "Ralph's voyeuristic gaze"; instead, she responds to his whispered comment that he loves her (Bentley 176; Walton 188). There are three other instances of Isabel's responses to being told she is loved, all of which are initially negative. In fact, in the scene when Gilbert Osmond (John Malkovich) first tells her, the camera moves back, circles around a statue, and then rushes forward to indicate panic—and the subsequent need for control—that such a pronouncement produces in her. Isabel's fears, yet lack of awareness of the traps offered by romanticized love, as well as her desire—and the connections between her experience and our current snares and entrapments—are made more apparent when these narrative scenes are understood in the context of the opening sequence. All of the sequences and scenes accumulate to provide increasingly complex preparation for Campion's female spectators to "view" Isabel's almost complete manipulation by Osmond.

Campion's sexual fantasy/voyeurism scene functions, too, as part of her intertextual dialogue with mainstream film, as well as her particular dialogue with Henry James who makes Ralph's "conscious observation of a lovely woman . . . the finest entertainment that the world had to offer" as the heart of his narrative vision (231). Campion's scene of Isabel's sexual fantasy, though, calls specific attention to her refusal to participate

in the appropriation of female desire by a male spectator constructed to assume that his right to voyeurism is inviolable. Instead, Campion shows such a male spectator inside the
cinematic frame, one whose presence exposes the construction
of Isabel's desire in James's narrative, as well as reveals the
ways female desire have been more generally constructed in
cinema. That is, Campion exposes mainstream techniques while
representing Isabel's desire from her perspective, even though
Isabel, unlike Campion's contemporary female spectators, is unaware of the problematic nature of the voyeurism.

Campion thus breaks the mimetic illusion of James's story
with the opening voice-over, portrait sequence, and Isabel's sexual fantasy—and later, with the silent-home-movie-like presentation of Isabel's journey—as strategies which disrupt and
destabilize the cinematic frame and which trouble, at the level
of narrative content, the portrait of a woman/lady who has neither the privilege of speaking desire nor escaping male constructions of female desire.[7] This disrupting and troubling of the
frame thus construct a contemporary female spectator who
views "against the grain" of sexual and cinematic constructions
and recognizes Campion's against-the-grain filmmaking. Campion may also be reminding feminist spectators that we may not
be free from romanticized notions of love and desire in heterosexual or lesbian relationships, not free, in other words, from
the problematic patterns that centuries of social inculcation
have produced, despite all the theorizing, we are trapped in our
"habitus" (Bourdieu).

In addition to the general preparation offered by the opening
voice-over that I have just discussed, Campion and her screenwriter Laura Jones more specifically construct and instruct a
contemporary female spectator of *Portrait*. For example, the
fourth voice says, "We're addicted to that being entwined with
each other, whether it was really positive, which it was at the
beginning, or negative." I see this comment as referring specifically to the film and Isabel's relationship to Gilbert Osmond.
The comment is marked, because it is the only one in the voice-
over that is in first-person plural "we" and because of the mid-
sentence shift in verb tenses. "We *are* addicted to love and being
intertwined," the voice states, then moves to the past tense—
"whether it *was* really positive, which it *was* at the beginning, or
negative" (my emphasis). All of the other comments are articulated in present tense to signify the continuing relationship of
the particular speaker to her description, as well as functioning

as descriptive and interpretive of the film's ensuing narrative. Therefore, whether the female spectator is already familiar with James's novel or whether her relationship to Isabel Archer will be the direct consequence of Campion's film, the fourth comment can prepare her for the desire for physical intertwining that remains in Isabel, generated by what seems so positive to her when she meets and is first kissed by Osmond, despite the purely negative turn their relationship takes following Osmond's commodified, legalized possession of Isabel and her inheritance through marriage.

The fourth comment also helps explain why, even after Gilbert's abuse, Isabel leans toward him, thinking (hoping) he might kiss her. Her desire, held hostage by the socially constructed romanticization of love and of desirous and desiring sexual partners, is complicated but not deterred by her experience of abuse, literally, at the hands of the man who professed, "I'm absolutely in love with you." One of the forms his abuse takes is pushing his head into hers, harshly forcing his beard into her skin, and later pushing her down on the floor. However, what Isabel seems to remember—to continue to hope for replication of—is that moment mentioned by the first speaker in the voice-over: "The best part of a kiss, I think, is when you see that head coming toward you, and you know that you are going to get kissed." Campion carefully represents those words in that fateful (for Isabel) moment when Osmond, unlike her other polite suitors, moves his head toward her and she knows she will be kissed. She is thrilled, clumsy at first, then lost in the actualization of what had only been sexual fantasies, and finally confused and obsessed with the memory.

Similarly, the last voice is significant: "It means finding a mirror and the clearest mirror and the most loyal mirror and that so when I love that person I know they are going to shine that back to me." Not only have many feminists theorized the problems of love-as-mirror, but have also drawn attention to the historical and social pattern of women having far more often functioned as the mirror for men to see themselves "at twice [their] natural size," as Virginia Woolf puts it, than seeing their own reflection (35). Yet, historically, women have been perceived as vain creatures, staring at themselves in mirrors, particularly in cinema. Since the 1970s, feminist alternative cinema has drawn attention to such mirror-scenes as further evidence of the power of the (white) male-gaze of the camera, in other words, recognizing that it is not the woman's looking at herself which has any consequence, but the male spectator's gaze directed by the camera to look at her looking. She sees not herself, but what she has been constructed to see, and the continuance of her self-objectification can be ensured by maintaining surveillance on her self-gazing.

Campion's direct reference to the mirror in the voice-over participates in the construction of her contemporary female spectator and prepares her actual historical female viewers for the repeated use of mirrors in *Portrait*, as well as for recognizing the obvious relationship between portraiture and mirrors. There are many instances, but one in particular occurs in the scene just before Isabel meets Madame Merle (Barbara Hershey). Isabel is watching the activities below her from a balcony in Gardencourt, but when she hears the piano, she descends the staircase. As she stands listening, her profile is reflected in a mirror. Isabel never turns to look into the mirror, eliminating a spectator's gaze at her gazing, but it is soon clear that Serena Merle becomes Isabel's mirror. What "shines back" to Isabel is as false as the constructed selves women have seen in portraits, in mainstream cinematic mirrors, as well as in advertising and television.

Campion's mirror-motif is also reflected in the symmetrical structure of her film with scenes mirroring other scenes, sometimes perversely, as, for example, in the two scenes of Madame Merle and Isabel Archer walking under their umbrellas in the rain, repeated with a variation when Isabel is protected and Serena stands soaked, oblivious to the rain. Mirroring scenes also include Isabel's sexual fantasy reproduced in Merle's experience of Osmond's groping of her—both women are completely passive—as well as the scenes of Osmond courting Isabel and, then, controlling and abusing her. In both scenes he circles her, as does the camera; and in the scenes of death—Mr. Touchett and Ralph's—and their consequences for Isabel, Campion's film also mirrors James' novel, yet that reflection is not perfect. Each production reflects its maker, its creator, and the portrait of Isabel Archer painted by each artist, though in different mediums, is just that: a portrait, a reflection, a representation, not a person, not a woman. As Dale Bauer puts it,

Campion's emphasis on the difficulty of reproduction is a metacommentary on her 'reproducing' the James novel. Ultimately, hers is no 'faithful' copy. Campion sheds no light on the Jamesian text, preferring to address her . . . vision about women's roles. The opening sequence in which young contemporary women offer comments and meet the camera's eye signal Campion's take on James: she refuses to play Isabel to Henry James' Osmond. As James himself writes, Osmond has "the hand of the master," and Campion has her own hand in refiguring James's mastery. (196)

THE PORTRAITS OF YOUNG "LADIES"

Campion further complicates the already complex disembodied voice-over, as it is connected with female spectators' relationship to the ensuing film narrative and to their own subject-positions, with the embodied portrait sequence of young, contemporary women. Several critics have discussed this short section; for example, Marc Bousquet grouses that the film "opens with a sequence like a Benetton advertisement, redolent of sixties flower power but glossier than the sixties ever were" (198). Nadel claims that the "models in this opening segment . . . often stare directly into the camera, a pose typical of TV commercials and print ads" (181). Likewise, a critic from *Entertainment Weekly* calls it a

> wordless parade of gravely lovely, anonymous girls, who look directly at the camera, and us—posed in trendy black-and-white natural-portraiture style. Campion's Madison Avenue-influenced intro has nothing whatever to do with James' exquisitely framed and plotted 1881 novel . . . [n]or, for that matter, does it have much to do with the rest of the director's full-color, full-costume production." (Schwarzbaum)

The critics' complaints notwithstanding, this mostly black-and-white portrait sequence (with a very brief middle section in color of two women dancing), like the voice-over, *can* be seen as having a great deal to do with the rest of the film and with James's portrait of Isabel in its construction of a contemporary female spectator and preparation/instruction for other historical female viewers. Moreover, the portrait-sequence *exposes* rather than utilizes advertising strategies: the film acknowledges the voyeurism of the gaze by having the portraited women return it and the film acknowledges its own complicity in portraiture, representations, reproductions, and mirroring. Or as one reviewer put it, "We literally see the reality of the social constraints of the earlier period being inscribed on the bodies of today's women" (McAlister). Also, as with the voice-over segment, viewers' attention in the portrait sequence is directed to the fact that the film's contemporary female spectator—and/or its actual, historical female viewer—may not be a white, heterosexual, privileged, young, extremely thin, independent but naive, and wealthy US citizen (like the portrait of Isabel Archer that will follow), or educated (and thus may not have read James, as Campion's academic viewers have, often viewing the film only to see what is missing or wrong). Moreover, Campion's spectator is certainly not living in the nineteenth-century or necessarily in the United States (between 18 October 1996, and 15 May 1997 the film was released in fourteen countries). Also, the women in the portrait sequence, shot in Sydney, Australia, are a diverse group—different races, sizes, faces, and, as it is implied, sexual orientations.

In the first shot of the sequence the women lie in the grass, their bodies framing the words, "a film by Jane Campion." As the sequence progresses, viewers see that all are casually dressed, some lie in the grass, some sit or lie on a tree that is a second cousin to the tree at Gardencourt (where we will first see Isabel), some dance or sway to music, some sit, some touch or talk to each other, and one has a dog resembling Ralph's that accompanies Isabel in most scenes at Gardencourt. As with the voice-over, Campion's portraits speak to a female audience.

Part of Campion's cinematic dialogue with her female spectator in the portrait sequence indirectly announces the absent presences that will follow in her film, since it is an adaptation of James's novel of the wealthy and their manners (or lack thereof). Issues of wealth, imperialism, colonialism, travel, education, medical care, multiple home ownership, power, and control are taken for granted in James's narrative, not themselves critiqued—unless they are in the hands of dilettantish, appropriative users/abusers of wealth; for example, Osmond and Merle. As Priscilla Walton tells us, "The opening frames emphasize the film's antipodean perspective and the credit sequence positions the ensuing Jamesian narrative on and through a post-colonial screen. The abrupt shift that then takes place from the Australian women to a close-up of Isabel Archer . . . as the young 'American girl' works to situate Isabel as a colonial heroine in an imperial setting" (188).[8] Campion's viewers thus receive warning that the film, as an adaptation of James's novel, will not foreground any characters who are not white, powerful, and wealthy. Gender mitigates the power of the female characters, but their freedom is immense when compared with those in the countries visited by Merle and Archer on their vacation and with the background figures in England and Italy: maids, nurses, servants, and drivers.

Some historical/actual spectators of Campion's film may be aware of—or, of necessity, may have developed the practices of—cultural film criticism like that of bell hooks who has discussed "the oppositional gaze": a "[c]ritical, interrogating" gaze directed at films in which "racial domination of blacks by whites overdetermine[s] representation" and those in which there is an absence of black female characters (200). As hooks argues, "[B]lack female spectators have had to develop looking relations within a cinematic context that constructs our presence as absence that denies the 'body' of the black female so as to perpetuate white supremacy and with it a phallocentric spectatorship where the woman to be looked at is 'white' " (201). In her recent book, *Reel to Real: Race, Sex, and Class at the Movies*, hooks has also discussed the problem of mainstream feminist film theory/criticism which

> in no way acknowledges black female spectatorship . . . not even . . . the possibility that women can construct an oppositional gaze via an understanding and awareness of the politics of race and racism. Feminist film theory rooted in an ahistorical psychoanalytic framework that privileges sexual difference actively suppresses recognition of race, reenacting and mirroring the erasure of black womanhood that occurs in films, silencing any discussion of racial difference—of racialized sexual difference . . . many feminist film critics continue to structure their discourse as though it speaks about 'women' when in actuality it speaks only about white women. (205)

In the later black-and-white, amateur silent-movie-like travel narrative of Merle and Archer's journey to northern Africa, Campion returns her contemporary and actual spectator's attention to the issues suggested in the opening portrait sequence. As Nadel explains, "Isabel's voyage is represented visually as an extreme fissure in the diegesis, disrupting the coherent cinematic gaze that creates a film's visual world" (180).[9] It also disrupts, even in its shift to black-and-white, the normalizing gaze of colonialism and privilege—further constructing a contemporary female spectator whose cultural/racial/gendered awareness may be matched by actual historical female viewers.

AND NOW, THE ENDING: "ON WHICH [WE] *LOOKED* UP AT [ISABEL]"

Despite the various possibilities I have raised in my reading of the opening sequence as Campion's complicating, alternative vision of filmmaking—particularly when the film is a re-portraiture of James's nineteenth-century portrait, it is no more possible to offer complex portraits of the young women in the opening sequence than it is possible to duplicate James's portrait of Isabel Archer in film or for James to have captured in a print-portrait the complexity of an American woman of his time. Bentley's pronouncement of the anachronistic travel sequence in the middle of the film is an apt description for the film in its entirety: "We are made aware . . . that we are seeing not a woman, but a portrait. Campion has made Isabel a portrait in flesh but not a naturalized portrait. The effect is to make female sexuality something ruptured, disjointed, but also something dynamic and open to change" (177). The key to reading Campion's decision to end the film several paragraphs before James's ending lies in recognizing this portraiture of female sexuality, making crucial connections with the ending to the opening sequences.

In the scenes prior to the last scene, Isabel's desire for kissing and touching is shown as no less present, though still deeply implicated in her romanticized vision of love: she simply chose the wrong friend and the wrong man. As Ralph says, "I don't believe that such a generous mistake as yours can hurt you for more than a little. And remember this, that if you have been hated, you have also been loved . . . adored." Isabel passionately embraces and kisses the dying Ralph, whom she seems to have realized as her ideal mirror, mentioned in the last comment in the voice-over. After his funeral, she repeats to herself Ralph's words that she was adored, as she heard earlier in her mind and repeated Osmond's words, "I'm absolutely in love with you." The passionate kissing of Ralph is then repeated with Caspar Goodwood, occurring under the tree where she refused Lord Warburton and where the film's narrative began. She suddenly breaks and runs from Goodwood, and as she nears the door of Gardencourt (the same door to which she walked so briskly after refusing Warburton), her movement is shown in slow motion, the camera focusing also on her bulky, confining skirts, quite unlike the clothing of the women in the portrait-sequence.

As Bruzzi notes about Campion's *Piano*: "Ada appears to be trapped and defeated by her clothes . . . [Campion's film explores] how women's sexuality, clothes, and lives interconnect" (232). The same interconnections function in *Portrait*, made apparent by the slow-motion shots.[10]

James' novel describes the scene as,

> She . . . darted away from the spot. There were lights in the windows of the house; they shown far across the lawn. In an extraordinarily short time—for the distance was considerable—she had moved through the darkness . . . and reached the door. Here only she paused. She looked all about her; she listened a little; then she put her hand on the latch. (544)

In Campion's closing shot, Isabel first grasps the latch, repeating almost exactly the shot of her hand on the latch of the door to the room where she meets Serena Merle—a portentious moment that will change her life's direction. Then she stops, turns her head slightly, looking just to her left. She looks forward next—stop-frame to a portrait. The novel, however, continues beyond this point: "She had not known where to turn; but she knew now. There was a very straight path" (544). Campion's closing shot could be interpreted as representing that decision in the movement of her head from the side to a straightforward look ahead, and in the repetition of the hand-on-the-latch shot as indicative of her re-entering her ultimately inescapable trap.

James ensures that his readers know that her straight path leads her back to Rome, Pansy, and Gilbert. His novel includes several more paragraphs in which Caspar goes to see Henrietta Stackpole (Mary-Louise Parker) in London to find Isabel and is informed that she has "started for Rome." Henrietta grabs his arm to stay him in his subsequent confusion, saying, " 'Look here, Mr. Goodwood . . . just you wait!' On which he looked up at her" (545). Whatever ambiguity has been claimed for these final sentences as they relate to the future of Goodwood or to James's meaning, there is no ambiguity about Isabel's path, its nature or consequences.

Campion's ending is far more ambiguous. Some critics have read it as Campion's further problematizing of the endings of nineteenth-century novels in which women die or marry, or as Isabel's escape from Osmond. In fact, it has been reported through "official" studio sites on the Internet that Campion "views [James's novel] as a fairy tale with Osmond representing

the underworld into which Madame Merle leads Isabel, who escapes at the end." Given the opening voice-over and portraits,
however, the ending seems to confirm the trap constructed by
romanticized notions of love, duty, marriage, and honor that Isabel cannot escape. Even her earlier independence is predeter-
mined, as are her "choices" as part of the grids of the symbolic
order—and certainly Isabel's desire remains a part of those constructions. There is nothing in the film narrative, nor in the
opening sequences, to suggest that Isabel Archer escapes from
the portrait James drew of her. Campion's film, articulating an
end-of-the-twentieth-century feminist perspective, foregrounds
the portraiture and the capturing of female subjectivity, sexuality, and desire in the lines drawn in print, paint, and film by
male artists. Campion never loses sight of, nor does her camera—nor does the contemporary spectator of her film ever
deny—the power of those portraits and the ways in which we all
remain implicated in them. Like James, though very differently,
Campion attempts to complicate the portrait of Isabel Archer
through the lens of her camera and through the eyes and ears
of her endlessly self-reflexive, intelligent female spectators who
watch, as Bentley has suggested, consciously, "holding in mind
. . . what it means to observe a woman in film" (179).

NOTES

1. Feminist film theories that have examined the positionality of the white,
heterosexual female spectator of mainstream cinema have been mainly focused on the subject/object dyad that is the consequence of seeing the camera's gaze as male and film as spectacle, that is, the [female] object of the look
[or gaze] . . . [as] possessed and controlled by the [male] subject of the look
(Mayne 13). As Sandy Flitterman-Lewis explains:

> Ever since Laura Mulvey's landmark article . . . the image of the woman in main-
> stream commercial cinema has been understood as a contradictory textual distur-
> bance which each film must work to resolve. . . . According to the lines traced out by
> Mulvey, the resolution of this crisis evoked by the woman's image is most often
> achieved in one of two ways: The female figure is either fetishized in the luminous
> isolation of an objectifying image, or made subject to the abusive mastery of some
> form of sadistic domination through the narrative" (2).

Judith Mayne complicates Mulvey's discussion when she argues that "[q]uite
obviously, no one can ignore the function of the look [or gaze] in film, but the
facile division of the (male) gaze from the (female) object of the gaze has led
to a kind of simplistic either/or—woman either foregrounds her objectification
or 'returns' the gaze" (42). Constance Penley, also discussing Mulvey, explains

that for the unconscious of the male spectator, "the female figure [in main-stream cinema] is associated with a potential danger . . . 'hence unpleasure' " (42).

2. I am certainly not the first to note Jane Campion's filmmaking as theoretically informed; for example, Patricia Mellencamp calls Campion an "acute critic/theorist" (177). Likewise, Bentley contends, "Campion shares the interest of theorists in the power relations of vision and in the erotic energies that may be generated along lines of sight" (175). Feminist alternative filmmakers—particularly Campion, Sally Potter, and Julie Dash—are also concerned with "rewriting history from a 90s perspective . . . [and] reinvent[ing] the costume drama in the process" (Cook xxii).

3. For example, Campion's crew included Laura Jones as screenwriter, Janet Patterson as production designer and costume designer, Veronika Jenet as film editor, Ann Wingate as co-producer, Maria G. Mona Bernal as production coordinator, Amanda Knight as make-up artist, Tasha Pym as assistant editor, Johanna Ray as casting director, and Jill Quertier as supervising set director (http://uk.imdb.com/Title?0117364).

4. The differences in the camera's gaze, in the film's articulation of desire, and in its focus on the screen itself construct a very different kind of hypothetical female spectator from that of mainstream film. Mary Ann Doane has claimed that the mainstream hypothetical female spectator is unable to achieve distance on the images of women, and thus cannot choose to have or not have the image, but psychically becomes it. The differences in Campion's films' female spectatorship have implications for the feminist critic and theorist of film who must, as Flitterman-Lewis has urged, "find a way to mediate between the social audience of a film (in which distinctions of class, race, and gender come into play) and the textual subject-positions constructed by it . . . [in other words,] a way to mediate between the social construction of feminine identity and the textual construction of 'female' viewing positions" (10).

5. See, for example, the spring 1997 issue of *Henry James Review*.

6. Linda Seger has discussed the exploration of "the perversity and complexity of sexuality in *The Piano*, also directed by Campion and produced by Jan Chapman, who has said, " 'It's a matter of creating a character and talking about what she might do. . . . Both Jane and I knew women who exhibited th[e] kind of womanly behavior which is contrived and capricious and perverse. In one scene Ada takes Stewart's hand knowing Baines is watching and gains enjoyment from his discomfort' " (214).

7. Nor does Isabel, for that matter, have the real choice of not marrying.

8. Campion herself was born and first educated in New Zealand, receiving a B.A. in anthropology, and, then, in Sydney, Australia, where she currently lives; she has another B.A. "with a painting major, [from] Sydney College of the Arts . . . [and] began filmmaking in the early 1980s, attending the Australian School of Film and Television" (Harrison).

9. See also: Bentley (176–77).

10. Even Kidman suffered from the clothing constraints. She was forced to wear "a corset while filming *Portrait of a Lady* to take her waist down to 19″." Moreover, she spent a couple of weeks in bed after filming was completed, "diagnosed as suffering from 'emotional stress' " (http://uk .imdb.com/BTrivia? Kidman, + Nicole).

Works Cited

Bauer, Dale. 1997. "Jane Campion's Symbolic *Portrait*." *HJR* 18: 194–96.

Bentley, Nancy. 1997. " 'Conscious Observation of a Lovely Woman': Jane Campion's *Portrait* in Film." *HJR* 18:174–179.

Bourdieu, Pierre. 1993. *The Field of Cultural Production: Essays on Art and Literature*. Edited by Randal Johnson. New York: Columbia University Press.

Bousquet, Marc. 1997. "I Don't Like Isabel Archer." *HJR* 18:197–99.

Bruzzi, Stella. 1993. "Jane Campion: Costume Drama and Reclaiming Women's Past." In *Women and Film: A Sight and Sound Reader*, edited by Pam Cook and Philip Dodd, 232–42. Philadelphia: Temple University Press.

Campion, Jane, dir. 1996. *The Portrait of a Lady*. Polygram, Gramercy.

Cook, Pam. 1993. "Border Crossings: Women and Film in Context." In *Women and Film: A Sight and Sound Reader*, edited by Pam Cook and Philip Dodd, ix–xxiii. Philadelphia: Temple University Press.

Doane, Mary Ann. 1988. "*Caught* and *Rebecca*: The Inscription of Femininity as Absence." *Feminism and Film Theory*, edited by Constance Penley, 196–215. New York: Routledge.

Flitterman-Lewis, Sandy. 1990. *To Desire Differently: Feminism and the French Cinema*. Urbana: University of Illinois Press.

hooks, bell. 1996. *Reel to Real: Race, Sex, and Class at the Movies*. New York: Routledge.

Harrison, Jennifer. "Biographical Information for Jane Campion." Internet Movie Database. <http://us.imdb.com/Bio?Campion + Jane>.

Interview with Campion. Internet Movie Database. <http://www.imdb.com>.

James, Henry. 1979. *The Portrait of a Lady*. 1881. Reprint, New York: New American Library.

Mayne, Judith. 1988. *The Woman at the Keyhole: Feminism and Women's Cinema*. Bloomington: Indiana University Press.

McAlister, Linda Lopez. 1998. "The Women's Show." WMNF-FM 88.5, Tampa, FL, January 4. <http://www.inform.umd.edu:8080/EdRes/Topic/Womens Studies /Film Reviews/ 1997-summary-best-feminist-films-mcalister>.

Mellencamp, Patricia. 1995. *A Fine Romance: Five Ages of Film Feminism*. Philadelphia: Temple University Press.

Nadel, Alan. 1997. "The Search for Cinematic Identity and a Good Man: Jane Campion's Appropriation of James's *Portrait*." *HJR* 18:180–83.

Penley, Constance. 1988. *The Future of an Illusion: Film, Feminism, and Psychoanalysis*. Minneapolis: University of Minnesota Press.

Premiere website. 1997. Online. Internet. 3 March. <http://www.premiermag. com/features/wih/campion/campion2.html>.

Schwarzbaum, Lisa . "Isabel Visible: Innocents Aground." *Entertainment Weekly*, Inc. <http://cgi.pathfinder.com/ew/archive/1,1798,1|19689|0|nicole_ kidman, 00.html?name1 = nicole + kidman&lastresult = 0&query = %22 nicole + kidman%22 + %3CIN%3E + MAJOR + %3CAND%3E + %5FSTYLE %3D%2Fexport%2Fverity%2Fcoll ections%2F ewlib%2Fstyle%2Fstyle %2Eddd&major_ref = ON&mtype = 0&list_size = 25&direction>.

Seger, Linda. 1996. *When Women Call the Shots*. New York: Henry Holt and Co.

Sklar, Robert. 1997. *Chronicle of Higher Education*. 14 February B7.

Walton, Priscilla. 1997. "Jane and James Go to the Movies: Post Colonial Portraits of a Lady." *HJR* 18:187–90.

Wexman, Virginia Wright. 1997. "The Portrait of a Body." *HJR* 18:184–86.

Woolf, Virginia. 1957. *A Room of One's Own*. Reprint, 1929. New York: Harcourt Brace Jovanovich.

Part 4
Politically Re-Correct

He Said *Che*, She Says *No:* Apocalyptic Discourse and Awakening from the Cuban Fantasy in Chely Lima's *Confesiones Nocturnas*

Mica Howe

> The new history is coming; it's not a dream, though it does extend beyond man's imagination, and for good reason. It's going to deprive them of their conceptual orthopedics, beginning with the destruction of their enticement machine.
>
> —Hélène Cixous, 253

It is believed by many that since his 1959 *coup,* Fidel Castro has maintained a political program based on civil restrictions, dominating innumerable aspects of Cuban culture and private society. Cuban author Chely Lima, in her novel *Confesiones nocturnas,*[1] portrays protagonist Ana Nury's personal struggle to conquer the negative effects of the repression exerted upon her by the controlling forces of Castro's dictatorship; Lima achieves her agenda through an "apocalyptic discourse" as she re-writes Castro's totalitarian text. Lima's novel underscores the Cuban individual and society in anguish and crisis, using apocalyptic discourse to subvert the mystic aura of Castro's revolution.

Apocalyptic discourse, as Marc Fonda theorizes, articulates feelings of crisis and anguish due to the recognition of impending doom; the discourse focuses upon the motifs of chaos upsetting the usual order of things. Apocalyptic discourse promotes the instigation of change as its rhetoric affirms that the traditional means of explaining the world are no longer adequate; the discourse may often promote a *revivalist* vision of the world and shares an affinity with other politically based discourses— such as feminism—that serve to promote social awareness.[2] In

Lima's novel, apocalyptic discourse promotes action and counters passive acceptance and apathy.

The apocalyptic discourse used throughout *Confesiones nocturnas* indicates that Castro's government in Cuba is deteriorating literally and figuratively. The Revolution, once the road to action, now signifies a dead end. The novel's protagonist, Ana Nury, personifies a segment of the younger generation who is discontented with a politics set in its ways and a complacent society that sees no reason to question the *status quo*. She describes the discontent, distress, and exigency in which Cuba finds itself, and how some Cubans cope with dissatisfaction by various means of escaping reality, a path that Ana refuses. She feels that the regime's means of explaining the world is no longer adequate—if it ever was; Ana upsets the usual order of things, and thus she does not fall prey to escapist tendencies or apathetic acceptance. Having been torn and confused by two worlds—the fantasy of the dictatorship and the reality that is Cuba—she rewrites Castro's script as a way of understanding herself. The re-envisioned Utopia that she describes is within herself as she breaks free from the political hold and embraces a new individuality that separates truth from fiction. It is by awakening from Cuba's dream and through individuality and the search for truth and feminist expression that Ana Nury is able to persevere.

Ana is a divorced free-lance writer who writes for a local newspaper; if she needs money she must write an acceptable article in order to obtain it. While living from check to check she is also writing a novel on the side—some chapters are included toward the end of *Confessiones*, a metafictional narrative strategy. There is not much hope of advancement for Ana after all, it is a communist society in which she lives, thus the novel relates Ana's internal journey to refute the *official* sociopolitical rhetoric of Castro's Cuba. Told in first person, the narrative is about the goings on in the life of one of the members of the younger generation at the end of the millennium in Havana, and most of the action takes place in the form of revealing conversations between Ana and her nucleus of friends and acquaintances in her apartment. This rhetoric is an *authentic* rhetoric; and the further away she looks beyond her apartment, the more she discovers the infiltration and infestation of the dictatorship.

Ana counteracts the inhumane ailments of an impersonal Cuban society by doing the only thing she can: assisting friends in need. She is always lending an ear and consoling people like,

for example, her friend Gordito who has just been found out by
more than one of the women he has been simultaneously seeing,
or Manuel who needs a place to stay after being kicked out of
his house for being gay, or Camila who has a *menage à trois*
going on with two men—both of whom consent to the relationship. These cases point to openness about sexuality and sexual
preferences that may differ from the norm banned by the regime. In contrast, another one of the lives represented in the
novel is that of Ana's neighbor, Cacha, a woman who is stuck in
an abusive relationship. Her husband hits her if he suspects that
she's been flirting with other men. After making a big scene in
the hallway, the next day they will reconcile only to know that it
is a cycle and will happen over and over again. This example of
the ills of *machismo* is only one of the many feelings of angst
that, taken together with the other apocalyptic motifs, form part
of the overall feel of impending doom of the general society.
Ana, however, remains grounded, partially with the help of her
grandmother who appears to her occasionally within her conscious. Her *abuela's* strong faith in *santería* is her link to pre-
Castroesque traditions and complements and strengthens Ana's
own faith. Finally, counterpoints dealing with economics, religion, and sexuality in the novel recreate for Ana a world which
she can live in—one that differs from that demanded by Castro's
political *machine*.

As mentioned previously, one element of apocalyptic discourse is the reference to a present state of crisis. The novel
presents a scene in which Ana and Agustín—Ana's friend of several years—get together over dinner and discuss Cuban life in
general. Agustín contends that the problem of the contemporary Cuban generation is that they live from one crisis to another, that crisis is a permanent state (61). On another occasion,
during a conversation between Ana Nury, Agustín, and his lady-
friend, the latter asserts that the world is going through a very
bad period and that it is falling apart. She asks if people have
always behaved so aggressively and wonders if the reason for
the aggression is because it is nearing the end of the century
(187). Ana's reply acknowledges the present state of chaos by
saying that, historically, there have always been wars and catas-
trophes at the end of the century (187).

This type of perception of crisis permeates the novel at the
microcosmic level of Cuban society as represented by the population of Ana's apartment complex. The individual crises of the
residents include attempted suicides, rejections due to sexual

preference, and spousal abuse. On a larger scale, these crises
reflect an ailing Cuba, a Cuba in which people walking down
the streets, remarks Ana, have empty looks, like fish: they don't
think; they limit themselves to just being there. She claims that
the contemporary youthful generation is worthless (164).
Whereas one of her friends counters that the youth seems to be
maintaining an adequate existence, Ana disagrees (205). She
stands in sharp contrast to the sheepish, brainwashed follower-
types that exemplify the Cuban youth she depicts. Ana is strong
and has the ability to think independently of the sociopolitical
forces that may attempt to sway her thoughts. By doing so, she
stands out as a contrast to the majority of Cubans portrayed in
the novel, and this independence is what endows her with the
ability to rewrite herself within the portrayed *fog* of problems
that surrounds her.

Nostalgic is a potent apocalyptic motif and it represents a
means of escapism. As Ana rejourneys through her childhood,
she finds herself reeling through cinematic images, provoking a
vertigo reaction in her; her vision is one of a different Cuba (25–
27). She complains that such nostalgic regressions give her a
headache; it is not where she wants to go: nostalgia is not a solution. Later on, Agustín asks Ana if she does, in fact, feel nostalgic about her past. She replies "no"; she refuses to indulge in
escapist nostalgia: it is a mortal disease, deathly (62). This indi-
vidualistic approach is a personal reinterpretation—and rejection—of Castro's philosophy, a politics that has been overtly
constructed upon the notion of nostalgia. Specifically, Cuban
politics were fabricated on a dream/vision initiated by Che
Guevara and continued on by Castro. Che, the idealistic guer-
rilla fighter, came to embody the aspirations and beliefs of a revolution seen as a success to the official party and a failure to
others. Guevara's philosophy helped shape the emergence of
the "new socialist man" in Cuba—a philosophy that is based on
moral not economic values. According to this idea, "Moral values could guide economic production as well as other social relations" (Leiner 10). One can derive from the novel that Castro
has used Che's mystic aura as an opiate for the Cuban people as
when, for example, Ana relates that her grandmother used to
tell her that if the newspaper has a martyr's face on it, you don't
throw it away (97). In no way, however, does Ana subscribe or
fall prey to this propagandic illusion; she understands the dangers of living under such false pretenses.

An integral portion of the crisis of Cuba's contemporary

youth, claims Ana, is anguish, an element of apocalyptic discourse. Her remedy for this anguish lies in the community and not the individual. It is communal compassion and communication that will heal—"the less you talk, the worse it is. The less crap you evacuate" (147)—an evocation of, for instance, Catherine Keller's feminist argument that the idea of self is interconnected to the surrounding world, a self that exists in community, a self that is in process, and a self that is diverse as well as multi-determined.[3] It is through community that the "self" finds a voice. Ana emphasizes that the people need to speak out. She argues that the people are suffering and they don't even realize it, a problem magnified by the fact that revolutionary Cuba lacks an independent press and the right to independent assembly, making it impossible to hear and debate issues.

In the novel, characters deal with anguish by escaping rather than by articulating their pain. Ana, however, sees that there are correct ways and incorrect ways of escapism; one of these negative avenues that she mentions is the "siesta" which she refers to as the "old national opiate" (28). She says the people "abandon themselves to the silk hand of dreaming and the poison runs through their blood and the future gets foggy" (28). Another victim of evading reality, Agustín's girlfriend, escapes through alcohol. She asks Ana how she makes her escape, to which Ana replies "I don't escape" (164). Ana consciously chooses to "awaken" herself in contrast to others in the Cuban society who need to wake up and take notice of reality.

Most of the novel takes place in Nury's six-story apartment complex. The reality for most Cubans living in similar apartment complexes is that of crumbling conditions and running water every other day (Guillermoprieto, "A Visit," 23). Ana and her friends resort to loaning each other books as monetary resources are not available to them to buy new ones. She also trades clothes with a friend because she cannot afford to buy new attire. Although neither particular focus nor attention is placed upon the residents' economic situation, the subtlety with which it is brought up underscores that, although painful, it is not her main concern. While Castro's economic and political slogan has been "socialism or death," Ana's is plainly "survival."

Castro's dependence on Russia and the Soviet Union for support has only prolonged economic strife, and now that market forces have changed, economic restructuring in Cuba is a must. The fall of the Berlin Wall, the loss of subsidized imports from the socialist bloc, as well as major markets for its exports, have all devastated the Cuban economy. In the '50s the island reached all-time levels of corruption and a widened gap between the very rich and the very poor, which all led to the overthrow of the Batista government. The revolution's effort to redistribute goods so that all may "have" has not been necessarily success-ful. Particularly in the '90s the food shortage was such that the population was hit hardest in the stomach: people were depen-dent on allotted quotas of such necessary goods as cooking oil, soap, or toothpaste. Some families, for example, are even now allowed ten ounces of beans and one pound of meat substitute per person per month (Guillermoprieto, "Love," 14).

This novel refers to the giant lines one needs to wait through in order to buy food (256). Ana criticizes the restaurant where reservations are unavailable unless you know someone. Yet the novel's focus is not on the shortages of food; instead, throughout the narrative are occasions that emphasize the reality of food as a social, communal phenomenon. Although food may be scarce, Ana Nury and her friends savor and celebrate food as if to make it clear that, in her reality, they are "living to eat" and not merely "eating to live," as may be most of her fellow citizens. Ana is able to combat her hunger by exalting in the *social* proc-ess of getting together with her friends and preparing and eating food. Her friend Gordito (meaning little fat one, used as a term of endearment) is the embodiment of cuisine satisfaction. When their friend is in the hospital and has lost the will to live, for example, Gordito gives him a reason to live: a long list of food items that occupies three of the novel's pages.

Ana also rejects Castro's mandate for an atheist society. She holds onto those sacred traditions that are a part of her "self." Attempts by the Castro regime to suppress religious practices in order to by-pass alternate possibilities of indoctrination failed. By destroying everything that we know as "self," Castro, theo-retically, would be able to re-brainwash his subjects with his own agenda. If the throne of God is empty then Castro can fill it with a system in which the Revolution would provide the people with their opium. Although religious repression in Cuba has had some "success" with some individuals, it seems that most Cubans have retained their original, pre-Revolutionary systems of belief in *Santería*, a blend of *Yoruba* (African) religions and Catholicism.[4]

Ana Nury is not willing to give up her religion for the man-dated censorship dictated by Castro's regime. Lima's religious text is central to the novel because it is yet another way for Ana to retain a part of herself that links her to pre-Castro Cuban tradition. *Santeros* believe in one god and a pantheon of deities called *orishas*. Ana's god, she says, is an all-inclusive one; her god has no specific race, is bisexual, and is both mother and father at the same time (252).

Through the image of her god we can see a feminist agenda. Like Catherine Keller's definition of a more unified feminism, this agenda is one that can "shake together more rhythmically, dancing out demons, dislocating sexual fates, unblocking spirits. Perhaps [they] might become public friends" (271). Similarly, Ana is looking for acceptance for all sexual choices and a peaceful cohabitation as well.

Again the moral rectitude of the dictatorship is deconstructed when Ana fantasizes about *Santería*. Her grandmother oftentimes appears to her in dreams; however, as she materializes, the world of the *orishas* or gods is transformed. The grandmother, disguised as *Obtalá*, who does not consume alcohol, was the first *orisha* created, is the god of peace and purity, and aids all heavy thinkers like doctors and lawyers. She is present along with *Yemayá*, the great mother who rules women; *Changó*, the Casanova of the *orishas*; and *Oyá*. The gods appear to Ana to be self-involved and are portrayed in erotic gestures to emphasize the power of moral freedom sought by Ana. These images of sex and independence reiterate against a dependent and deprived script for Cubans.

Santería lives under the premise that this world is a magical one and that this magic is really quite natural. Though not a prominent theme of the novel, the magic is expressed in relation to the story of the old dying man in the upstairs apartment to whom Ana agrees to bring up some soup. He tells her things he ordinarily couldn't have known, including things about the Sphinx, the man on whom she has a crush; however, on the whole, magic is not a fully developed topic in *Confesiones* as in other Latin American novels.[5] Perhaps magic is kept to a minimum in this particular novel because the focus is on the realities of life under the regime. It is as if Lima were saying that magic doesn't really happen and certainly doesn't work when applied to the ends of the Revolution in Cuba. Unfortunately, the Revolution has not worked its magic!

Deeply connected to Ana's feminism is her expression of sexuality. As evidenced by suppressed prostitution and a ban on homosexuality, Castro's Cuba has struggled to create a barrier against sexual freedom of expression. Homosexuality, for example, goes against the image of the postrevolutionary "new man" who is to be a person of high morals and a strong and virile revolutionary, in contrast to the "weak homosexual" (Leiner 34). To be homosexual in Cuba is to make an anti-authoritarian statement whether you intend to or not.

However, Ana encourages sexual freedom, diversity, and equality among the sexes. For example, Ana's gay friend, Miguel, comes to her in desperation. After he tells his parents he is gay his father beats him up and makes comments like, "we gave you a good education and you do this? . . . You must have a mental disease" (120). He has nowhere to go. He and his lover can't afford a place of their own so they have nowhere to be a couple. Ana breaks the traditional sexual script by defining her own, which is closely tied to her own personal reality. As she defines it, reality for her is to masturbate, eat and aspire to buy a car (39). Probably in that order, she says. When talking about sex, Ana refers to men as objects, she is like a kid in a candy store, and men are the candies. Each flavor is a different skin color: brown, blond, golden brown (12).

Indeed, sexuality is a means of empowerment and liberation for Ana. She uses active (as opposed to passive, escapist) sexual fantasies, and when having sex she takes on a domineering role. She imagines Alejandro, one of her soon-to-be-lovers, dancing for her alone; a reverse strip-tease, and she kills him with pleasure: she will make him scream, she says. He will be completely consumed by her (92–93). By writing her own sexual script Ana is able to free herself from the traditional, male models of female sexual behavior by, paradoxically, emulating those roles. Adhering to her domineering role, she plays the warrior. There is a mystery man whom she fantasizes about often; she calls him the "Sphinx." In her imagination she fights off the enemy who attacks him. She refers to herself as his knight in shining armor and wants to know if she may slay the dragon or carry out a holy war for him.

The ultimate battlefield for Ana Nury *is* in the bedroom; in this novel the sexual experience is referred to in apocalyptic terms as "Armageddon." Not only does Ana's friend Camila use images of the angel blowing the trumpet and use terms like "the Final Judgment" to describe her newfound pleasures with a threesome, Ana, in bed with the Sphinx, describes his moans as those before Armageddon (216, 218). The images of impending doom are the power words she needs to express her sexual pleasure. They are related to the apocalyptic discourse used to dis-

close the pictured demise of the, what is now, Castroesque
empire. It is by expressing her sexuality and "returning to the
body" that Ana takes back what was "confiscated from her"
(Cixous 250). Ana is able to write her-self by writing her-body,
a self that was taken from her by Castro'/man's phallocentric
society.

For Ana, Utopia will be most definitely found beyond Armageddon. Lima re-possesses the traditionally male images of the
Apocalypse with a feminist agenda. As Catherine Keller states:
"Apocalypse always charges its batteries with sex/gender images, not originally as 'essences' or 'separate spheres' but as primal abhorrence: a male fantasy of a cosmic holocaust of other
males, the oppressors, satisfyingly symbolized as whore-queen
and purged of female agency" (Apocalypse 253).

The novel comes to an end with the inclusion of the first chapters of Ana Nury's novel, a novel that she has a hard time finish-
ing due to writer's block. The postmodern open-endedness of
the meta-novel is hope that there may be a new/different history
approaching that negates the current oppressive one, and that
Cubans might be open/aware to/of it. Ana Nury claims she
doesn't know how she will end her novel; in fact, she says, she
really doesn't know if it's a novel at all. She implies here that
the meta-novel is more factual than fiction, giving legitimacy to
the interpretation of it as historical text relating to Castro's
politics of power and domination.

Ana's novel is about a man who dreams his friend is lost and
starts to search for him. He is led to a cave where he finds two
cages and he is placed inside the unoccupied cage. He witnesses
a Verdugo (Executioner) who sodomizes and tortures the other
captive. He attempts to rescue the other prisoner; however, as
he approaches, he sees that the other victim is, in actuality, himself. The Executioner has a conversation with a "gigante ca-
noso" (giant gray-haired man) who functions very much like a
teacher. The Executioner asks the giant if he's carrying out the
torture properly, to which he replies that he's behaving pretty
macho-like but that he still needs work and that he must be
tough and not give into "girly" emotions.

This meta-novel is analogous to the political repression that
has been going on in Cuba. The giant gray-haired man symbolizes Che; the Executioner is Castro. Through this analogy, Lima
is representing Castro as he truly is: a suppressive tyrant whose
goal is to follow the teachings of a giant has-been whose idyllic
goals don't function in reality. She points her finger at Castro's

enticement machine: an ideology that has been built on the nostalgia of the Revolution, on the martyrdom of Che Guevara, and upon promoting the false notion that the Revolution has been successful, that it has "worked." The victim, of course, is Cuban society; several characters in the novel, including Miguel and Ana, feel trapped liked the victim in the cage (161–62), and Ana, like the victim, increasingly becomes aware of her own position. Metaphorically, Ana is describing her vision of Cuban reality. The victim/observer originally escapes the reality of his own torture by projecting it upon another, but cannot, in the end, truly escape the recognition of his own victimhood. Ana suggests that Cuban society is evading reality with dangerous and painful consequences. In Ana's re-version of the myth, Castro becomes changed from the liberator into the oppressor, and Cubans— once they *truly perceive* their predicament instead of resorting to escapist strategies—become freed from the oppression. Cubans are the victims of a fantasy-promise for equality and economic and political well-being, and, unlike Ana, they suffer with their mouths shut and their eyes closed.

This passage not only has a political connotation, but a feminist one as well. Lima here is deconstructing the traditional masculine hero. As Richard Tarnas suggests in his book *The Passion of the Western Mind,* the days of the masculine-hero paradigm that has existed by feeding upon the repressed feminine are numbered.[6] This, he says, is because we are much more interested in hearing what the dragon, or the feminine has to say in regard to how our myths or paradigms construct the world. If so, Ana Nury becomes the feminist heroine. She does so by erasing for herself all that Castro stands for. She won't stand to be a second-class citizen. She insists on sexual equality and she also validates the forbidden religious traditions of pre-Castro Cuba.

In sum, Castro's text of chaos and crisis, political incorrectness, heterosexism, economic challenges, and religious repression surround/make Ana. As she rewrites this text she reveals the truth: according to her, life is all there is and there are no hidden meanings. One day at a time, she attempts to see things as they really are. She calls it a type of mental gymnastics (71). Her goal, she says, is to obtain through other means what drunks get through alcohol and drug addicts get through drugs. And ultimately it is through Ana Nury's struggle to deconstruct the Cuban Apocalypse that surrounds her that she is able to escape from it and reveal the political restraints present in her surroundings.

NOTES

1. Portions of the text of *Confesiones nocturnas* have been translated into English by Mica Howe.

2. These ideas are presented in Fonda's unpublished essay, "Postmodernity and the Imagination of the Apocalypse," presented on 22 April 1994 at a panel entitled: "Religious Studies and the Apocalypse" at the Eastern Regional Meeting of the American Academy of Religion in Montréal. In his paper the author uses these terms to compare millennial movements and postmodern thought.

3. In her book, *From a Broken Web*, Keller discusses *theoria*: "seeing" within the feminist sensibility: that is, a vision through seeing relations and a quest for connection. She explains the emerging feminist vision that "drives beyond the sphere of interpersonal, seeking a broader context . . . a 'panrelational whole' " (157–58).

4. With the slave trade coming to the New World also came the *orishas*. The slaves were mostly from western Africa in what today we call Nigeria, and from a tribe called *Yoruba*. As slaves, the *Yoruba* people were expected to adopt the customs and traditions of their Spanish masters. This involved not only speaking the Spanish language but also adopting Catholicism as their religion, presenting a problem to the *Yoruba* people who insisted on holding on to their traditions. Thus, in the New World much of the slaves' religion was hidden behind a façade of Catholicism with the *orishas* themselves represented by various saints. In this manner when their Spanish masters observed their slaves worshipping, for example, St. Barbara, the people were secretly worshipping *Chango*, the god of thunder. See *Santería: The Religion* by Migene González-Wippler (Harmony Books: New York, 1989).

5. I am referring to the genre of "Magical Realism" as portrayed by such authors as García Márquez, Carlos Fuentes, and Laura Esquivel.

6. Tarnas contends that "postmodern critical thought has encouraged a vigorous rejection of the entire Western intellectual 'canon'. . . . Received truths concerning 'man,' reason,' civilization,' and progress are indicted as intellectually and morally bankrupt." (400)

WORKS CITED

Cixous, Hélene. 1980. "The Laugh of the Medusa." In *New French Feminisms: An Anthology*, edited by Elaine Marks and Isabelle de Courtivron, 245–264. Amherst: The University of Massachusetts Press.

Fonda, Marc. 1996. "The Postmodern Apocalypse." 1994. http://www.clas.ufl.edu/users/gthursby/fonda/dragon.html (April 22).

Guillermoprieto, Alma. 1998. "A Visit to Havana." *The New York Review*, 26 March. 19–24.

————. 1998. "Love and Misery in Cuba." *The New York Review*, 11 June. 10–14.

Keller, Catherine. 1986. *From a Broken Web*. Boston: Beacon Press.

————. 1996. *Apocalypse Now and Then*. Boston: Beacon Press,.

Leiner, Marvin. 1994. *Sexual Politics in Cuba*. Westview Press.

Lima, Chely. 1994. *Confesiones nocturnas*. Mexico: Planeta.

Tarnas, Richard. 1991. *The Passion of the Western Mind*. New York: Ballantine Books.

Purloining *The Scarlet Letter*: Bharati Mukherjee and the Apocryphal Imagination

CHRISTIAN MORARU

[A]bove all it is necessary to read and reread those in whose wake I write, the "books" in whose margins and between whose lines I mark out and read a text simultaneously almost identical and entirely other.

—Derrida, *Positions* 4

[T]he "American" literature I am talking about is no more than a vaguely apprehended "other," but a futural other, to which the actual literary texts we have and study are kinds of prefaces or notes toward; prologues written both after and before the fact, before the letter. They are necessarily written, then, in the old received letter, in the old words and forms, and are in a sense quotations of them. But they are no less, by a kind of ironic reinscription, quotations of the future, of their potential otherness. The 'America' letter, which so much American writing is condemned to describe by anticipation, is a letter never yet written, a metaleptic letter.

—Riddel 21

"IMAGINATION FEEDS ON PREVIOUS IMAGINATION," ROBERT Scholes provocatively insists (214) in his account of the "fabulative movement" that has got under way, he reminds us, with Nabokov and Borges and continued with Pynchon, Doctorow, Coover, Barth, Sukenick, Federman, and other postmodern "fabulators." If, against romanticism's and, to a certain extent, modernism's major tenets on creativity, this holds true, then, odd as it may seem, the literary imagination should be seized upon "in terms of plagiarism." And since there is no way around the latter, we might as well relax and, *pace* Harold Bloom, even "enjoy it": "Away with anxiety"! (Scholes 215).

Needless to say, there is nothing wrong with "enjoying" the

metafictional games of the bookish, wittily "parasitic" or "plagiaristic" imagination. What I find truly fascinating and worthwhile of closer scrutiny at present, though, is primarily the kind of postmodern plagiarism where rewriting of past works steps beyond the jocular antics of earlier metafiction to fulfill culturally and politically specific functions. Late twentieth-century authors such as Toni Morrison, Ishmael Reed, Charles Johnson, Samuel R. Delany, Kathy Acker, Maxine Hong Kingston, Louise Erdrich, and Gerald Vizenor, to give only a few examples, "parasitize" canonical, mostly white and male works to take on the values, hierarchies, and ideologies ingrained in them and lay out aesthetic and political alternatives. Simply put, the rewriting they perform often turns out to be counterwriting, "writing otherwise": a polemical agenda-driven form of intertextuality.

True, some critics have argued that such a "program" is inherent to any intertextual operations, including those whose "meanings" appear at first glance to merely "repeat" the model's. As Romita Choudhury maintains apropos of "postcolonial intertextuality," "no text is self-contained. Neither is it an obedient follower of its predecessors." "The conception of meaning as produced through repetition and difference," she specifies, "has become an important base for challenging hierarchical notions of the unity, authorship, authority and sanctity of the literary text" (315). Choudhury's argument on the "differential" politics of narrative "repetition" trades upon the tradition of poetics-based analysis of intertextuality and "second-degree literature," to quote the subtitle of Gérard Genette's fundamental contribution, *Palimpsests*. But critics from Mikhail M. Bakhtin to Julia Kristeva, Roland Barthes, and John Frow have struggled to overcome the "formalism" of this sort of analysis. Michael Worton and Judith Still, whom Choudhury also mentions, follow in the latter line of critical thought as they have shown great interest in the broader bearings of intertextuality. Significantly, they claim that the phenomenon and, by implication, its critical analysis are "inevitably political. . . . The practice of intertextual interpretation"—as much as literary intertextual practices at large—"is an attempt to struggle against both complicity and exclusion—perhaps something, some shifting of barriers, can thus be achieved even if, in general, none of our thinking can escape constructing identity against differences" (Worton and Still 33).

As one can see, the two critics stress that intertextuality is unavoidably political. But they are less precise as to how writers

and critics may achieve political goals while "doing" or "analyzing" intertexts since we all are already enmeshed in a web of
preexistent sociocultural intertextuality and therefore everything we may undertake is bound to be carried out within preset
norms, languages, structures, texts, and other "formations."
Thus, as Worton and Still themselves point out à la Derrida,
much though "the 'textual' and the 'extra-textual' inhabit each
other"—which makes "the 'extra-textual' " "another kind of
text"—"there is a need to draw out further the relations between social formations (one kind of text) and texts in the conventional sense" (33).

To explain exactly how and why literature's "feeding" on previous literature is a political act, we do need, it seems to me, to
demonstrate how reworking of extant texts redoes the sociocultural textuality, the con-textual "formations" surrounding and
soaking through intertextual constructs. Again, merely postu-
lating the "politics"—one implies, naturally, a "progressive"
politics—of this process will not do. As I argue, one must ascertain how re-forming available literary forms would impact "social formations" such as discourses and representations of
gender, sexuality, class, race, ethnicity, or belief, around which
we usually organize and enact our identities. One has to spell
out, for example, how, its own social "construction" notwithstanding, the *re-storying* of a former story resists the *restoring* of
these categories and, by the same token, the reproduction of the
inherited power configurations based on them: how, in other
words, writing as *re*writing encroaches upon the "traditional"
space of political agon.

In what follows, I want to propose a way of undertaking this
critical task by focusing on Bharati Mukherjee's 1993 novel *The
Holder of the World* as a reworking of an emblematic text of
American letters. Specifically, what I am setting out to do is
show how, in "purloining" a letter of our foundational cultural
alphabet, Mukherjee spells out an entire politics of gender and,
in doing so, engenders an alternative history of empire as well
as of the canon—the "empire of letters" and its hierarchies.

Mukherjee presents us with an ambitious rewriting: an "apocryphal" response to *The Scarlet Letter*, one of the most intensely
revisited works in contemporary fiction.[1] Appropriating the celebrated romance, *The Holder of the World* critically engages with
a whole array of Western, British, and Puritan images, notions,
and ideals, fancifully displacing them onto a "defamiliarizing,"
as the Russian Formalists might say, indeed, "subversive" con-

text. What comes out of this polemical re-narrativization is, bluntly put, a "postcolonial" or, even better, a "transnational" Hawthorne with a bold, original twist on feminine agency and history. In Mukherjee's "re-lettered" *Letter*, various discourses of gender, race, religion, and ethnicity clash, intersect, and coalesce as to dynamically multiply, decenter, and complicate the textual and ideological structure of the Hawthornian "matrix" and, through it, a whole paradigm of power, cultural authority, and representation.

The Holder of the World tells a double-layered story. Beigh Masters, the narrating protagonist, uncovers this structure from the outset when she points up "the past, the present, and the future" in which she is simultaneously living (5). But this is not just the worn-out device allowing sci-fi heroes to shuttle back and forth between distinct time periods and places. It pinpoints, rather, a sort of "informational" time-space, a "continuum" whose prototype is the computer "grid" the narrator's boyfriend, an Indian immigrant named Venn, works on at MIT. Yet technological verisimilitude and hi-tech details are, it seems to me, less consequential than what they hint at in Mukherjee's novel: a model, metafictional as much as metapolitical, for the palimpsest-like structure, for the "interconnectedness" characteristic of the global age in general and *The Holder of the World* as a cultural document of this age in particular.

In this view, one has to grasp this interconnectedness in terms of the intertextual and cross-cultural dynamics the novel itself draws from and thematizes. For, to emphasize this process, the book sets up a transformative dialogue between itself and previous texts, primarily the *Letter*. Mukherjee recirculates and remakes Hawthorne to foreground our time's unprecedented circulation and refashioning of cultural products, ideas, styles, symbols, and people. In fact, at the novel's very end, Beigh Masters, once again Bharati Mukherjee's transparent mouthpiece, flaunts her intertextual/rewriterly *modus operandi*, specifically, the *Letter* as *The Holder of the World*'s "source" along with other materials such as the main characters' fictitious diaries, late seventeenth-century Mughal paintings, Puritan embroideries, and all sorts of other documents: "We have," she revealingly confesses, "the shipping and housing records, we have the letters and journals and the *Memoirs*, and of course we have *The Scarlet Letter*" (284). And, as the narrator goes on to ask rhetorically: "Who can blame Nathaniel Hawthorne for shying away from the real story of the brave Salem mother and her illegitimate daughter?" (284)

The Holder of the World purports precisely to make up for this "lack" and recount the "real story" of Hester Prynne and her daughter Pearl. "I write," Gloria Anzaldua confesses, "to rewrite the stories others have miswritten about me," and Mukherjee could say the same (Anzaldua and Moraga 169). In effect, she is saying it, in various ways, throughout her book. *The Holder of the World* rewrites the *Letter*, its "shy" "prototype," to counter the alleged Hawthornian "miswriting." To do this, it reinterprets, rereads Hawthorne's text and reads between its lines, even writes between those lines, wedging its own "parasite" narrative body in and between them, as it were. Mukherjee interpolates and develops the Hawthornian story, so much so that one could seize *The Holder of the World* as an apocryphal refurbishing and "spin-off" of the Hawthorne classic. It should be clear, though, that I am here using the term rather loosely: Mukherjee's is certainly a "postmodern" apocrypha. She does not pretend that her book actually recovers or is somehow inspired by a possibly forgotten or heretofore unknown Hawthornian text. Nonetheless, "people and their property often get separated," as Beigh Masters remarks, and her author does not hesitate to "appropriate" that which used to be Hawthorne's exclusive property.

Appropriating and "ironically 'doubling' "[2] a real work by Hawthorne, though, she works it into a "pseudo-Hawthornian" narrative that contains stuff Hawthorne might have—better put, "has"—"left out" or "miswritten" (5). This way, the unspoken and the unwritten in Hawthorne's letter(s) come to the fore in the rewrite. The latter is the *Letter*'s "futural other," to recall Joseph Riddel's phrase. Or, conversely, Hawthorne's *Letter* is, to Mukherjee's, the "prologue" written "before the fact, before the letter," awaiting—and now spectacularly receiving—its postmodern sequel. But this sequel does not pastiche or mimic the "style" of the classic precursor: Hawthorne provides mainly plot, characters, and, above all, a cultural mythology—quite a bit, actually. For, as it turns out, this is more than what an astoundingly inventive writer like Mukherjee needs to rewrite Hawthorne's story and, along with it, its transcultural and transhistorical problematics.

If Hawthorne supplies narrative materials, a story to retell, Thomas Pynchon may well be the one to furnish literary tools and themes Mukherjee makes her own and employs to "retool"

Hawthorne: pastiche, dazzling amalgamation, geographical, geopolitical, and cross-cultural dynamic of mysterious femininity. "Pynchon" represents the postmodern marker re-marking (re-lettering) pre-modern history as accounted for in the *Letter*. In *The Holder of the World*, he stands for the generic functioning of the stylistic machine that rewrites history, literary and otherwise. This intertextual apparatus takes in and turns that (hi)story upside down and inside out, much like Pynchon's mysterious letter "V," from his 1963 novel having this letter as its title, "upsets" and repositions, according to Mukherjee's genuinely Borgesian imagination, Hawthorne's own "A." As she tellingly writes about her character Hannah Easton, "her life is at the crossroads of many worlds. If Thomas Pynchon, perhaps one of the descendants of her failed suitor [Solomon Pynchon], had not already written V., I would call her a V., a woman who was everywhere, the encoder of a secret history" (60).

De-coding (rereading), re-encoding (rewriting) Hawthorne: this "encoding" frenzy permeates and links up the two major stories within Mukherjee's narrative. The "frame" and the "enframed" story are tightly interwoven and, together, worked into the novel's textually oversaturated fabric, which is modeled, half ironically half in earnest, after the MIT time-space, virtual reality-based computer grid. Thus, Beigh Masters, a Massachusetts "asset-hunter," gets hired by a "Hollywood mogul," Bugs Kilken of Bel Air, to locate a famous gem called "The Emperor's Tear." Beigh finds the precious stone embedded, so to speak, in the bloody history of late seventeenth-century southern India. She is assisted in the search by her Hindu boyfriend, a computer wiz who is developing a software capable of "recapturing of past reality . . . [by] absorb[ing] my manuscript and all the documents, the travelogues and computerized East India records, the lavishly illustrated *namas*, or chronicles, of the emperors of the Mughal" (280). Accessing the past by virtual reality technology, Beigh witnesses crucial scenes of Indian history and, ultimately, tracks down the famous diamond.

This is the part sci-fi, part travel story, part thriller "outer edge" of Mukherjee's novel. I might point out, too, that, remarkably enough, the plot of this narrative also "recycles" two well-known stories: Hermann Hesse's 1922 novel *Siddharta*, which revolves around the retrieval of a diamond and the Hindu culture this comes from, and possibly one of John Updike's own rewritings of Hawthorne's *Letter*, *S* (1988), where the woman protagonist joins a Hindu religious community in Arizona. But as I am suggesting here, the intertextual/rewriting operation is far more spectacular at a deeper level. There, Mukherjee manipulates Hawthorne to develop her own cross-culturally/cross-textually allusive plot, or in her own words, "transcultural adumbrations" (230). At this level, she feeds the *Letter* into her own rewriting machine, *The Holder of the World*, inscribing Hawthorne's characters into a (hi)story that, as Mukherjee insists, "was already rewriting [their] fate" (207). If the *Letter* recuperates an essential moment of North American history, the "story of [India's] Coromandel Coast" as chronicled by *The Holder of the World* is "the story of North America turned inside out" (160). And this is exactly what Mukherjee's rewrite does: it turns its narrative "model" inside out, thereby uprooting ("purloining") and relocating its "insiders" and "outsiders" in what has come to be one of the most startling replies to Hawthorne and his world.

For all its intertextual de-centeredness, *The Holder of the World* turns on Mukherjee's mobile, ubicuous Hannah Easton as Hester Prynne and on the imaginary New Salem of ancient India's Coromandel coast as the (Old) Salem of the "New" World. Indeed, one might ask, what is "new" and what is "old" here? What is the "model" and what is the "replica," the "prologue" and the "afterward," the rewritten and the rewrite? What happens to the "prototype"—to how we read the *Letter*—following its revisionary "misspelling" by Mukherjee? At any rate, Hawthorne, his book, and universe supply the narrative chart, or, once again, "grid" for mapping out the Indian territory based on the commonality ("coincidence") of a fundamental cultural and historical experience affecting them at the same time: colonization and the subsequent encounter between the British and the "Indian" natives, either Native Americans or Hindus. Hannah plays the role of the female agent connecting—without leveling out—the newly "discovered" Extreme West and Extreme West, two intertwined stories of conquest and desire. At both ends of the expanding British Empire, in the New England of John Hathorne, Nathaniel's ancestor, and in India alike, she bumps against race-, gender-, and religion- based purist if not always Puritan orthodoxies.

Interestingly, in New Salem she comes to be known as the Salem *Bibi*, the nonconformist white concubine of the fearless ruler of Devgad, Raja Singh, whose child she will actually bear—an ultimate yet proudly borne stigma. Thus, as Beigh seems to suggest, Hindustan may be seized as a vast Puritan analogy. It sets in motion similar mechanisms of exclusion, marginalization, and control as the same "discourse operations"[3] typical of colonialism "write," in both cases, people into "subaltern" positions. The "Indian" becomes the culturally, ethnically, and racially ambiguous signifier or "metaphor"[4]—both critique-wielding and lending itself to critique—that Mukherjee "wields" to legitimate and deploy this analogy.

Notably, though, this parallel entails no symmetry or cultural synonymy, blindness to the painfully actual differences. Mukherjee builds a sophisticated, quasi-Borgesian analogical narrative apparatus that reproduces and filters Indian history and mythology through the lenses of the *Letter* and, I should add, the 1682 *Narrative of the Captivity and Restoration of Mrs. Mary Rowlandson*. As a matter of fact, the story of Rebecca Easton, Hannah's mother, which recapitulates the 1675 Native American uprising led by Metacomet, also known as King Philip, and Beigh's rendition of the episode devoted to Sita, Rama's wife, in the classical Hindu epic poem *Ramayana*, are equally patterned after Mary Rowlandson's narrative. Now, as we recall, Siva's chastity is questioned in *Ramayana* by the people and Rama himself following her abduction by Ravanna, the demon-king of Lanka. After giving birth to Rama's two sons, Siva passes the trial of fire and exiles herself in the forest, where she eventually meets her courageous end (she will be swallowed by earth after refusing to take the fire test again).

It is true we do not have, as Beigh Masters reminds us, "Sita's version of captivity in Lanka" (177). We do not have her words, to be more precise. But we do have Hannah's, that is, the Salem *Bibi*'s—Mukherjee's "apocryphal Hawthorne." And Beigh does contend that he knows—from Hannah's captivity—what Sita would have written. Thus, what Mukherjee's transculturally intertextual games of conversions, translations, adaptations, and permutations lay out is a polyphonic narrative where *Ramayana* is reinterpreted through—or "with"—the *Letter* and where, conversely, the latter is "contaminated" by Hindu epic literature, mythology, and history, and turned into the Salem *Bibi* story: Mukherjee's own book. To quote Beigh, here again an authorial alter-ego, underlying all this is "a hunger for connectedness, a belief that with sufficient passion and intelligences we can deconstruct the barriers of time and geography." This "deconstruction" may lead, she hopes, "circuitously, to Venn. And to the Salem Bibi and the tangled lines of India and New England" (11). Tangled and interrupted, hardly visible as they might have been rendered by a convulsive history, these lines are being retraced and worked into a pretty compelling and coherent narrative of "connectedness" in *The Holder of the World*. And what unifies, what holds together the *Holder*, I might say one more time, is the Hawthornian narrative body—references, puns, allusions, and other intertexts with various degrees of visibility—shrewdly scattered throughout Mukherjee's novel. Definitely, *The Holder of the World* is structurally marked by Hawthorne's presence and, as noted above, re-marks this "source" insistently as unreels its own story.

Speaking of marks, one could retrace this presence by looking for how Mukherjee demarcates—playfully repeats, reinscribes, or, on the contrary, blurs, disfigures—the emblematic mark of the *Letter*: the Hawthornian, ambiguous and dynamic "A." Taking up the shifty symbolism of the letter, Muhkerjee "disseminates" it all over her novel. At times, this operation is easily recognizable. Other times, though, you have to step back, distance yourself from the text to make out the contour of the purloined symbol. For, as Derrida insists in his critique of Lacan's interpretation of Poe's "The Purloined Letter," the appropriated letter—or letters, literary works, that is—might not be hidden at all, but widely written across the textual body of the appropriating text, which may render it perhaps *too* remarkable, *too self-evident* to be seen and read ("The Purveyor of Truth," Muller and Richardson, 176). At any rate, Mukherjee's "model" is, so to speak, marked for rewriting—and *The Holder of the World* is marked as a rewrite—from the first to the last page.

The novel begins, for example, with Beigh Masters tellingly reading *A & A*, namely, the *Auctions and Acquisitions* magazine. Here, she comes across a story about a museum of antiquities located between (Old) Salem and Marblehead, a museum which has acquired a big gem. As she admits, it is not the stone itself that interests her, but the "inscription"—the "script" or original "intertext," I would add—inscribed, marked on the gem, and in general anything having to do with Mughal India and the legendary Salem *Bibi*. More often than not, this inscription is literally—I am tempted to say, "letterally"—performed on bodies and works as an exclusionary mark exactly like in Hawthorne. Scalped survivors of the King Philip upheaval display bodily stigmas that cast them out as much as many a "disreputable fellow with one of the several possible letters of the sinner's alphabet—Adulterer, Blasphemer, Thief, Incest breeder—branded to his forehead, or an Indian patch sewn to a woman's sleeve for miscegenation" (41). But if Hester Prynne is forced, in the *Letter*, to wear the infamous veil, Hannah, one of her reincarnations in the *Holder*, takes up "needlework" on her own. This gives her fame and her author another opportunity to flaunt the intertextual makeup of the novel.

One of Hannah's embroideries, for instance, plays in great detail on the "rag of scarlet cloth" the authorial narrator discovers in the Custom-House in the "introductory" chapter of the *Letter* (Hawthorne 31). As we may recall, the "embroidery" bearing the infamous "A" "had been twisted" around a "small roll of dingy paper . . . containing many particulars respecting the life and conversation of one Hester Prynne"—the "groundwork of a tale," the romance itself (31–33). Rolled around Hawthorne's own "roll," Mukherjee's tale and, within it, the *mise-en-abyme* motif of the cloth retextualize Hawthorne's text, dazzlingly complicating its cultural fabric. Hannah's "little embroidery" weaves together, symbolically, the West and the East. It features verses from Psalms "emblazoned" in colors "so tropical" that the "threads Hannah used had to have been brought over from a mysterious place with a musical name: Bandar Abbas, Batavia, Bimlipatam," and thus represents "one of the great colonial samplers" (44). The needlepoint, which Hannah took with her to England and India, Mukherjee writes,

> is a pure vision. It is the first native American response to a world that could be African or Indian or anything not American. It employs the same economy, the same apparently naive sophistication as the Mughal paintings that would later feature her. Thomas [Fitch, but it might as well have been Pynchon] framed her handiwork in the finest cherrywood left over from a chest he had made for the fearsome old magistrate, the twisted John Hathorne (whose excesses in the witch trials would so torment his descendant, Nathaniel Hawthorne). (44–45)

This *textum*, this *textual* "vision" is a superb "embodiment of desire." It appears to body forth, illustrate ethnocentric and patriarchal paradigms by featuring the biblical lines about "desire" understood as the worship of the true God, "heathens," and earthly "possessions."

However, much like Mukherjee's reweaving of Hawthorne's narrative texture, what this embroidery does is overhaul this paradigm in a fundamentally political move: desire means un-

censored physical desire where woman finds freedom and fulfillment through sexual initiative. Likewise, possession no
longer designates "possession of the earth" by the right believ-
ers, but, again, and against both and Puritan patriarchal appre-
hensions, physical possession of the male partner—and a
"heathen" partner to that Hindu (Iyer 38).[5] Indeed, Hannah's
work seems "like a clash of the sexes, a triumph of pioneer virility" (Mukherjee 43), with the proviso that virility becomes, odd
as it may sound, a feature of the female protagonist, while being
a pioneer—a woman pioneer, to be more precise—entails a new,
rather nonimperial relation to the "unknown or the unex-
plored" (100).

It is true, Mukherjee does not cover up her character's inescapable "complicity . . . in imperialism" (Iyer 40). I would nevertheless argue that, through the same plagiaristic games,
Mukherjee rather stresses Hannah's resistance to empire,
which remains in the novel an essentially masculine, indeed
masculinist project. Thus, the author lays strong emphasis on
the conflict between Hannah-as-Hester Prynne, one of the novel's intertextual reincarnations of Hester, and one Cephus
Prynne, East India Company's Chief Factor (107) and "customs
officer" (112). Obviously lifted from the same Hawthornian rep-
ertoire, the latter epitomizes the cynical, racist colonizer and,
generally speaking, the self-sufficient, monological story of gen-
der- and race-based oppression *The Holder of the World* seeks to
retell "otherwise." Hannah, however, is mainly the female agent
of this pluralist and enabling retelling where the imperial narrative of domination, acquisition, and assimilation is displaced
through a narrative of interaction, "translation" and cross-cultural solidarity (100, 118). Revealingly, Mukherjee plays upon
the identical motif of the stigmatizing letter(s) to mysteriously
"write" Cephus Prynne's collective guilt all over his corpse. As
we learn,

> Very little flesh remained [on the letter when it was found], but for
> the tight skin of the forehead, upon which the letter *H* in a Roman
> script had been slashed. And on parts of the body the pariah dogs
> and buzzards and hyenas had not carried away, other letters were
> faintly discernible—an *A*, a *C*, an *E*—as though the Hindus or Mus-
> lims had thought by a promiscuous imitation of the English alpha-
> bet they were pointing the finger of guilt away from them, instead
> of directly at their hearts. (157)

Symbolically completing the circular trajectory of the purloined letter through history and stories, *The Holder of the World*

ends with—or rather *at*—its source, by re-marking its textual origin. Hannah, now called Pearl, like Hester Prynne's daughter, sails back to New England to join her ostracized mother, and is about to give birth to her own daughter, also named Pearl—Pearl Singh, after her father, the Raja. Hannah's Indian (Hindu) lover reiterates her mother's stigmatizing relationship with her Indian (Native American) lover and, of course, foreshadows Beigh's own relationship with Venn, the Indian immigrant. And here we are, come full circle; here is Hawthorne's letter sanctioning this transhistorical and transcultural analogy: Hannah returns to North America to find her mother wearing her "outmoded woolens with the shameful *I*"—"[I]t meant 'Indian lover' "—sewn in red to her sleeve" (283).

Remarkably, only nine years old when Hannah ("White Pearl"), Pearl ("Black Pearl"), and Rebecca Easton, the "Ur-Hester Prynne," get back to New England's Salem and son of John Hathorne the famous witchcraft judge, Joseph Hathorne is deeply affected by the stories that White Pearl storyteller "related as she sewed" (284). He even "goes to sea" under the spell of these stories, apparently carrying on, rounding off, and rewriting a story that his great-grandson, Nathaniel Hawthorne, was to provide the "model" ("preface") for—retroactively as it were. Yet this is a paradox Mukherjee is fully aware of: a paradox of literary history, of history itself, of time finally. "Time, O Time!" reads the closing, remarkable lines of the novel, where Mukherjee reinscribes her "model." "Time to tincture the lurid colors, time for the local understudies to learn their foreign lines, time only to touch and briefly bring alive the first letter of an alphabet of hope and of horror stretching out, and back to the uttermost shore" (285). Time, indeed, to revivify the "branded letters of sin: *E* for English, Extraordinary, Ethical" (127). Time for irony, of course, but also for "relettering" games that result in a "subversive alphabet" (54) in which "*A* is for Act ... *B* is for Boldness ... *C* is for Character ... *D* is for Dissent, *E* is for Ecstasy, *F* is for Forage ... [a]nd *I* is for ... Indian lover," according to Hester, a friend of Hannah's, or rather "Independence," as Hannah herself insists (54). The relation between this "subversive" cultural alphabet and Hawthorne's letter(s) is fairly obvious. Mukherjee's symbolic acronyms spell out and cherish a whole paradigm that Hawthorne's world—if not always Hawthorne's own story—tones down, represses, marks for control, stigmatization, and colonization: desire, sexu-

ality in general, the female body and power, the "menacing,"
mysterious native, and so on.

Intertwined with and growing from this intertextual dialogue
are other relations and tensions, where the politics of intertextuality comes even more forcefully to the fore. First, there is a
problematized, increasingly ambivalent rapport between center
and margin, metropolis and colony, by virtue of which we get
increasingly unsure which one comes first. Is Old Salem a
model for New Salem or vice versa? Do the "Indians" come before the Hindus or the other way around? Mukherjee's postmodern rewriting of history disrupts linearity, priorities, cause-
and-effect and model-and-copy narratives. And second, but in
conjunction with this, what also obtains in *The Holder of the
World* is an intensely revised relation between the canonical
"precursor" (Hawthorne)[6] and "imitator" (Mukherjee herself),
through which the former Bengali, South Asian Canadian, Indian American, and currently American author authoritatively
reclaims the tradition of the American letters as hers and, for
herself, a place of honor in this tradition.

NOTES

1. John Updike (*A Month of Sundays, Roger's Version, S*), Kathy Acker
(*Blood and Guts in High School*), Samuel R. Delany (*Neveryóna*), Toni Morrison
(*Sula, Beloved*), and Margaret Atwood (*The Handmaid's Tale*) are among the
most striking rewritings of *The Scarlet Letter*.

2. Low analyzes Mukherjee's notion of narrative mimicking in other stories
and essays such as *The Middleman and Other Stories, Jasmine*, and *Wife*. The
critic relates Mukherjee's essay "Mimicry and Reinvention" to Homi Bhab-
ha's theory of mimicry as "imitative performance" that "disturbs an originary
essence of identity by returning a *different* and strange image of the self" (Low
13).

3. "Colonialism (like its counterpart, racism) . . . is an operation of discourse, and as an operation of discourse it interpellates colonial subjects by
incorporating them in a system of representation. They are always written by
the same system of representation" (Tiffin and Lawson 3).

4. To Mukherjee, "Indianness is now a metaphor, a particular way of partially comprehending the world," as she writes in *Darkness* (qtd. in Iyer 29).

5. *The Holder of the World*, Iyer observes, "also rewrites the Raj narrative
popular in British literature. These colonial narratives often tell tales of forbidden relationships between white women and native men, which the English characters perceive as rape, and such alleged rape of the English woman
is a central trope of these narratives. . . . In *The Holder of the World*, Mukherjee
rewrites the Raj narrative by making the English woman (Hannah is seen as
English in India) an agent in her sexual life rather than a passive subject" (42).

6. As Fakrul Alam observes,

by inscribing Hawthorne into *The Holder of the World* ... and by taking every opportunity to associate her novel with *The Scarlet Letter*, Bharati Mukherjee is making two points: she is asking her readers to place *The Holder of the World* in the tradition of American romance inaugurated by Hawthorne and is emphasizing the historical dimension of her novel. (129)

Along the same lines, Nalini Iyer insists that, in taking on a "Great American Novel," Mukherjee "challenges the exclusivity of the American canon and interrogates the process of literary canon formation" that tends to reinforce distinctions and disparities between "mainstream" and "marginal"—"postcolonial," "ethnic," "female," and so on—figures (32).

WORKS CITED

Alam, Fakrul. 1996. *Bharati Mukherjee*. New York: Twayne Publishers, Prentice Hall International.

Anzaldua, Gloria, and Moraga Cheerie, eds. 1983. *This Bridge Called My Back*. New York: Kitchen Table.

Choudhury, Romita. 1992. " 'Is there a ghost, a zombie there?' Postcolonial Intertextuality and Jean Rhys's *Wide Sargasso Sea*." *Textual Practice* 10, no. 2:315–27.

Derrida, Jacques. 1995. *Positions*. Translated and annotated by Alan Bass. 1981. Reprint, Chicago: University of Chicago Press.

———. "The Purveyor of Truth." In Muller and Richardson 173–212.

Hawthorne, Nathaniel. 1990. *The Scarlet Letter*. With an introduction by Harold Bloom. New York: Vintage Books / The Library of America.

Iyer, Nalini. 1996. "American/Indian: Metaphors of the Self in Bharati Mukherjee's *The Holder of the World*." *ARIEL* 27, no. 4 (October): 29–44.

Low, Gail Ching-Liang. 1993. "In a Free State: Post-Colonialism and Postmodernism in Bharati Mukherjee's Fiction." *Women: A Cultural Review* 4, no. 1 (spring): 8–17.

Mukherjee, Bharati. 1994. *The Holder of the World*. 1993. Reprint, New York: Fawcett Columbine.

Muller, John P., and William J. Richardson, eds. 1988. *The Purloined Poe. Lacan, Derrida, and Psychoanalytic Reading*. Baltimore and London: The Johns Hopkins University Press.

Riddel, Joseph N. 1995. *Purloined Letters. Originality and Repetition in American Literature*. Edited by Mark Bauerlein, Baton Rouge and London: Louisiana State University Press.

Scholes, Robert. 1979. *Fabulation and Metafiction*. Urbana: University of Illinois Press.

Tiffin, Chris, and Alan Lawson, eds. 1994. *De-Scribing Empire. Post-Colonialism and Textuality*. New York: Routledge,.

Warton, Michael, and Judith Still, eds. 1990. *Intertextuality, Theory and Practice*. Manchester: Manchester University Press.

To Speak with the Voices of Others: Kathy Acker and the Avant-Garde

SVETLANA MINTCHEVA

> Being born into and part of a male world, she had speech of her own. All she could do was read male texts which weren't hers.
>
> —Acker, *Don Quixote* 39

IN THE SIXTIES, IT WAS CHARLES OLSON AND THE REST OF THE BLACK mountain poets who offered, for Kathy Acker, the most influential model of innovative writing.[1] However, even though compelled by their imperative to discover her individual poetic voice, faced with a blank page, Acker could not find "a speech of her own." So she started by copying texts and later developed that into an aesthetic method. The practice of copying texts became Kathy Acker's rebellious response to her poetic "fathers."

Acker's "failure" in terms of the originality valued by modernism was a condition widely experienced by writers and artists in the sixties and seventies. Postmodernism came to be defined, to a large extent, precisely by the method of borrowing from high and low culture, from myth and history, by a raiding of the past for images and styles. Acker, in her flight from the Black Mountain "fathers," pushed postmodern unoriginality to the extreme of plagiarism, while, at the same time gendering it, whereas male postmodern writers played boisterously with the past and present, reality and fantasy, or high and low, Acker was struggling with a need to express a pain and anger and love, for which, however, there was no available language.

Although *Great Expectations* programmatically announces Acker's new technique with its first section entitled "Plagiarism," the term plagiarism is inadequate in describing Acker's agonistic use of other texts; the passive connotations of plagiarism are at odds with her active disturbance of textual elements. The critical foregrounding of the fact of plagiarism in Acker's

267

reputation as experimental writer is most certainly due to the prominence of the work of appropriation artists in the late 70s, whose influence she admits,[2] as well as to the general tendency toward pastiche, stylistic and image raiding in postmodern fiction. "Plagiarism" then, as a method, both gives her writing an appropriately transgressive postmodern cache and conveniently packages her work. Consequently, the various functions of "plagiarism" as an element in Acker's writing that critics have pointed out do little to distinguish Acker's practice from postmodern fiction in general whether they refer to the unstable identity of the narrative self (Martina Sciolino), the resulting fragmentation of the narrative, or the method of scandalously re-contextualizing familiar texts (Larry McCaffery). Interpretations that note the combination of critical reading and feminist writing in Acker's texts, where plagiarism constitutes simultaneously "feminist critique and gynocritics," come closer to locating the specificity of her method (Sciolino, "Kathy Acker," 442).[3] Acker's re-writing of texts is both a form of exposure of their gender and power dynamics and a way of finding means of expression.

After *Don Quixote*, however, critical readings become less central to Acker's work. Toward the late eighties, she affirms a necessity to construct a positive alternative to what she has been heretofore only reacting to. Yet the struggle to break away from patriarchal capitalist power structures is at every turn haunted by these very structures. And the language used to form the lines of this struggle is not a pure, true, magical language but carries a baggage which any artist has to drag along consciously or not. A closer analysis of the relationship between original text and Acker's use reveals a much more agonistic relationship than has so far been noted. For, in her quest for an alternative, Acker's intellectual sources come from an avant-garde tradition which is exclusively male. This is the tradition of Sade, Baudelaire, Rimbaud, Lautreamont, Jarry, the surrealists and dadaists, Bataille, Artaud, Genet, Burroughs, Johnny Rotten, Patti Smith, and Charles Bukowski, with which Acker identifies as it shares a "deeply sexual perspective, which insists upon the connections between power and sexuality . . . also the use of non-social realist language and imagery that is very involved with areas of the mind, which are not rational" (McCaffery, "The Path," 20). Acker's aesthetic method, where the power structures of late capitalism are invariably expressed in terms of sexuality, does form part of this tradition.

Sexuality for Acker, as well as for the representatives of this particular avant-garde tradition, gives expression to and reinforces power relations within the social system; hence, for them, a critique of power relations can be framed in terms of sexuality. However, this critique, as exemplified by a male avant-garde, has itself been gender biased. As my analysis of the texts proves, Acker is both affected by the writing of these men and needs to wrestle a place for herself as woman within a line of thought for which woman is the imagined other and material women are better ignored. We are confronted here with an intellectual struggle that introduces further complexities in the earlier combination of gynocritics and feminist critique.

Taking as my object of analysis Acker's use of borrowed text in her three last novels: *In Memoriam to Identity*, *My Mother: Demonology*, and *Pussy: King of the Pirates*, I concentrate on the differential of personal re-workings, namely, the curve created when Acker copies texts, interrupting them, possessing them and being possessed by them. Acker cries across and through the "plagiarized" texts, re-reading them for a new situation, using them as a language with whose otherness of meanings she struggles, and in that struggle reveals an essential belief in the expressiveness of language, of literature, of the texts she iterates. However, she never loses sight of the material reminders of gendered power and ownership where the imagination of freedom functions differently for women than it does for men, even the self-marginalized men of the avant-garde.

Arthur Rimbaud, the visionary poet, tortured but defiant, transforming the ordinary into the marvelous, is a model for writing that "will change things magically."[4] A persisting faith, which Kathy Acker shares, namely that the material and materialistic fallen world can be recreated through the imagination, is still experienced in the late twentieth-century as the legacy of Arthur Rimbaud. Hence, in her search for positive alternatives, Acker naturally turns to his work. However, always critical of her own visions of transformation and their viability when confronted with the real world of ownership and power, Acker explores/explodes the myth of Rimbaud in *In Memoriam*, which she partly bases on his life and poetry.

The first section of *In Memoriam to Identity* is dedicated to re-telling the life of Arthur Rimbaud through a mixture of biographical reference and strategically modified translations of his poems. What results is an assemblage combining poetic metaphor with fragments of the prose narrative of Rimbaud's life.

"Rimbaud's" initial response to the pain of his life is a turn away toward the imagination: "Unable to stop these tortures, R moved into the imaginary. The infinity and clarity of desire in the imaginative made normal society's insanity disappear" (5). However, brutal physical realities undermine poetic vision at the very moment it risks transcendence: the descent into the "dirty recesses of being" (6) is both a liberating transgression of repressive social constraints (as it was for a French tradition of avant-garde art and writing from Baudelaire to Bataille), and all too literal an expression of real power relationships where teacher, as representative of a disciplinary educational system, fucks student. "This society isn't France; it's America" (6), Acker reminds us, and, moreover, a late capitalist America of the 1980s, where avant-garde transgression is easily received by a late capitalist cynical marketplace. Thus it is only possible for her to write about pain, transgression, and poetic vision by evoking a wartime France (later, when the novel moves to America it is only through the dark Southern modernism of Faulkner).

In the chapter based on Rimbaud's *The Morning of Drunkenness*, Rimbaud and Verlaine are trying to escape the joint forces of mothers, wife, and cops. Yet Rimbaud is constantly in fear of Verlaine's betrayal. The section breaks R's poems into a dialogue with V. I quote that passage at some length so as to make the breaks apparent. The original French of Rimbaud's text is in brackets.

> R to the cops: "ALCOHOLISM (IN HONOR OF MY *FORMER LOVER V*)
> "My good! My beauty. Love! Torture! You are the atrocious fanfare who prevents me from making a mistake. You are torturing me."
> [Ô mon Bien! Ô mon Beau! Fanfare atroce où je ne trébuche point! Chevalet féerique ! Hourra pour l'oeuvre/ inouïe et pour le corps merveilleux, pour la première fois !]
> "We began, V, in the laughter of children. We'll end in that innocence."
> [Cela commença sous les rires des enfants, cela finira par/ eux.]
> V who knew he wanted to go back to his wife: "How?"
> R: "When the fanfare turns—it is doing that now—and when I'm (now) returning to my old discord, your poison will be in my veins, I, in you."
> [Ce poison va rester dans toutes nos veines même quand, la fanfare tournant, nous serons rendus à l'ancienne/ inharmonie.]
> "And now that we are worthy of the torture through which we've

put each other, we can reap the results of that promise we made to
the body and soul we created. A promise, a belief made in madness!
Through madness we've survived!"
[Ô maintenant, nous si dignes de ces tortures! rassemblons fervem-
ment cette promesse surhumaine faite/ à notre corps et à notre âme
créés: cette promesse, cette démence !]
"As R babbled, the cops led these boys out of the train. . . .
R: "Our relationship began with certain disgusting acts and it has
ended—"
V wanted to return to his wife.
R:"—since at this moment we no longer believe in its eternity—"
"Looking around in the disgusting cop station.
R:—and it is ending as the perfume of your cock disperses."
[Cela commença par quelques dégoûts et cela finit,—ne pouvant
nous saisir/ sur-le-champ de cette éternité, — cela finit par une dé-
bandade de parfums.]
V: "I'm going back to my wife. I hate art."
(Acker, *In Memoriam*, 62–63)

Rimbaud wrote "The Morning of Drunkenness" about the experience of smoking hashish. Kathy Acker entirely disregards
this ostensible subject to turn the poem into an expression of
Rimbaud's tortured relationship with Paul Verlaine. Thus she
can amplify the clash between poetic vision and the drab reality
of the everyday. The poetic diction of Rimbaud's text trans-
posed into an insistently prosaic context is out of place, exorbi-
tant and absurd. Poetic figure strains the generic boundaries of
narrative prose to the point where a fissure appears between
the narrative voice ("V wanted to return to his wife."; "As R
babbled, the cops led these boys out of the train") and Rimbaud's intensity of affect. If we look for narrative, we find it interrupted by a hysterical amplification of affect. If we change
focus and try to read the poetry, we find it interrupted by the
prosaic yet threatening pull of domesticity where mother, wife,
and cops are conflated. We can then recognize the repetition of
Acker's obsessive themes of mothers and institutions of state
power (the cops) emerging as symptoms of insidious and un-
graspable networks of state and family, power and money. The
material exigencies of bourgeois life emerge traumatically, that
is, as incongruous but consistent interruptions of Rimbaud's affective speech. While the temptation is to read here two levels
of existence that have no common ground, one of the bourgeois
and another of the avant-garde poet, Acker's writing holds them
together where a mutual disregard can only result in the return
of the repressed as traumatic symptom.

The poetic writing is itself desublimated through subtle changes in the translations of Rimbaud's texts. Acker's translation substitutes a personal pronoun, "we," ("You are the atrocious fanfare who prevents me from making a mistake. You are torturing me."; "We began, V, in the laughter of children. We'll end in that innocence") for the impersonal one in the standard translation. Introducing Verlaine's more and more aloof presence as well as turning the poem, through the introduction of a personal pronoun, toward another, spelling out its suppressed relationality, Acker underscores the pain on which its triumph of liberation is based, the underlying loss. She is thus desublimating the pain, revealing poetry as speech to another, and the figures of poetry as screams of affect. A similar function is played here by the explicit sexual references that border on the obscene. What in Rimbaud remains coded and disembodied is pushed back into matter. The indomitable materiality of mothers, the wife, cops, the disgusting police station and the smell of V's cock is both ground and terrible weight to Rimbaud's poetry which transfigures it in the imagination, in a delirium that cannot be integrated into the narrative. The struggle of the visionary with material realities, as re-written by Acker, doesn't even manage to sustain the sublime of its tragic pain but is constantly on the verge of the ridiculous. Matter here is not the heroic visceral which in its sublimity justifies the pain. It is, rather, the material unredeemed, banal, truly obscene.

Although it is never directly represented, Acker's narrative of Rimbaud's life is haunted by the failure of poetic vision enacted when Rimbaud, in real life, returned into the social fold as a merchant and gave up poetry. Acker's fiction explores the struggle of poetic vision with economic reality, where poetic efforts to transform the world repeatedly crash. The narrative of *In Memoriam*, which focuses on Rimbaud's relationship with Verlaine, emphasizes Verlaine's insistence on a return to bourgeois domesticity. In later sections of *In Memoriam* Rimbaud appears as Faulkner's Jason, the dehumanization of capitalist free enterprise thus effectively both separated and informing the struggles of the imagination. An almost Manichean vision emerges where the visionary poet struggles with the interiorized pressures of bourgeois as moneymaking capitalist. Rimbaud's poetic vision traces a line of imaginative flight repetitively interrupted by Verlaine's bourgeois guilt or by literal banalities which undermine the romanticism of transcending capitalist economic values through debasement. Even as the only hope is the imagination, reality as a nexus between property-poverty-education and family disrupts the transcendent impulse as it materializes.

The subversive plunge into the taboo and excremental as that which threatens systems characterizing the Rimbaud section of *In Memoriam* is evocative of Bataille's writing of transgression. Georges Bataille's assault on beauty and dignity is, in fact, the most obvious source of Acker's anti-aesthetics, yet, in Bataille this constituted a coherent philosophical position, a systematic subversion of the grand systems of Christianity or Hegelianism. As part of a philosophical position, the details of the lowly and excremental are inevitably subsumed into philosophical abstraction, much as Bataille resisted this. Acker short circuits that flight toward the abstract by inserting details that refuse any reading but the literal. Alongside the efforts to transfigure the world—the move into the imaginary—there are, viscerally present, literal, banal details like "The filthy brat picked his nose;" or questions like: "How can I be free if I am broke?" (Acker, *In Memoriam*, 24). The literal demonstrates the resistance of material reality where the imagination fails.

In *My Mother: Demonology*, Acker turns explicitly to the work of Georges Bataille and his one time lover, Laure (Colette Peignot),[5] because, as she explains in an interview, of the failure, now as then (in the 30s), of both the democratic and post-Leninist models. Acker identifies with Bataille and Laure in their search for "something else" which makes them turn to anthropological work, myth, and sacrifice so as to "come up with a new ground for a new social model," where "irrationality would not be just a matter of mental functions, and sexuality would be something more than just the repressed." What attracts Acker to Laure, more than to Bataille, is, that in her search, Laure is consciously a woman (Rickels 61).

The letters Acker is reworking are love letters. However, in spite of the affective amplification of the texts, or rather through it, the relational aspects are opened beyond the personal toward the exploration of an emphatically female political subject, who is, however, disappointed with politics. References to current politics constitute asides in the text where Acker blasts at President Bush or at the American position in the Gulf War. Thus, the text is structured around the topical-political on the one hand, and the metaphysical search of ways to revolutionize selfhood on the other. The latter implies a suspicion that the powers that be in America, with Bush (the rapist father in the novel) as metaphorical representative, cannot be directly opposed either through the democratic mechanism, or through a Marxist revolution. Acker can only rage at the state of affairs in contemporary America; her actual quest for a positive program leads her farther and farther away from party politics toward the search of a new ground for a social model: a ground sought in the sexual and in a metaphysical exploration of the limits of the self (Sirius). Acker is attracted to Bataille's exploration of the theme of the loss of self, where "specific, controlling, imprisoning 'I' " (Sirius) of bourgeois individualism is given up along with capitalist modes of economic and social organization.

Acker's translations of Laure's letters are simultaneously a commentary on the letters' repressed content and an amplification and critique. As Bataille is the addressee of these letters, as well as Laure's partner in the search for a new ground for a social model, his presence is felt throughout. Acker's interaction with the letters is no simple gender critique: she joins Laure and Bataille on a quest, tests out the validity of their answers, and examines their implications for women. In this process, as we shall see, Acker and Laure have various degrees of identification—from possession, to a mother-daughter relationship, to a final defiant distancing.

> Malgré l'écriture due à de mauvaises conditions matérielles, il y a longtemps que je n'avais été si ferme—si assurée. (Laure 248)

> "Despite my profound and continuing fascination with decadence and decay, with where dead humans lose their bones, I'm more stable than I've been in a very long time." (Acker, *My Mother*, 247)

The stoic assurance of calm in the face of adverse circumstances of the original is revealed as denial and repression. The repressed text underlying the "normality" of the original sentence is brought out as a symptom, that is, as a distortion of the symbolic constituted in the incongruity of what the sentence is insisting on, emotional stability, and what the bulk of it is dedicated to, the fascination with decay threatening to proliferate until it drowns the proclaimed stability. Acker's ironic rewriting partly constitutes an interpretation of Laure's letter in the context of what Acker knows about her life and interests; namely, Laure's fascination with death and emotional feverishness, of which there is ample evidence elsewhere. In this light Laure's professed strength and assurance appear convincingly as strategies of repression and denial. However, in spite of the possibility to read Acker's version as interpretative, the language of "bones," "dead humans," "decadence," and "decay," which clash with both Laure's sentiment and style, are all too often encountered in Acker's own writing to be just an interpretation. The ironic bringing out of the incongruity in Laure's text also contains, in its language of repugnance, a moment of defiance toward any "proper" way of containing female pain. Yet, the "fascination with decadence and decay" calls to mind Bataille, the addressee of Laure's letters. For Bataille, the goal of this violent imagery is to "rescue being from profound boredom" ("The Lugubrious Game," 27). This is boredom understood as a felt incapacity to affect social structures. What Bataille seeks in the lowly and ugly is a certain potency, a virility he associates with the lower classes. Criticizing Andre Breton for his elevation of the lowly into the spiritual, and redeeming it as knowledge (as idea, as spirit), Bataille redeems it as power, or a myth of power. Although profoundly seduced by Bataille, Acker's gender difference precludes the possibility of assuming the position of male bestiality: spoken by Laure, the language of decay speaks of female pain, of self-destructiveness.

C'est trés beau mais dans la vie même cela ne donne rien si on n'a pas atteint une sorte de maîtrise complète de soi-même. J'en suis bien loin. Je me sens toute émiettée. J'ai cru qu'il était bon de réaliser *tout* ce qui est en soi . . . et je suis arrivée à une cacophonie monstre et si quelque chose (votre amour par example) me rappelle ma fierté initiale je sens surtout ma misère actuelle. (Laure 251)

This sounds romantic—actually I don't care if I have any mastery. I've no mastery of myself. I'm crumbling. I used to believe that I must understand and realize everything that constitutes me . . . and on this journey of realization, I came upon, just as Ulysses must have done, a monstrous cacophony.
    I had no Penelope.
    If there's anything that can and is returning me to the arrogance in which I began this journey, such as your love, B, most of all it is this suffering I now know. I am crumbling. (Acker, *My Mother*, 249)

Laure fails in her quest for a full realization of the self because she can claim no control over her identity. As a result the quest ends in the "monstrous cacophony" of multiple affect, a crumbling self. Acker interprets the failure of control as indifference to it: "I don't care if I have any mastery." The full realization of self actually requires this indifference to mastery over one's identity. However, the stakes for men and women are strikingly different as Acker demonstrates through the introduction of the archetypal Western quest hero: if woman as faithful wife can guarantee the self-identity of man, woman herself has no such guarantee. The modern male lover (Bataille) is no guarantee of self the way Penelope's recognition of Ulysses was.

The same monstrous cacophony Laure encounters in the journey of self-discovery is the condition of Acker's textual experiments: textual circumstance mirrors the plight of self. The text, like the self, is shot through with the words of others in a cacophony which refuses the mastery of an authorial consciousness that would guarantee its identity. This passage demonstrates the degree to which Acker's text is "possessed" by Laure: the theme of the crumbling self is developed further toward the end of the section and the novel; but, more than that, the cacophony of Laure's consciousness reflected in Acker's books marks the continuity between the two women both struggling within the male context of the twentieth-century avant-garde.

At the end of *My Mother*, which is also the end of the section including Laure's letters, there is a mystical vision of nothingness, preceded by the attempt to lose the self so as to regain life. The triumphant success of this attempt, however, leaves the narrator (Laure) voiceless, a "nothing." Paralyzed, Laure is reduced to an animal scream, to "bestial howling," her rejection of political activity as devoid of value succeeded by a metaphysical quest into the limits of the self. Political intervention is superseded by an attempt to cut into the tissue of life and death, ultimately into any recognizable reality: "It's necessary to cut life into bits, for neither the butcher store not the bed of a woman who's giving birth is as bloody as this." "Absurdity, blessed insolence that saves, and connivance are found in these cuts, the cuts into 'veracity' " (Acker, *My Mother*, 267).

Although Laure's paralysis and becoming nothing cede in *My Mother* to an active feminist defiance, the issue of the loss of a social and constraining self persists in Acker's writing.[6] At this point of Acker's search for social alternatives, however, the desire to lose the self, arrested by the realization of the different stakes involved for woman, turns into aggressive defiance:

Avez-vous vu comme j'entre dans le role ignoble, vulgaire d'une femme qui *ment*—ça ne m'était pas arrive de ma vie. J'avais toujours pensé et je pense encore qui si je mentais *de cette manière-là* juste-

ment *comme* ça la vie, ma vie perdait toute raison d'être—Je ne sup-
porte pas le mensonge—

. . . C'est bien ainsi—je devrais même en mourir de savoir *moi
aussi* mentir ignoblement superbement, triomphalement— (Laure
255)

Do you see how easy it is for me to ask to be regarded as low and
dirty? To ask to be spat upon? This isn't . . . the sluttishness . . . but
the language of a woman who thinks: it's a role. I've always thought
for myself. I'm a woman who's alone, outside the accepted. Outside
the Law, which is language. This is the only role that allows me to
be as intelligent as I am and to avoid persecution.

My life's disintegrating under me so I'll not bear the lie of
meaning.

My inability to bear that lie is what's giving me strength. Even
when I believed in meaning, when I felt defined by opposition and
this opposition between desire and the search for self-knowledge
and self-reclamation was tearing me apart, even back than I knew I
was only lying, that I was lying superbly, disgustingly, triomphally.

Life doesn't exist inside language: too bad for me. (Acker, *My
Mother*, 253)

The distance between Laure and Acker is expressed in terms
of the years of feminist analysis of the relationship between
woman, language, and the law, implicit in the later author's interpretation of the earlier one. Acker detects the defiance implicit in Laure's complex staging of guilt, abasement, abjection,
and perverse pleasure. In her exegetic rewriting which triples
the original the self-abasement in Laure's text is justified as
masquerade, a defense of the Woman outside the Law, a means
of survival for the intelligent woman. Where meaning is a lie
and there is no "life outside language," one must lie "superbly,
disgustingly, triomphally."

Laure's abject admission of her lying is transformed into
anger and overt defiance. Acker-Laure turns the terms of abjection, being "low and dirty" and "spat upon," into weapons
against the authority of the patriarchal system of meaning that
excludes her. And this leads us to Acker's feminist variation on
punk which finds its unlikely predecessor in the figure of the
anarchic carnal desiring feminine of Surrealism and early feminism. In *My Mother*, Acker quotes Elizabeth Roudinesco's description of this figure: "The rebellious, criminal, insane, or gay
woman is no longer perceived as a slave to her symptoms." Instead, "in the negative idealization of crime [she] discovers the

means to struggle against a society [that disgusts]"(30). This powerful and threatening, almost monstrous figure may be an expression of male anxiety, but could also be used as a weapon of upsetting social space.

The process of identification is striking here: the speaking voice is a Laure that can look back and say "Even when I believed in meaning . . . I was lying superbly, disgustingly, triumphally." The repetition of the exact words from the original letters in the past tense signal that what we have is a remembrance of the period when the letter was written, and not a translation. But who is the remembering Laure, who knows about meaning, and language, and the lies of male language? It has to be Acker herself. In spite of the mother-daughter centrality in the novel, it is not a mother-daughter relationship that brings Acker and Laure together, or at least not a conventional one.

Acker is learning from Laure, but also talking back to her, becoming her, but retaining her present knowledge and experience. While previously I noted a moment where Laure "possessed" Acker, here the relationship is reversed and Laure's writing is made aggressive and positive at the expense of her original self-doubt and contradictory feelings of debasement and triumph. This is a deliberate demystification of "high" suffering, the suffering of the lapsed bourgeois and Catholic overwhelmed by guilt and indulging in existential angst.

In one of the final returns to Laure's texts there is a deliberate flattening of the complexity of the love relationship turned into power game. What follows is inverted by Acker and what is a plea and an assurance in Laure turns into open revolt.

> Georges, maintenant c'est si clair. Tu penses avoir asservi à jamais *mon existence*—tu la vois toute enfermée, finie, délimitée—les limites que tu prévois,
>   qui te sont connues et puis tu pars . . . vivre vrai et secret—ou du moms tu croix à cela. . . . Comme si le vrai en toi pouvait m'être étranger (Laure 260)

> B, everything is clear. You believe that you've put me into servitude because I'm living shut off from society, devoid of intercourse. But what is true is false to me. (Acker, *My Mother*, 258)

Acker's exploration of the feminist political subject in Laure's letters finally recuperates Laure (somewhat against herself) to an aggressive female stance where the added imagery of decay and the repugnant dares a monstrosity Laure shies from. Yet the defiance of the monstrous feminine is itself interrupted: the coherence of its fledgling narrative is soon broken into fragments carrying reminders of a banal daily materiality as incommensurable with Laure's intensity of disembodied desire as it is with Acker's dirt-hurling feminism. The material details of daily unheroic female existence, kitchens, toilet seats, drunks, in their inescapable thereness open the intensity of Laure and Acker's quest to the world which floods in fragmenting the narrative.

In Bataille the existence of the bourgeois individual is based on an awareness of discontinuity. The fracture of discontinuity informs notions of the individual, of self-possession, the object and its separateness. Bataille turns his attention to the space between discontinuous existence and the continuous where he finds madness or eroticism, death, violence, and revolution. It is similar spaces that Acker's fiction occupies: those spaces that are taboo to any particular cultural system. It is precisely the flesh which, in Bataille, testifies to the continuity between animal and man, organic and inorganic. Thus eroticism, emphasizing the flesh, reminds of the continuity discontinuous individuality is torn from and, consequently, threatens its stability.

Acker places Bataille's mysticism squarely within socioeconomic reality where the critique launched by his "base materialism" onto Marxist "reality" is reversed: if Marxism fails to take into consideration base materialism, base materialism itself falls victim to socioeconomic structures of power. An individual's quest for a mystical loss of self (itself a paradox) is caught up within objectively existing economic power structures: both Laure in *My Mother* and O. in *Pussy*, rather than liberated from a bourgeois self, end up further subjugated by male economic power. In other words, if the flesh in Bataille speaks most clearly of the tear from animal nature and the inorganic that individuation accomplishes, it also, according to Acker, in its needs, most powerfully entangles us in networks of sociality as economic exchange. Acker is both critical of Bataille and strongly attracted to his writing. In her novels, the weight of economic power constantly pulls back the impulse to experiment with the loss of self. The mystically celebrated loss of self loses its liberatory potential when it is sought by a woman who is still economically dependent. O. in *Pussy* seeks to become nothing so that she can have vision only to end up as an object of ownership in a whorehouse.[7]

Acker's last book, *Pussy: King of the Pirates*, thematically marks her departure from the world of the male avant-garde. Antonin Artaud, one of Acker's most admired models, is one of the narrators in the first part of *Pussy*. Acker uses parts of Artaud's letters while emphasizing his fascination with Gerard de Nerval and the latter's suicide. Nerval hung himself on an apron string, a trivial object of domestic femininity. This suicide is consequently rewritten by Acker's "Artaud" as a symbolic self-castration: "Gerard cut off his own head with a woman's apron string, so now he is a woman, so now he has a hole between his arms" (20). Nerval's suicide is a "protest against control"(21): as a symbolic act of self-castration, it is a denial of phallic authority in its different forms as the tyranny of divine power, as pure rationality, as masculine containment. As a result of that polysemic cutting of the head a different kind of language emerges, or, rather, "spurts out," "pours out" (*Pussy* 20–21). A language of the body replaces the male language of control.

In "Critical Languages" Acker traces her ideas of nonpatriarchal language as a language of the body to the "Acephale" society of which Bataille was one of the founding members. The acephalian god which the group adopted as its symbol has self-decapitated so as to release the "fleshy passions" or "jouissance." Thus a renewed awareness of death and the materiality of the body would shift the center from the head to the labyrinth of the colon. It is this labyrinth of the self, inextricably and untranscendably linked to the flesh, which can generate nonauthoritarian languages (89–91). In *Pussy*, through the figures of Artaud and Nerval, Acker tests out this myth of the acephalian god as the origin of a new language.

So far Acker is actually following the logic of avant-garde men, where the figure of woman is appropriated as that of the other (real women have no place in this system). When Gilles Deleuze, for instance, claims that writing is "becoming woman," he is referring not to actual women, but to men becoming another. The symbolic act of writing, becoming woman, has no effect on the system of ownership of real women by men—in the novel "Artaud" still wants to own O., to protect her (*Pussy* 21, 23). The grid of meaning organized around property relations traumatizes the mystical quest for the loss of the bourgeois self (becoming woman) and emerges symptomatically in the power structure of the love relationship as a desire for ownership. Neither can a confusion of sexual roles be consistently liberating. In a world of revolution O. and a masochistic "Artaud" make love exchanging roles. But gender fluidity becomes impossible to maintain. Where O. wants pleasure only, Artaud, even in his abjection, wants to protect her, wants mastery, love. Thus the philosophical or aesthetic act of refusing mastery changes nothing while human relations remain relations of ownership, that is while society is divided along property lines. Even so, Artaud, with his tortured consciousness of self and body presents a literary precursor whom Acker can most closely identify with. The fragments from his writing used in *Pussy* remain almost unchanged (200–201). It is rather through the impossibility of Artaud's survival than through his participation in a male economy of possession, that Acker realizes her critique: "At the moment of his death, his language split into forgettable, unreadable fragments" (202).

The last of the white men in *Pussy* are the punk boys, Artaud's followers in the world of multinational corporations. In this world, Acker argues, the extreme concentration of capital and simultaneous concentration of power has led to the passing away of the patriarchy of the bourgeois industrial world. The punk boys, a force of pure negativity, are the disenfranchised creatures of this new world. They are, Acker claims, the "descendants of Heliogabalus of Alexandria," the young emperor of murder and horror of whom Artaud wrote. The women in *Pussy*, themselves similarly disenfranchised, are attracted to these violent boys, much in the way Acker herself was attracted to the punk scene. The only possible avenue for action left for the punk boys is terror, where the only possible freedom lies. These are the contemporary avatars of the boys of the avant-garde tradition forming an unbroken line from Rimbaud to Johnny Rotten. The women, however, for whom horror has been a material part of history, refuse terror as a solution. Acker's writing constantly pulls back the impulse to transcend material realities into the weight of economic power: the philosophical experimentation with the loss of self is tangibly different from the economic loss of self experienced by O. in *Pussy*. The author/narrator being woman, and economically unfree cannot but run against the father-property machine. The weight of culture is not so easily lost. To have a free world it is not sufficient to kill or behead the father. He always comes to haunt the future. *Pussy* recapitulates Acker's intellectual biography, her attraction and struggles with an avant-garde tradition. Departing from the world offered by the punk boys, the women in *Pussy* offer a glimpse of a new world without men, a world of pleasure.

The world of anarchic female pleasure echoes the revaluation of female sexuality in the work of French feminists in the late 70s, notably Irigaray and Cixous, but is more directly influenced by "these crazy wild girls who are part of the San Francisco scene," where Acker was living and teaching while writing the book. In an interview with Laurence Rickels, she talks with exhilaration about the girls' society in San Francisco and its presence in *Pussy*:

> Here's a tremendous freedom in daily living that I've never had anywhere else. My strongest desire (it's beyond desire, it's a need) is to make it possible for people like me to be in society. Perhaps it'll have to be a different society. . . . What I'm seeing in San Francisco is the emergence of a community of younger women that seems revolutionary, and also a relation to the body that I've never seen before with women. (103)

Elsewhere Acker expresses her belief in the demise of the old art worlds of "cowboys and financiers" in favor of a new, grass roots emergent women's culture produced within networks of friendship. Her examples are the computer artists of VNS Matrix and the anarchic feminist punk of Tribe 8 (Acker, "After the End"). For both these groups an aggressive and transgressive sexuality is a political weapon,[8] but it is the ways in which they redefine art production as community and friendship based that has the potential of changing the very idea of art world.

It is this generation of girls that the narrator in *Pussy* watches in awe as they abandon the pirate treasure so as to go on "pirating." But that new world of pirate girls is a hopeful new world, which the narrator/Acker can only admire. If she cannot quite imagine the material realities of that new world, as a writer, she can devise its language. It is a language of the body, of wonder and discovery, not of judgment and categories.[9] In *Pussy*, Acker literally wrote with the rhythms of the flesh: the text follows the rhythms of the body building up toward orgasm.[10] Language is organized to resonate with the quickening breath of sexual arousal: syntactic organization cedes to fragments of sentences corresponding to the contractions of excited flesh. With this Acker's always sexualized writing leaves the deconstructions of male texts and becomes a writing of female erotism.[11]

In the Alexandria whorehouse section of *Pussy* Acker imagines a world without men, a world of female sexuality, not of profit but of touch. Such a world entails a different kind of language, a visceral, affective language:

> the whores learned that if language or words whose meanings seem definite are dissolved into a substance of multiple gestures and cries, a substance which has a more direct, a more visceral capacity for expression, then all the weight that the current social, political, and religious forms of expression carry will be questioned. Become questionable. Finally, lost. (Acker, *Pussy* 31)

Meaning is dissolved into nonsense, but that nonsense makes sense to the body, viscerally. *Pussy* speaks, in its rhythms and metaphors, of the pleasures of the female body. Masturbatory writing is an attempt to flee the subject as subject of ideology, to shake off the weight of "current social, political, and religious forms of expression." This is the fantasy Acker opposes to domesticity: dreams of pleasure, of desiring flesh dissolving a selfhood defined by property and Oedipal relationships.

In reading Acker's flesh writing, I have emphasized its continuity and break with an avant-garde male (and, most frequently, misogynistic) line. However, an argument could be made that she is closer to Hélène Cixous's self-actualizing prophesy of feminine writing. After all, while writing *Pussy*, Acker was actually teaching Cixous's texts. Acker's writing with the rhythms of the body certainly seems inspired by the dizzying, "flesh and blood," affirmative flow of feminine writing Cixous celebrates together with a prediscursive feminine essentially bisexual libidinal economy. And as Gabrielle Dane argues, Hélène Cixous and Kathy Acker both seek to establish an alternative yet intelligible discourse outside of the phallocentric one ("Hysteria"). Yet Cixous' celebration of a prediscursive maternal space from where feminine writing would originate seems to be too quick a resolution of the conflict woman is cast into by her acculturation into the symbolic order. Moreover, it might be simply reversing the values perpetuated by the symbolic order, rather than going beyond them: by locating Woman prior to the symbolic order and prior to language Cixous is upholding the opposition nature—culture, even as she is reversing its underlying hierarchy. As Luce Irigaray insists, "there is no simple manageable way to leap to the outside of phallogocentrism, *nor any possible way to situate oneself there, that would re-*

sult from the simple fact of being a woman" (*This Sex* 162). Acker, as Irigaray, moves back systematically through a masculine imaginary—for Irigaray this is the imaginary of Freudian psychoanalysis and a classical philosophical tradition, for Acker it is the imaginary of the male avant-garde.

However, Irigaray is in search of a place outside a dominant system, while Acker is exploring a tradition already on the margins of the dominant. The male avant-garde itself seeks to exceed the limits of the dominant and subvert it. Thus Acker both uses its weapons against systems of power and ideological control and critiques the implications of these weapons from a gendered and economically marked position, where to be female, for her, means to be economically dependent. Toward the end of *Pussy*, her last novel, Acker gestures toward a new development, emerging from under the shadow of a male avant-garde with which she has been obsessively struggling.

NOTES

1. See: "The Path of Abjection" and "Dead Doll Prophecy."

2. The first instance of using borrowed text practice Acker refers to is the use of Jean Genet in the last part of *Blood and Guts in High School*, at a time when she was influenced by Sherrie Levine, Richard Prince, and David Salle (Lotringer 10). In an interview with Ellen Friedman in 1988, Acker explains her work by analogy with the appropriation art of Sherrie Levine (Friedman 12).

3. See also Rod Phillips and his comparison between *The Scarlet Letter* and Acker's use of it in *Blood and Guts in High School*. Phillips argues that Acker both criticizes Hawthorne's framing of Hester Prynne and uses his text as a way of speaking about the imprisoned condition of women and their desire in the Puritan past as well as in the Punk present. Also see Sciolino, "Confessions of a Kleptoparasite."

4. In "A Few Notes on Two of my Books," Acker writes of the necessity for political change and of her simultaneous skepticism as to the possibility of writing to accomplish this change. She concludes "If writing cannot and writing must change things, writing *will* change things magically"(8). The essay dates from 1989—precisely when she was working on *In Memoriam to Identity*.

5. Laure (Colette Peignot) was the one woman in the Bataille-Klossowski circle, mistress of Boris Souvarine, lapsed catholic, member of the communist party, writer, and sexual anarchist. In a series of radical existential moves she went to postrevolutionary Russia to live (and almost die) as a worker on a cooperative farm, rejected political activity as devoid of value after a period of intense involvement, and lived turbulently with Bataille for the last four years of her life. In her desperate quest and internal conflict Laure is a point where the contradictions of Modernist avant-garde politics and gender inflection are

staged in all their complexity. We have Bataille's memoir of her—*Vie de Laure*, and his edition of her letters and fragments of political and philosophical texts.

6. In *Pussy*, for instance, the exhilaration and horror of this loss are figured in a doubling of the self: Ostracism, one of the novel's girls, splits in two with one part (the name bearing one) preserving her selfhood, cutting herself off from the possibility of merging with another, preventing the possibility of losing one's self. The other part "was nameless and wild. Was never to be touched, just like the winds cannot be grasped. That part felt joy when she was as open as the air, as that invisible *not there*" (*Pussy* 121). The latter wildness and joy terrifies the named selfhood of the "I."

7. A similar contrast between what is possible for women in their struggle with the system of power and what is possible for men is a conscious part of Acker's search for a myth to live by in the previous novels as well. In the "Airplane" section of *In Memoriam*, for instance, the myth of romantic love explored in that text is emphatically gendered: men dream of love, women dream of survival. The subordinate economic and social position of women determines the stakes of romantic love as a matter of life and death.

8. VNS Matrix, a collective of Australian feminists producing art for the Intemet, have electronically disseminated a "Cyberfeminist Manifesto for the Twenty-first Century" which reads: "We are the modem cunt positive antireason unbounded unleashed unforgiving . . ."; Tribe 8, San Francisco's militant lesbian S&M warriors write political hardcore tailored for the slam pit. (See Ray Rogers, "QUEER PUNK comes out of the closet—loudly," *Rolling Stone Magazine*, 18 May 1995).

9. See also "Critical Languages."

10. The passages are too long to quote in length here, but see, for instance *Pussy*, 32–33.

11. The pleasures of female erotism are actualized only in masturbation, never interpersonally in sex between subjects—male or female—where power, masochism, pain, fear of abandonment, and desperate desire always get in the way. However, as masturbation *writing*, the text invites the reader to participate erotically in the text. Thus it is the relationship between writer, text, and reader that offers the hope of an erotism free of social pressures.

WORKS CITED

Acker, Kathy. 1995. "After the End of the Art World." In *The Multimedia Text*, edited by Nicholas Zurbrugg. *Art and Design Profile* 45:3.

———. 1984. *Blood and Guts in High School*. New York: Grove.

———. "Critical Languages." In *Bodies of Work*, 81–92. London: Serpent's Tail.

———. 1994. "Dead Doll Prophecy." In *The Subversive Imagination: Artists, Society, and Social Responsibility*, edited by Carol Becker. New York: Routledge.

———. 1987. *Don Quixote*. New York: Grove Press.

———. 1997. "A Few Notes on Two of my Books." In *Bodies of Work*, 6–13. London: Serpent's Tail.

———. 1983. *Great Expectations*. New York: Grove Press.

————. 1990. *In Memoriam to Identity*. London: Pandora.

————. 1994. *My Mother: Demonology*. New York: Grove.

————. 1996. *Pussy: King of the Pirates*. New York: Grove.

Bataille, Georges. 1986. *Erotism: Death and Sensuality*. Translated by Mary Dalwood. San Francisco: City Lights Books.

————. "The Lugubrious Game." *Visions of Excess: Selected Writings, 1927–1939*. Edited by Allan Stoekl, translated by Allan Stoekl. Minneapolis: University of Minnesota Press, 24–30.

Cixous, Hélène. 1986. "Sorties." In *The Newly Born Woman*, edited by Hélène Cixous and Catherine Clément, translated by Betty Wing, 61–132. Minneapolis: University of Minnesota Press.

Dane, Gabrielle. 1994. "Hysteria as a Feminist Protest: Dora, Cixous, Acker." *Women's Studies* 23:231–56.

Irigaray, Luce. 1986. *This Sex Which Is Not One*. Translated by Catherine Porter. Ithaca: Cornell University Press.

Friedman, Ellen G. 1989. "A Conversation with Kathy Acker." *The Review of Contemporary Fiction* 9, no. 3:12–22.

Laure. 1977. *Écrits, fragments, lettres*. Paris: J.-J. Pauvert.

Lotringer, Sylvère. 1991. "Devoured by Myths (Interview with Kathy Acker)." In *Hannibal Lecter, My Father* by Kathy Acker, 1–24. New York: Semiotext(e).

McCaffery, Larry. 1993. "The Path of Abjection: An Interview with Kathy Acker." *Some Other Frequency: Interviews with Innovative American Authors*. Philadelphia: University of Pennsylvania Press.

Phillips, Rod. 1994. "Purloined Letters: 'The Scarlet Letter' in Kathy Acker's *Blood and Guts In High School*." *CRITIQUE: Studies in Contemporary Fiction* 35, no. 3:173–91.

Rickels, Laurence. 1994. "Body Building." Interview with Kathy Acker. *Artforum* 32, no. 6:60.

Rimbaud, Arthur. 1967. *Illuminations*. Genève: Droz.

Sciolino, Martina. 1990. "Kathy Acker and the Postmodern Subject of Feminism." *College English* 52:437–45.

————. 1989. "Confessions of a Kleptoparasite." *The Review of Contemporary Fiction* 9, no. 3:63–67.

Sirius, R. U. "Where Does She Get Off?" Interview with Kathy Acker. *io magazine: The digital magazine of literary culture* 2: 7pp. Online. 9 December 1997. http://www.altx.com/io/acker1.html

Contributors

SARAH APPLETON AGUIAR is an associate professor of American and women's literature at Murray State University and received her Ph.D. from the University of Connecticut. She is the author of *The Bitch Is Back: Wicked Women in Literature*. She has also published articles in the *Journal of Contemporary Thought* and other journals.

LYNN M. ALEXANDER is a professor of English at The University of Tennessee Martin. She received her Ph.D from the University of Tulsa. She is co-editor of *The Slaughter-House of Mammon*, and the author of numerous articles on women and work.

JAMIE BARLOWE is an associate professor of English and women's studies and director of undergraduate studies in English at the University of Toledo. Her essays have appeared in *Novel*, *American Literary History*, *Women and Language*, *Studies in the American Renaissance*, and *The Hemingway Review*, as well as in other journals and collections on feminist theory, feminist pedagogy, and women's scholarship. Her book, *The Scarlet Mob of Scribblers: ReReading Hester Prynne*, is forthcoming from Southern Illinois University Press, and her current book-project is titled, *Viewer, I Married Him: The Construction of the Female Spectator in Cinematic Adaptations of 19th- and Early 20th-Century Novels by British and American Women*.

RUTH BIENSTOCK ANOLIK teaches in the freshman English program at Haverford College. She is completing her dissertation, "Possessions: Property and Propriety in the Gothic Mode," at Bryn Mawr College. She has written on the English and American gothic, including the ethnic gothic, and on immigrant literatures. The essay included in this volume has won the NEMLA's Women's Caucus of the Modern Language Association 1999 Best Essay in Women's Language and Literature Award.

LINDA JOYCE BYRD has been teaching composition and literature at Sam Houston State University in Huntsville, Texas, for twelve years. She received her Ph.D. in American literature from Texas A&M University in College Station, Texas; the title of her dissertation was: *Sexuality and Motherhood in the Novels of Lee Smith: A Divine Integration*. She has published widely on Lee Smith and several other southern writers and presents papers regularly at conferences all over the south. The highlight of her career was when she flew to North Carolina and did a personal interview with Lee Smith. The interview may be found in the Summer 1997 issue of *Shenandoah: The Washington and Lee University Review*. Dr. Byrd is currently working with a publisher on the book manuscript of her dissertation.

BEVERLEY CURRAN is an associate professor of English at Aichi Shukutoku College in Nagoya, Japan. She is the author of many essays published in Japan and internationally in such journals as *Canadian Literature*.

ELISE EARTHMAN is a professor of English at San Francisco State University. She has published numerous articles in such journals as *English Journal* and *Research in the Teaching of English*.

CONNIE D. GRIFFIN received her Ph.D. in English and American literature from The University of Massachusetts. She currently teaches in the Department of English at Boston College.

MICA HOWE is a Spanish professor at Murray State University. She received her Ph.D. from the University of Nebraska in 1995 and has published in *Revista de estudios hispánicos* and *Nueva Revista del Pacífico*. Her other current book project is *Paravicino: vida y verso* based on Spanish Golden Age poetry.

MERRIE LISA JOHNSON is a Ph.D. candidate in English at SUNY Binghamton, with an emphasis in women's writing and feminist theory. Her work has appeared in *Sexuality and Culture* and *Inquiry: Critical Thinking Across the Disciplines*, and she contributes regularly to the webzine *Women's Writing* on subjects at the intersection of American literature and feminism.

BRACHA LICHTENBERG ETTINGER is an internationally recognized artist and psychoanalytic feminist theorist. She received her Ph.D. in aesthetics from the University of Paris VIII, a D.E.A. in psychoanalysis from the University of ParisVII, and an M.A. in clinical psychology from the Hebrew University in Jerusalem.

Her paintings have been exhibited in major museums throughout the world, and she is the author of numerous books, including *The Matrixial Gaze*, and an extensive collection of essays.

TIMOTHY MCCRACKEN is a senior professor at Union County College in New Jersey and has published and presented widely on comparative literature. His most recent publication was on the nature of music for the *University of Toronto Quarterly*. His work on Lolita comes out of fellowships at Princeton and the University of Rochester and is part of his planned book, *Domestic Nymphs: The Framing of Salome, Lolita, and Their Suburban Sisters*.

SVETLANA MINTCHEVA is working on her Ph.D in literature at Duke University. She has presented a number of papers on John Barth and Kathy Acker, and she is author of the forthcoming "The Paralyzing Tensions of Radical Art in a Postmodern World: Kathy Acker's Last Novels as Exploratory Fiction."

CHRISTIAN MORARU holds a double Ph.D. in English and comparative literature from Indiana University. He is an assistant professor of American literature and literary theory at the University of North Carolina, Greensboro. He is an associate editor of *Symploke*. A chapter of his 1990 book on mimetic ideologies in twentieth-century critical theory, *The Archeology of Mimesis*, has recently been reprinted in a SUNY P anthology, *The Play of the Self*. He is the author of the forthcoming *The Rewriting Machine: Narrative and Cultural Revisionism in the Age of Recycling* and also of numerous articles that have appeared in journals such as *The Journal of Narrative Technique*, *Studies in the Humanities*, and *Studies in the Novel*.

ELLEN PEEL is an associate professor of comparative literature at San Francisco State University and holds a Ph. D. from Yale University. She has published numerous articles in such publications as *Reader*, *American Literature*, and *Comparative Literature Studies*. She is also the author of the forthcoming *Beyond Utopia: Feminism, Persuasion, and Narrative*.

Index

290